Routledge Revivals

THE RISE OF LOUIS NAPOLEON

THE RISE OF LOUIS NAPOLEON

BY
F. A. SIMPSON

First published in 1909 by Longmans, Green and Co. Ltd.

This edition first published in 2018 by Routledge
2 Park Square, Milton Park, Abingdon, Oxon, OX14 4RN
and by Routledge
52 Vanderbilt Avenue, New York, NY 10017, USA

Routledge is an imprint of the Taylor & Francis Group, an informa business

© 1909 by Taylor and Francis

All rights reserved. No part of this book may be reprinted or reproduced or utilised in any form or by any electronic, mechanical, or other means, now known or hereafter invented, including photocopying and recording, or in any information storage or retrieval system, without permission in writing from the publishers.

Publisher's Note
The publisher has gone to great lengths to ensure the quality of this reprint but points out that some imperfections in the original copies may be apparent.

Disclaimer
The publisher has made every effort to trace copyright holders and welcomes correspondence from those they have been unable to contact.
A Library of Congress record exists under ISBN: 66078716

ISBN 13: 978-0-367-14632-0 (hbk)
ISBN 13: 978-0-367-14635-1 (pbk)
ISBN 13: 978-0-429-05281-1 (ebk)

THE RISE OF LOUIS NAPOLEON

LOUIS NAPOLEON BONAPARTE
From an engraving by Hall after a drawing by Stewart

THE RISE OF
LOUIS NAPOLEON

BY

F. A. SIMPSON
FELLOW OF TRINITY COLLEGE, CAMBRIDGE

LONGMANS, GREEN AND CO
LONDON · NEW YORK · TORONTO

LONGMANS, GREEN AND CO LTD
6 & 7 CLIFFORD STREET LONDON W 1
ALSO AT MELBOURNE AND CAPE TOWN

LONGMANS, GREEN AND CO INC
55 FIFTH AVENUE NEW YORK 3

LONGMANS, GREEN AND CO
215 VICTORIA STREET TORONTO 1

ORIENT LONGMANS LTD
BOMBAY CALCUTTA MADRAS

FIRST PUBLISHED . .	1909
SECOND EDITION . . .	1925
NEW IMPRESSION . . .	1929
THIRD EDITION . . .	1950

Ο ΘΑΥΜΑΣΑΣ ΒΑΣΙΛΕΥΣΕΙ.

FROM THE PREFACE TO THE FIRST EDITION

OF the two great French historians of the Second Empire, Ollivier devotes one chapter to the story of Louis Napoleon's life before 1848, while La Gorce is content to introduce his hero in less ceremonious fashion; his four-page summary would hardly be an adequate, even if it were altogether an accurate, account of forty years of a life singularly crowded with incident and interest. Ordinarily, the historian might well plead that it is in no way incumbent on him to preface his history of any reign with a biography of the monarch up to the time of his accession. Indeed such a task would usually appear strangely unprofitable. The record of a royal upbringing must always in the telling of it seem to lack the elements of emulation and competition, the slight achievements and distinctions, which redeem from utter dullness the narrative of an orthodox education. Nor would there be any very apparent interest in the early career of one who from his position must share the limitations of royalty, while debarred from truly regal activities. For while hardly any man has a larger opportunity of expressing what is in him than the modern king, hardly any man has less opportunity for so doing than the modern prince. In fact, of the ordinary modern monarch it would hardly be too much to say that from his accession to the throne dates not only the history of his reign, but the history of his life. But Louis Napoleon was not an ordinary modern monarch; in the phrase of Elizabeth Barrett Browning, he was no 'common king-born king.' Before his accession to power he was not merely a prince, but a pretender. And for this reason his career demands exceptional treatment. For when the king owes his crown in great part to his own prolonged exertions, then indeed his accession is preceded by a very essential portion of his life. And when, further, the exertions which have brought him to the throne have so affected his character as to have a profound and abiding influence on his conduct of affairs as king, then some acquaintance with these early adventures becomes a necessary preliminary to the right understanding not merely of his life, but of his reign. To those, then, who would study the history of the Second Empire, I offer this book without further apology. I venture also to hope that the larger band, which is more generally or more vaguely interested in Napoleonic literature, may find in it an account in some ways more adequate than any yet existing in this language, of the process by which the gulf between the two great Napoleonic experiments was bridged.

There remains a third class of reader—possibly not the smallest of the three—to whom an account of the early career of Louis Napoleon may conceivably be of interest. To many the adventures of a pretender possess a certain romantic interest all their own. The bearer of a great name, fallen on evil days, who dauntlessly and desperately endeavours to win his way back to the throne of his ancestors—such a man may not amount to much in his own generation, but he is assured of a certain sympathetic attention at the hands of posterity. Now Louis Napoleon was almost the ideal pretender. Other exiled princes have been restored: foreign pressure, native enthusiasm, or the intervention of some king-maker have replaced or recalled the descendants of other fallen dynasties. On occasion, brute force has won back for the son what brute force had taken away from the father. But of hardly any other pretender in history can it be maintained that by the persistent parade of his claims, by the incessant exploitation of his name, by the sheer importunity of his suit, he himself succeeded in inducing his countrymen to confide to his hands the dominion of which his dynasty had been deprived. And it is here, perhaps, that a word of apology is due to those who make a study of pretenders. Just because Louis Napoleon was an ideal pretender, his career was not quite typical of the ordinary pretender's career; for while they all eventually failed, he alone eventually succeeded. But if the connoisseur will pardon this one irregularity, if he will forgive Louis Napoleon for failing to fail, then we can undertake that in no other feature of his profession will he be found wanting. A royal birth, a princely heritage, an imperial name; a king for his father, queens for his nursing mothers, a cardinal to christen him, emperor and empress to stand his sponsors; early exile, puerile persecution, youthful wanderings in search of a home; headstrong resolutions, reckless invasions, miraculous escapes, transportation, imprisonments, flights in disguise: these for circumstances, and for central figure a dreamer, an adventurer, a conspirator, a suspect in his teens, a rebel in arms while still a beardless boy, thrice the leader of forlorn hopes whence no ordinary man had once escaped with his life—if we have not here the stock-in-trade of a pretender, we confess we should despair of any further quest of him.

It is this aspect of the incidents here narrated which must be the author's excuse for thus presenting them in separate and independent form. For though it is to the momentous consequences which flowed from them that the events recounted in this volume owe their importance to the historian, yet it is not to these, or to anything outside themselves, that they are indebted for their great intrinsic interest. Nor do they lack a sufficient artistic completeness as they stand; for they form not the first act in a tragedy, but the first drama of a trilogy. Or, more properly

—since the early portion, at any rate, of Louis Napoleon's career was epic rather than dramatic—they compose the Odyssey of a man who on his home-coming had still an Achilleid in front of him. Louis Napoleon was not the only man who had laid on him that double task; nor was he the only man who emerged triumphantly from the first, only to perish miserably in the second. But it may safely be said that no man in the first half of his career attained so striking a triumph by the road of such dismal failure, and in the latter portion of his life prefaced such overwhelming disaster by so brilliant a promise of success.

A word is necessary in conclusion with regard to the sources drawn upon for this volume, and the method adopted in employing them. Although I have generally attempted to trace every questionable fact back to its first printed source, and though in case of conflicting evidence I have always endeavoured to give the better attested statement its due, yet I have purposely refrained as far as possible from footnote reference to published authorities. Such references, to be used consistently, must often have been half a dozen deep to the page—a parade of industry which might have been more distracting to the reader than helpful to the student. The latter will, I hope, find in the fairly full bibliographical appendix a sufficient indication of the printed sources of information. Since no bibliography of the subject treated in this volume is yet in existence, I have endeavoured to give some indication of the relative value and importance of the authorities enumerated. By this disposition of it, such information will at least be inoffensive to those to whom it is useless: easily accessible to the explorer, it yet will not obtrude itself on the wayfarer. Doubtless no appendix of this kind can ever quite take the place of systematic marginal reference; but I trust that an arrangement, which certainly does not lack some compensation of convenience, may in this case have entailed no very appreciable sacrifice of scholarship.

Marginal reference has, however, been consistently employed in the citation of unpublished authorities. For here, if nowhere else, reference to chapter and verse is indispensable. The writer who claims for his work that it is based on research, claims in effect that he has made some contribution to the available information on a certain period— either by bringing to light facts or details not yet known at all, or at least by confirming what was before conjectural, by disproving what hitherto could only be denied. But unless he inform his readers what are the exact points on which his labours have shed light, and what is the exact source from which that light is derived, he makes it impossible for his successors either to identify or to verify his results.

The French Government does not yet permit the examination of any judicial documents in its possession relating to the Strasburg and Boulogne affairs. However, the surviving documents are probably of no great value. Not that the grapes are sour, but the best of them have almost certainly been plucked long ago. Within a week of his election to the Presidency, Louis Napoleon wrote to M. de Malleville, his Minister of the Interior, demanding the dossiers of both the Strasburg and the Boulogne affairs. The fact that, in order to obtain them, the President was ready to face a ministerial crisis at the very outset of his term of office, suggests that those dossiers contained, or might be expected to contain, important information which the Orleanist Government had not allowed to come to light; but as Louis Napoleon's anxiety to obtain the papers was doubtless due to a desire to destroy all portions of them which might compromise his friends, this is a testimony to the past rather than to the present value of the documents.

The English Government, however, does under certain restrictions allow the examination of the diplomatic correspondence of its agents during this period. The documents utilised for this volume consist of correspondence between the Foreign Office and the British Embassy in Paris, reports from English Consuls in France, and despatches from the British legations in Switzerland, Tuscany, and the other states through which Louis Napoleon wandered during his long exile. In this connexion I have to thank Mr Hubert Hall, of the Record Office, for much courtesy and kindness.

The few unpublished letters of Louis Napoleon

quoted in this volume are contained in various collections in the Additional MSS. department of the British Museum : by permission of the curators, one of these letters has been reproduced in facsimile. For a similar permission, in the case of documents preserved among the Municipal Archives of Geneva, I am indebted to the *Conseil Administratif* of that city.

LONDON, 1909.

NOTE TO SECOND EDITION

The present edition has been revised in the light of such small additions as recent years have made to the sources for Louis Napoleon's early life. A few new letters have been added to the first appendix, and the bibliography has been brought up to date.

CAMBRIDGE, 1924.

NOTE TO NEW IMPRESSION

The text remains unchanged, but the bibliography has again been brought up to date.

STANDING STONE, 1929.

NOTE TO THIRD EDITION

Apart from the removal of a few surviving misprints, the only change made in the present edition is the inclusion of a third appendix, dealing with the effects upon Louis Napoleon's later policy of his early intensive study of his uncle's career. This material originally appeared in a special supplement of *The Times*, produced on the centenary of Napoleon's death : it is here reprinted by kind permission of the publishers.

CAMBRIDGE, 1949.

CONTENTS

CHAP.		PAGE
I.	THE BIRTH OF THE NAPOLEONIC LEGEND	1
II.	THE BIRTH OF LOUIS NAPOLEON	20
III.	EXILE AND EDUCATION	34
IV.	THE FIRST ATTEMPT TO DELIVER ITALY	62
V.	LOUIS NAPOLEON A POLITICAL APPRENTICE	79
VI.	THE FIRST CLAIM TO THE INHERITANCE	101
VII.	LOUIS NAPOLEON A POLITICAL PRETENDER	132
VIII.	THE SECOND CLAIM TO THE INHERITANCE	167
IX.	LOUIS NAPOLEON A POLITICAL PRISONER	196
X.	LOUIS NAPOLEON REGAINS HIS LIBERTY	235
XI.	LOUIS NAPOLEON REGAINS HIS CITIZENSHIP	267
XII.	AFTER MANY DAYS	296

APPENDIX A
SOME EARLY LETTERS OF LOUIS NAPOLEON . . . 331

APPENDIX B
BIBLIOGRAPHY 354

APPENDIX C
LOUIS NAPOLEON AND THE FIRST EMPIRE . . . 373

INDEX 389

ILLUSTRATIONS

	FACE PAGE
Louis Napoleon in 1836, *ætat.* 28 . .	*Frontispiece*
Facsimile of Letter from Louis Napoleon to General Sir Robert Wilson in 1836	92, 93
Facsimile of Louis Napoleon's Proclamation to the Inhabitants of Pas-de-Calais in 1840 . . .	172
Porte de Calais, Boulogne	182
Louis Napoleon's Prison at Boulogne	183
La Grosse Tour, Ham	198
Facsimile of Opening Clauses of Louis Napoleon's Draft for Treaty of Alliance with the Duke of Brunswick . .	238
Louis Napoleon's Prison at Ham	248
Facsimile of Smith's Attested Copy of Louis Napoleon's Draft for Treaty with the Duke of Brunswick .	368, 369

THE RISE OF LOUIS NAPOLEON

CHAPTER I

THE BIRTH OF THE NAPOLEONIC LEGEND

O bienheureux malheur plein de tant d'advantage
Qu'il rende le vaincu des ans victorieux!
Philippe Desportes.

THE close of the year 1814 saw what was to all appearance the definite conclusion of an epoch without parallel in the history of modern Europe. Since the beginning of the century, that history had been in effect the biography of one man. And now at last the man had fallen, with every circumstance of finality. Neither Napoleon himself nor any of his name or race was ever again to ascend the throne of France. The representatives of the ancient dynasties, in taking up once more the task of governing Europe for themselves, had readily and unanimously come to this decision. A little less easily, with not quite such unbroken unanimity, but still with perfect confidence that their decision once reached would be conclusive and incontestable, they were now proceeding to the political reconstruction of Europe—in other words, to the division of the spoils of victory.

A few months later the Congress of Vienna was rudely reminded that the man after all was not yet exhausted. The news of Napoleon's return from Elba was received by the assembled potentates with very pardonable surprise; for never had his star seemed lower than at this time. The final collapse of his power, in spite of the brilliant winter campaign of 1814, had been unexpectedly sudden. France had not rallied to him in his dark days as she had to Louis XIV a hundred years before. The truth is that even in France, during the period of his actual rule, Napoleon never enjoyed anything approaching to the unanimous hero worship of which he afterwards became the object. In the year 1814 nothing had occurred to obscure the magnitude and importance of the discontent to which Napoleon's rule had given rise in France itself. If later these discontents have been generally unrecognised, or realised very imperfectly, this may in part be due to the fact that, while a vast literature has grown up round the Napoleonic campaigns, the internal history of France under the First Empire has to this day hardly received its fair share of attention. But chiefly it is owing to the impression produced by Napoleon's striking and apparently overwhelming success in the spring of 1815. In remembering the triumphant march from Grenoble to Paris, it is easy to forget that from large portions of France Napoleon could count at no time on more than a passive acquiescence in his rule; that towards the end of his reign he was, outside the army and certain localities such as the eastern provinces, positively unpopular, actively disliked. Even the army seemed to have failed him at the end. Indeed the solemn sanction, with which Europe forbade any restoration of his power, appeared for a moment almost unnecessary; for France seemed voluntarily to have abandoned him. The restoration of the Bourbons had been represented as the act of the French nation; the allies, and especially Alexander of Russia, posed as liberators and not conquerors. France had acquiesced in the restoration—without enthusiasm, it is true, but without visible protest—and in Paris itself there was show enough of popular welcome to make the rôle of Louis and of the allies not altogether incredible. There was no great love for King Log, but the memories of King Stork were too recent for his depredations to be forgotten; and many, who did not pretend to rejoice at the restoration of the Bourbons, were yet unfeignedly relieved at the cessation of the ceaseless drain of men and money which the later and more fantastic of Napoleon's schemes had imposed on them. There was moreover in France, as in the rest of Europe, a sturdy and genuine spirit of constitutional liberalism afloat; and at this time France, like the rest of Europe, still regarded the overthrow of the Napoleonic despotism as a preliminary to the attainment of some form of self-government. Little wonder that the general impression of the Congress of Vienna, on hearing the first news of Napoleon's return, was one of almost incredulous surprise; when even Wellington, who had but recently come to the congress from Paris after some months' service as British ambassador to the restored Bourbon court, could only conclude that Napoleon 'had acted on false or no information, and that the king would destroy him without difficulty in a short time.'

This prophecy was signally falsified: but those who regard it merely as a portentous blunder, arguing a complete lack of insight into popular feeling, misunderstand the true nature of Napoleon's achievement in the spring of 1815. That achievement, dramatic and unprecedented as it was, was the personal triumph of a great general whom his troops hail as *imperator* even on the morning after defeat, not the welcome of a sovereign whom his longing subjects greet on his return as the saviour of his country.[1] The *bourgeois* population for the most part stood aside in indifference or in sullen silence. Napoleon might have found it harder to maintain his seat on the French throne

[1] This title was actually proposed for Napoleon by a member of the newly assembled Chamber of Deputies (Felix Lepelletier), and expressly negatived by an overwhelming majority of the assembly. Nothing could be more significant of the true attitude of thoughtful contemporary opinion in France towards the returned emperor than the temper of the deputies as revealed in their debates during this short session of June 1815.

than to win his way back to it, even had no foreign hand been raised to pull him down. For when he set forth on his last campaign, he left behind him many who feared the consequences of his possible success even more than those of his probable failure.

But the ease with which he overran France on his return from Elba deceived Europe then, as it was to deceive France itself in the future; and the seeming change in the attitude of France towards Napoleon brought with it a real change in the attitude of Europe towards France. There could be no illusion as to the method of the second restoration of the Bourbons. This time it was frankly as part of the allies' baggage that they were dumped down once more on the throne of their ancestors. The powers were no longer, even by courtesy, mere benevolent spectators. They had imposed the Bourbons as they had imposed the indemnity. And to France, looking back on the event, acceptance of the Bourbon rule became a sign of dependence. It was not Alexander who was remembered as the liberator, but Napoleon himself, whose last appearance on the scene of practical politics had thus gained all the tactical advantage of opposition to the powers that be.

Contemporary observers were for the most part quite unconscious of the great historical significance of 'the hundred days.' To the majority of the statesmen of the period the incidents which culminated in Waterloo appeared to form a brief episode which delayed, without materially modifying, the European settlement of 1815. Even the historians of the following generation persisted in regarding 'the hundred days' as a mere epilogue to the great drama of the First Empire's fall, not realising that it was in point of fact a prologue to the strange romance of the Second Empire's rise. A similar attitude is revealed in the most interesting English study of Napoleon's captivity at St Helena. To Lord Rosebery that captivity is '*The Last Phase*,' and nothing more. But we shall not rightly appreciate the importance of this phase if we ignore the constructive work of Napoleon during his captivity. For St Helena saw not only the end of a great career, but the beginning of a great creation; it was the scene not merely of the death of Napoleon, but of the birth of the Napoleonic Legend. Indirectly, we have here another and still more important result of 'the hundred days.' Great service, as we have seen already, was rendered to the Napoleonic tradition by Napoleon's initial success in 1815 : a greater benefit still was to result to it from the punishment which befell him for his final failure.

At Elba, Napoleon's kingdom must have remained limited to the small territory over which he actually bore rule. So long as he remained there, his horizon seemed to be completely bounded by the narrow straits and shallow seas which swept the few leagues of his island empire. There was something almost toylike in the mimic court, the petty sway in which 'the Emperor'—for he was still suffered to retain the title—affected to take such interest; as in some new Trianon, in which the founder of the empire should imitate the relaxation of the *ancien régime*, when the grandeur of Versailles had grown oppressive. The whole affair smacked too much of the pastoral play. At best, the central figure could not be much more than the exiled duke in the Forest of Arden. If Napoleon had relinquished perforce the painted pomp of Paris, he still affected a philosophic preference for the soothing calm of Porto Ferrajo. This was hardly the rôle on which to base a vindication of his great past; hardly in character with a clamorous appeal for the future of his family. Out of Elba could have come no dynastic resurrection.

But on St Helena all was different. Unwittingly his victorious foes had presented their captive with a singularly effective background for the closing scene of his career. Posed on a solitary rock, alone in mid-Atlantic, he could gather to himself once more an empire world-wide and universal. For Napoleon, to own little was to court contempt; to have nothing was to hold the world in fee. Half a century later the bearer of another great name ceased to rule over a petty Italian principality. Here too an effort was made to turn a small material loss into a great moral gain. But the prisoner of the rock was a cleverer actor than the prisoner of the garden, and, it may be added, was happier in his audience. For if Napoleon was wiser in his generation than Pio Nono, it must be admitted that he was also more fortunate in it.

It is not easy for us to enter into the spirit of that strange age which followed the Congress of Vienna. Yet if we are to understand what came after, it is essential that we should make the attempt. Here was a generation which believed itself to have witnessed one of the most tremendous dramas in all history. It had seen nation after nation go down before Napoleon; coalition after coalition burst asunder and flung in fragmentary confusion by the mere sweep of his great arm: an arm whose strength seemed to grow greater as its weight grew heavier with each successful defiance of international law. To many the very idea of successful opposition had come to appear an idle dream. 'You may strain at your chains, but the man will be too much for you.' This was all Goethe had to say to the authors of the War of Liberation—the sole comment of Germany's greatest mind on the inception of Germany's greatest effort and greatest achievement hitherto. Yet the chains were broken and the man was fallen after all. Little wonder that as before the event there had been many who regarded it as beyond the power of human effort to bring about, so after it there should be some who saw in its unexpected accomplishment a direct intervention of divine providence. Alike in the slow annihilation of the grand army on its retreat from Moscow, and in the swift climax and sudden catastrophe of the Waterloo campaign, was discerned the plain intervention of a God who ruled, and did not merely reign. Nor was this all. Such a reading of the past could not but affect men's expectation for the future. Surely there was now to be inaugurated that golden age of which the older centuries had dreamed, for history might grow dim indeed ere such another prologue could be found for the millennium. Speculations such as these, though far of course from universal, were yet curiously prevalent; it is not easy to peruse the memoirs, the correspondence, the very journalism of the age without finding traces of them —occurring occasionally in most unexpected quarters.

Indeed for a brief moment it seemed as though these vague aspirations might find some sort of fulfilment. Two nations stood out at the close of the Titanic struggle as Napoleon's victors by sea and land. In their power it had been to demand almost any return for their victory. Yet England showed herself at the Congress of Vienna more anxious to secure the abolition of the slave trade than to obtain any adequate commercial or territorial returns for the sacrifices of her long and costly campaigns. And Russia, as personified by Alexander—for the Tsar at this time was the absolute personification of his state—though far from neglectful of such advantages, was engrossed with the idea of establishing a reign of universal peace. The arbitrament of war was to give place to the just award of a brotherhood of Christian kings—who recognised 'that the Christian nation of which they and their peoples form part has really no other sovereign than the sole rightful owner of all power . . . our divine God and Saviour Jesus Christ'; and agreed 'to recommend to their peoples the principles and duties He had committed to mankind.' For some years, indeed, Alexander not only set the example of liberal reform in Poland, but threw the shield of his great influence over the liberal movements of Spain and Italy. Even in Prussia, Frederick William's edict promising a constitution to his people seemed to foreshow the fulfilment of the hopes which the war of liberation had inspired. One alone of the great powers was unmoved by any of the high and generous hopes of the period: Austria dreamed no dreams either of free nations or of free citizenship; Metternich saw no vision, but only vain visionaries whose dangerous imaginings it must be his task to dispel. To that task he set himself with but too swift success.

The weak, well-meaning King of Prussia was the first to succumb. A few hundred students met at the Wartburg to celebrate a double anniversary which appealed to Protestant and patriotic sentiment: at once Frederick William was convinced that repression alone could save Prussia from revolution. Alexander himself was the next to yield to the spell of Metternich, who played so dexterously on the fears that his own cunning had created. England under Castlereagh, and even Canning, turned as it were its face to the wall, and in contemplating the grinding hardships of its own domestic lot—the result in great part of reaction from the vast effort spent on the Napoleonic campaigns—had little pity and no help to extend to the disappointed liberals of the Continent.

Thus it was that throughout Europe those new forces, whose uneasy stirrings kings had turned to their purpose, found themselves after a brief moment of fitful expression once more voiceless and ventless. The Holy Alliance itself—that very band of Christian princes which was to lead in a new reign of enlightenment and peace—took after 1818 the form of a definitely reactionary alliance of governments against the governed. Slowly on the newly risen peoples, great with the consciousness of an unprecedented achievement in the past, great with high hopes of they knew not what vague splendour for the future, settled the heavy pall of Metternich's tyranny. And as one by one the lesser lights died down beneath that dull extinguisher, men's eyes turned slowly to the solitary beacon on the Atlantic rock, and their hearts went out again to the man alone on St Helena.

With such a stage and such an audience, a less consummate actor than Napoleon might have been successful. Mournfully over the ocean rolled the majestic utterances, the mild and beneficent meditations of this latter-day Marcus Aurelius. The halo of unbounded success was exchanged now for the subtler glamour of unmerited failure. Fate and the gods had decreed his fall at Waterloo: true; but he would show them that appeal was yet possible to a higher judgment-court than theirs. Cato might still prefer the beaten cause: and never was appeal made to him more sonorous, more insistent, or more successful. The second Alexander had failed in his great scheme for the foundation of a vast Oriental empire, wherein the rejuvenated peoples of the East should sun themselves in the light of a more than Alexandrine Hellenism. The latter-day Charlemagne had failed in his majestic design for the federation of all Western Europe in a higher harmony than it yet had known. And East and West alike had reason to lament that failure.

Such was the purport of the studied utterances borne to Europe from St Helena; and the liberals of Europe received them gladly. They had been mistaken, it seemed, in imagining that Napoleon's overthrow would be their deliverance: might they not also have been mistaken in supposing that his triumph would have been their undoing? How should they disbelieve his statement that his victory would have been the victory of their own noble hopes, when his defeat had proved their defeat, when his very punishment was in a measure their punishment? Men against whom were directed the irksome restrictions of the Carlsbad Decrees, and the petty intrusions of the Mainz Commissioners, could sympathise with the victim of Sir Hudson Lowe. For as such Napoleon was regarded by his unsuspecting admirers. A new rôle was thus opened to the great actor. Surely he too must have had something of the divine fire in gift for man, that he should thus be chained like a second Prometheus to his rock. But not even the most pathetic conception of all heathen mythology seemed adequate to the promoters of the cult of Napoleon. The French press freely compared his sufferings to those of our Lord. No lesser similitude would now suffice for one in whom ten years earlier many had discerned the visible incarnation of the Antichrist. The transition is more amazing in appearance than in reality. For, admitting the superhuman proportions of the central figure, there could be no intermediate stage : ceasing to be devilish, Napoleon straightway became divine. And if we find the last comparison so startling as to be offensive, we must remember that fifty years later it was employed with even greater freedom by *la bonne presse*, both in France and out of it, when the attempt was being made to launch on a less credulous age the legend of the Prisoner of the Vatican.

The age on which the Napoleonic Legend was sprung was, on the contrary, a curiously credulous one. It was the age of a recurrence towards mediæval ideals in Religion, of a legitimatist restoration in Politics, of the Gothic revival in Architecture, of the romantic reaction in Literature. It was an age which, if it prided itself on anything, was proud that it was not as its predecessor, 'an age of common sense.' And indeed it was not; for in general it was more anxious to avoid the obvious than to attain the truth; or, rather, it was only willing to recognise the truth in the uncommon, and too readily mistook anything uncommon for the truth. In one respect, certainly, it was inferior to its much despised predecessor. The age which rewrote Shakespeare in its own more refined verse, or introduced into Gothic masterpieces the amenities of eighteenth century architecture—this age, whatever else it lacked, possessed a sturdy spirit of self-reliance, a most hardy confidence in its own enlightenment and good judgment. Now the romantic reaction, whatever else it possessed, suffered from a morbid self-depreciation, an excessive mistrust of its own powers. Politically we may now look back on it if we will as a period of respite, a space wherein an overwrought Europe might take breath between the Napoleonic wars and those which were involved in the great national movements which lay before it. But to the contemporary observer no such consolation was forthcoming: to him the age could only appear a period of bathos, a time of small men and little things succeeding to one of great men and tremendous events. So it was that a generation curiously deficient in the historic sense was yet sincerely devoted to the study of history. From the realities of a not very glorious present, men turned eagerly to the glories of a not very real past. And of these, none was more glorious—or less real—than the legendary Napoleon.

The actual Napoleon was not blind to the advantages of his position, though he was careful never wholly to admit them, even to his own followers. 'Our situation here may even have its attractions,' he remarked in one of those studied confidences with which at times he favoured his disciples at St Helena. 'If I had died on the throne amid the clouds of my omnipotence, I should have remained a problem to many; to-day, thanks to my misfortune, they can judge of me naked as I am.' This remark has often been quoted as an admission of the truth on Napoleon's part. It is indeed noteworthy; not, however, as an admission, but as a perversion of the truth. For it stands in precise contradiction to the fact. The clouds which obscured men's judgment of Napoleon were due to the greatness, not of his former power, but of his final misfortune. It was to his actual use of power when he was all-powerful that his critics should have looked, had they wished to see him 'naked as he was.' Had he died in the clear noonday of his fortune, Napoleon might indeed have been remembered as he really was—cruel, brilliant, pitiless. It was precisely the dark clouds which surrounded the setting of his sun that his genius contrived to tinge with every glorious hue.. these were the gorgeous mists which baffled criticism, and enabled him—in his own phrase —'to remain a problem to many.' It is true that the years spent at St Helena were of immense service to the Napoleonic tradition. But this was not because, stripped of the trappings of power, he could there be seen in utter nakedness. On the contrary, it was because he was there able to wrap himself in a mantle far more mystic and majestic, and far less penetrable to the shafts of criticism, than any external circumstance of power; because he there succeeded in evading the light of common day—the most serviceable light after all for those who would see things as they are. By a deliberately eclectic representation or misrepresentation of his own past, part of his career was brought into prominence, while part of it was withdrawn into obscurity. Consciously or unconsciously, Napoleon availed himself in this process of a habit of men's minds which was as beneficial to the tradition of the First Empire as it has since proved disastrous to the memory of the second. It is the fact that it is to the beginning or the ending of an institution that men are apt to look, when they seek to pronounce judgment on its nature. Now the beginning of Napoleon's career was on the whole its least vulnerable point. Never was his military genius more brilliantly displayed than in the Italian campaign of 1796. Nor did any of his later triumphs appeal more strongly to the imagination of France than his half-accomplished Egyptian exploit of 1799. Napoleon here had comparatively little to do with his facts save to direct attention to them. But with the close of the empire it was not so. The motives which inspired the hundred days' raid were selfish; the methods of its execution were faulty; the results of its failure were disastrous to France. The political innovations of Constant's framing, which Napoleon flung as a sop to liberal opinion, were palpably insincere: the military tactics of the concluding campaign were not free from grave error. With deliberate purpose and extraordinary success he now proceeded to explain away the latter, and to enhance the importance of the former. The mistakes which lost Waterloo were those of subordinates; the steps he had taken in the path of liberal reform were as nothing to the progress he had really intended in that direction.

The legend took the form its author and subject had desired. He was remembered as the 'little corporal,' the hero of the Italian campaign, the husband of the humble Josephine, not yet allied in marriage to one of the ancient dynasties of Europe. Or else, he was the Emperor of 1815, with his pale, haunted face; deserted now by his Austrian queen, granting liberal reforms in France, turning grandly at bay to face the banded forces of reactionary Europe, and finally,

> 'Broken in a strain of fate
> And leagued kings at Waterloo,
> When the people's hands let go.'

And so, in recollecting the real glory of the empire's inception and the fictitious glamour of its close, Europe began to forget the insolent oppression of the heyday of the imperial rule. France too forgot—what only by forgetting could she have forgiven—that it was Napoleon and none other who had lost her her natural frontiers, the Rhine and the Alps : forgot in fact the vast abuse of his unparalleled power ; remembering only the glory of its acquisition and the tragedy of its loss.

This then was the heritage which after Napoleon's death in 1821 lay waiting, till one of his proscribed name and race should be found courageous enough to lay claim to it. It was a task from which the boldest might well shrink. It was not merely that the claimant must be willing to take his life in his hand, ready if need were that his death should be his sole contribution to the imperial cause. This was true, but it would only be the beginning of his troubles. In such an enterprise initial success was only a degree less hazardous than initial failure. For the name of Napoleon, admirable as a stepping-stone to power, might become a mere embarrassment when power was won.[1] In the nature of things, it was a name reserved for ever to its first holder : any other who bore it must challenge comparison with the greatest general in history. But even this was not all. The subtle alchemy which had been applied to all Napoleon's motives and actions had reduced the wars themselves to

[1] For a detailed consideration of the ways in which a contemplation of Napoleon's career was later to mislead his nephew, making his study of the History of the First Empire a chief contributory cause to the ultimate downfall of the Second, see Appendix C, page 373 below.

DIFFICULTIES OF NAPOLEON'S SUCCESSOR

the position of mere by-products: glorious as they were, they had only been his ineffectual strivings after a yet more glorious peace. And it was the tradition of this idealised Napoleon that his would-be successor must take up; the tradition of a man whose greatness had escaped exaggeration only where exaggeration was impossible, whose faults had been forgotten, whose aims had been idealised, whose achievements had been transcended in the light of an uncritical legend. Not even Napoleon risen from the dead could have been certain of success in such an enterprise. The prophet himself, allowed to descend from his chariot of fire, might have found his mantle grown too large for him.

CHAPTER II

THE BIRTH OF LOUIS NAPOLEON

> In vera nescis nullum fore morte alium te
> Qui possit vivus tibi te lugere peremptum
> Stansque jacentem.
>
> LUCRETIUS.

> Thou know'st not there shall not be other thou
> When thou art dead indeed that can tell how
> Alive to waile thee dying,
> Standing to waile thee lying.
>
> JOHN FLORIO.

IT is time that we turn from the heritage to the heir, from the mantle to the man who was destined to wear it, and to do so we must go back to the halcyon days of the First Empire. On April 20, 1808, Queen Hortense, wife of Louis, King of Holland, gave birth in the early morning to her third son, the future founder of the Second Empire. He was the first child of the imperial house who was born a prince, for Napoleon was still faithful to his childless empress; and Louis had not yet been promoted to his uneasy throne when his other two sons were born. Of these the elder had already died, so that one life alone—that of his four-year-old brother, Napoleon Louis—stood between the infant born in the centre of Paris, and the ultimate succession to the vast empire of which that city was then the capital.

His birth was a source of lively satisfaction to the imperial house. Napoleon on the Spanish frontier, on the point of adding a new kingdom to the dominions of his dynasty, rejoiced at the timely birth of a new heir. From Bayonne he wrote to congratulate Hortense; and along the whole Spanish frontier French cannon saluted the birth of a child, who might as easily have become King of Spain as Emperor of the French. A still warmer letter, breathing a yet greater delight, came to Hortense from her mother Josephine. For to her the news was of more than dynastic importance. Herself beyond hope of bearing an heir to Napoleon, she lived already in perpetual fear of the fate which soon afterwards befell her. For the unhappy marriage of Hortense to Louis Napoleon she had herself been mainly responsible. Alone among her husband's family, Louis had seemed to bear her no ill-will, and she hoped by marrying him to her daughter to secure the powerful support of Napoleon's favourite brother.

Regarded as a political alliance, there had been much to recommend the marriage. It formed a fresh link between the two families of Beauharnais and Bonaparte; and if Napoleon himself were to be denied a son, it might well seem that he could hope for no better heir than one who should unite the many excellent qualities of Louis and Hortense.

At the time of her marriage, in January 1802, Hortense was a beautiful girl of nineteen, whose grace and charm had already won her golden opinions in Paris, and whose stirring songs—for she was a musician of no small merit—were soon to be heard throughout the length and breadth of France. Louis, her husband, though not the ablest, was in many ways the most estimable of Napoleon's brothers. By nature quiet, studious, retiring, he had been forced by Napoleon to adopt a military life. In this capacity he had shown himself in Italy a brave but unambitious soldier; a strict but unsympathetic disciplinarian. But his military career was already closed at the time of his marriage. Indeed, since his return from the Egyptian expedition in 1799, his health had rendered active military service impossible for him. After occupying a series of important civil positions, he was placed by his brother, in June 1806, on the throne of Holland. For Napoleon was at this time engaged in converting a polite fiction into a substantial truth: henceforth when saluting a fellow-monarch as *Sire, mon frère*, he would allude to a physical fact. His brother of Holland retained his regal style for something less than four years. Louis' brief reign was marked by a conscientious attempt to govern in the interests of his subjects, but his position was from the first an impossible one.

Ever behind him loomed his inexorable brother, sternly demanding the levies of men, money, and munitions, which his incessant campaigns entailed.

Sincerely desirous of being king by the will of his people, and for their good, Louis was not long suffered to forget that he was in fact king by grace of Napoleon, and at his pleasure. From the first the two titles could hardly be reconciled; they became plainly incompatible when Napoleon began to enforce strictly the observance of his Berlin Decrees. To an essentially commercial community, inhabiting a country with a long coast-line facing the continental ports of England, any interruption of the English trade spelt misery, any absolute cessation of it meant sheer ruin. Louis might hope to mitigate the other Napoleonic exactions, nor were they in themselves insupportable. But nothing short of the complete abrogation of the Continental System could save Holland, and nothing less than its most rigorous enforcement could satisfy Napoleon. For it was a characteristic feature of the fantastic scheme that its entire success depended on the completeness with which it was put into execution; one gap would render useless the whole hedge so laboriously constructed. The natural result followed. In the summer of 1810, Louis, who had already some two years earlier refused promotion to the throne of Spain, resigned his thankless office in Holland, abdicating in favour of his elder son, or in his default, of the future Napoleon III. In accepting the kingdom, in the first instance, he had shown a weakness which betrayed his better judgment; nor had his actual reign been free from certain ineptitudes and absurdities which gave point to his brother's merciless criticisms. But the manner of its close was not undignified: the calm surrender of an office which he could not hope to hold with honour, and the fearless protest against the annexation of his kingdom to the French Empire, serve to stamp the character of the King of Holland as that of a highminded and honest man. 'From the throne he had mounted amid the curses of his people, he descended amid their tears,' says Landor; and indeed, his subjects could not but recognise the sincerity of the goodwill which had cost their sovereign his crown.

When Louis left Holland to lead a life of retirement at Toeplitz, Hortense did not accompany him, but returned with her children to her old home at St Leu. For his brief reign had cost Louis the affection not only of his brother but of his wife.

Hortense—as her songs bear witness—was an enthusiastic admirer of Napoleon, and no less attached than her soldier brother, Eugène, to the military glory of France. She could not in the least sympathise with the process of acclimatisation by which patriotism came to her husband to mean loyalty to his adopted country, Holland. To her there could only be one *patrie*, and any opposition to the imperious demands which came from Paris was an act of treachery to Napoleon and disloyalty to France.

Her impetuous nature caused Hortense to make no secret of her opinions; she became the head of the French party in the little court at the Hague, as her husband was of the Dutch. As early as 1807, Napoleon warned his brother that this open antagonism threatened to give public scandal. Unfortunately, the political differences of Hortense and her husband were not the sole cause of their estrangement. Personal misunderstandings were already making cordial relations between them impossible. It is improbable that either had ever really loved the other; certainly Hortense had never pretended to regard her husband with more than dutiful attachment. His good qualities—like her own—were many, but they were not such as she could appreciate: his faults were precisely those which she could not endure. There was too much truth in Napoleon's stricture: 'You treat a young woman as though you were drilling a regiment'; and Hortense was the last woman in the world to tolerate a martinet for a husband. At no time a very ardent lover, Louis grew ever more taciturn and unapproachable as he grew older; he suffered from a chronic rheumatism contracted in Egypt, and the settled melancholy of his later years was possibly a consequence—indeed, a symptom—of the disease with which he was afflicted. It would be a fruitless task to seek to apportion the blame of the breach between the two; but Hortense's own explanation seems the true one: each had just the faults which rendered fatal the faults of the other. The real blame must rest elsewhere: with the brother who had over-ruled Louis' protests; still more with the mother who sacrificed to her own hopes and fears the happiness of her child.

For Josephine, indeed, the hopes had already been disappointed, the fears already fulfilled, even before the practical dissolution of her daughter's marriage in 1810. At no time after the death of Hortense's eldest son had there been any real doubt of Napoleon's intention to seek a new wife; and when in November 1810 the state christening of the future Napoleon III took place at Fontainebleau, it was the new Empress, Marie Louise of Austria, who acted with Napoleon as godparent. At the Emperor's request the child had been named Charles Louis Napoleon, but the first of these names was soon dropped, and it was as Louis Napoleon that the prince was generally known for the next forty years.

The year which followed the christening, though without incident of any kind in the life of the infant prince, saw the birth of two children whose careers could not but affect materially his future fortunes. In March a son was born to Napoleon himself, and the magnificent ceremony of the preceding year was thrown into the shade by that attending the baptism of the ill-starred King of Rome. Prince Louis' chance of becoming Napoleon's heir was thus already greatly diminished, and his prospects were not improved by the birth, in October, of another son to Hortense, whose father was not Louis of Holland but the Comte de Flahaut. Under the title of the Duc de

Morny, this child was destined to win European fame as one of the most statesmanlike of the supporters of the Second Empire. But great as were the services he was to render to his half-brother in his life, they were hardly greater than the disservice his birth could not but occasion him. For it gave point and circumstance to an assertion freely made by the enemies of his house in later years; that Napoleon III had in his veins no drop of Napoleonic blood, that his undoubted dissimilarity of feature and physique to other members of the Napoleonic family was to be accounted for by attributing his fatherhood to a certain Admiral Verhuel, an acquaintance of Hortense; and that the absence of the King of Holland at the birth and baptism of the child was a tacit disavowal of paternity. It has even been asserted that King Louis *explicitly* denied it in a letter addressed to the Pope in 1831; but a single sentence from an apocryphal letter, unsupported by documentary evidence, cannot claim serious attention when in flat contradiction to it stand numerous authentic avowals made by King Louis at every period of his subsequent life, that the boy was indeed his son. As his son he announced his birth to his people assembled in his capital, with all the formality usual on such an occasion. As his son he addressed him, or alluded to him, in many letters of undoubted authenticity; and, finally, to 'my sole surviving son, Louis Napoleon,' he left in his will his entire property. That the king was himself in error as to the child's parentage is not contended even by those who have raised the question ; their assumption is that he was prevailed upon to conceal his knowledge. But, apart from the fact that Louis of Holland was certainly incapable of successful concealment, it is most improbable that any inducement, personal or political, would have prevailed on him to attempt concealment in such a case. As a matter of fact no such inducements existed. The child was a weakling, seemingly little likely to survive his sturdy elder brother. After 1811 his political prospects were of the scantiest, while Louis' personal relations with his wife and brother were not such as to induce him to recognise the child through any consideration of their feelings. The very fact which has served as the basis for the whole assertion — the known faithlessness of Hortense after 1810—is itself a most cogent argument against the supposition that King Louis could either have been himself deceived, or desirous of deceiving others in this matter.[1]

The author of this unhappy marriage did not long survive the double indignity of her own divorce and her daughter's disgrace. The calamities of the closing years of the empire, which passed serenely over the unconscious head of Prince Louis, weighed all too heavily on Josephine. A year before her death the haggard remnant of the Grand

---

[1] For a further discussion of this question, see Appendix B, p. 358.

Army made its way back to France; and in their stony faces Paris must have read something of the message which Athens learned from the scattered survivors of the Sicilian Expedition. Hortense was present when Napoleon bade farewell to his National Guard, before starting for his brilliant defensive campaign of 1814. And when that campaign was over and the allies were at the gates of Paris, it was Hortense who vainly endeavoured to persuade the Empress to hold the city to the last. In this she failed: Marie Louise fled, the city was pronounced untenable; and Hortense was forced to seek safety for her children by taking refuge with her mother at her estate in Navarre. After Napoleon had been installed in his island empire at Elba, they returned to Malmaison; and there it was that Josephine, unable to share the Emperor's exile, died before his return.

The allied princes treated Hortense and her family with great respect. Among her visitors at this time was the King of Prussia, who brought his two boys to see her children. The incident, trivial enough in itself, acquires a curious interest in the light of later history. For the younger son of King William was to become the first German Emperor; and the younger son of Queen Hortense seems likely long to be known as the last Emperor of the French. No omens of the portentous future are recorded of this their first meeting; but we can imagine—and half envy—the delight with which the mediæval chronicler would have seized and embellished this nursery encounter of the victor and the victim of Sedan. At times the modern historian is tempted to regret the lost privileges of his predecessors; tempted even to regard as perverse the code which still permits him to point a moral, but no longer suffers him to adorn a tale.

Another and more frequent royal visitor at Malmaison was the Tsar Alexander, who displayed towards Hortense and her children all that chivalrous tenderness of which his nature was capable. At this time he was still liberal in his political views. Thus he refused to attend a solemn Te Deum which was celebrated in the presence of the allies for the return of the Bourbons; instead, he left Paris for the occasion, and spent the day at Malmaison with Queen Hortense.[1] Often he discussed with her the future prospects of France; and always he expressed the conviction that 'the restoration of the Bourbons was a great mistake, and that France ought to have been left free to choose its own sovereign.'[2] His sympathy towards Hortense took more practical form. Not only did he shield her from any annoyance at the hands of the restored Bourbons,

[1] Reported in unpublished portions of Queen Hortense's Memoirs, and quoted from them by Louis Napoleon in a letter written to remonstrate with the Tsar Nicholas on his opposition to the assumption of the title Napoleon III. This letter Louis Napoleon read to Cowley, the British Ambassador, on the 24th of January 1853. 'It is perhaps as able a document as ever came from the emperor's pen,' was Cowley's comment, 'and as far as my humble opinion is of any weight, this is no mean praise.'—(Cowley to Lord John Russell, 25th January 1853.)

[2] *Ibid.*

but he secured for her the estate of St Leu as a duchy, to be held by her under the title she had already adopted since her husband's abdication of the crown of Holland. Her position, notwithstanding, was not an easy one. To the returned *émigrés* she was an object of suspicion and dislike, while the less fortunate Bonapartists looked with some disfavour on her cordial relations with Napoleon's conquerors. Nor was she free from private troubles. As a result of proceedings instituted by King Louis in the French law-courts in 1814, an award was made by which the elder son was handed over to his father's care, though the younger was allowed to remain with Hortense. The result was a great grief to her; but other news which reached her on the same day (6th March) as the award, left her little time to mourn her domestic misfortunes. Napoleon had landed in France. A fortnight later he was in Paris.

In the hurried events of the hundred days Hortense and her children played a prominent part, for Napoleon's own son, with the Empress Marie Louise, was in the hands of the allies. It was therefore the two sons of Hortense whom Napoleon presented to his reassembled legions in the Place du Carrousel. Together they were present at the brilliant but unconvincing ceremony with which Napoleon inaugurated his liberal constitution, on the Champ de Mars. Together they visited the Emperor to bid him good-bye on the eve of his departure for the Waterloo campaign.

The account of Louis' last interview with his uncle is well known, though it rests on poor authority.[1] The Emperor—for the story is at any rate worthy of repetition—was in consultation with Marshal Soult, deep in the study of the coming campaign. To him ran a seven-year-old boy, who flung his tearful face in his uncle's lap. 'What ails you, Louis?' said Napoleon, little pleased to be so interrupted at such a moment. 'Sir, my governess tells me you are going to the war. Oh do not go, do not go.' Softened a little, the Emperor answered more kindly, 'Why not, child? It is not the first time I have been to the wars. What is there to cry about? I shall be back again directly.' 'Uncle dear, the wicked allies want to kill you. Please uncle, please let me go with you.' The grim warrior was touched now, and silent for a moment, as he kissed his favourite nephew. Then calling the child's mother to him he said, 'Take the boy, and scold his governess for working on his feelings.' And again more tenderly to Marshal Soult, who had been visibly touched by the scene: 'There, Marshal, kiss the boy: he will have a good heart and a lofty soul . . . Perhaps after all he is the hope of my race.'

If these were not the words with which Napoleon I bade farewell to Napoleon III— and it is far from certain that they were—at least they ought to have been. For indeed

[1] See Appendix B, p. 360.

the frail child whom he left behind at Paris was to pick up the crown let fall at Waterloo, to wear it longer than his uncle himself had done, and only after a yet more strange eventful history than his, himself to drop it in the still deeper downfall of Sedan. And when all deductions have been made, and all detractions taken into account, there still remains proof enough of an essential kindliness of heart and loftiness of conception displayed by Louis Napoleon at every portion of his career.

CHAPTER III

EXILE AND EDUCATION

Travel, in the younger sort, is a part of education. BACON.

Time may be employed to more advantage from nineteen to twenty-four almost in any way than in travelling. . . . How much more would a young man improve if he were to study during those years. DR JOHNSON.

IN the misfortunes which Napoleon's raid brought upon France Hortense had her full share. After the second restoration Alexander was no longer disposed to screen her from the attacks of the Bourbons; and the memory of his former favours only served to increase their animosity towards her. On July 19, 1815, she was informed that she must leave Paris immediately with her children, and withdraw from French territory.

The exiles were accompanied to the frontier by a guard of Austrian troops, and before the end of their journey had reason to be glad of their escort. For since the second overthrow of Napoleon large districts in the south of France had been given over to a royalist and clerical reign of terror. At Dijon, a hostile mob surrounded Hortense's carriage, and royalist officers broke into her apartment, demanding her arrest. Thus it was, indebted to foreign troops for their safe passage out of their own country, that Hortense and her sons passed into exile.

Their troubles were not at an end when they had left French soil behind them, for the narrowed frontier of France did not mark the limits of the Bourbon power for persecution. With difficulty the fugitives obtained permission to tarry a few days at Geneva, before proceeding to Aix in Savoy. Here Hortense was allowed to remain for a little time; and it was during her short sojourn at Aix that her husband sent for his elder son, whom the French law-courts had awarded to his custody. The parting was a sad one for both mother and brother, and to young Louis it was a real misfortune. Already deprived of a father's care, he was now to lose the companionship of his brother. It is true that his mother's affection for him was increased by the severance of these other ties. But this was hardly a compensation for the other loss; indeed, in a sense, it was an aggravation of it. Louis at this time was a shy, delicate boy, whose occasional shrewd remarks alone gave promise of an intellect of any unusual capacity. It is possible that the paternal guidance of even so eccentric a father as King Louis of Holland might have been of value, in the development of an intelligence as curiously precocious in some ways as it was unaccountably backward in others. Beyond question, it was the society of other boys, rather than the concentration upon him of his mother's well-meaning but somewhat absurd precautions, which he needed to give vigour to a disposition naturally the reverse of robust.

In October 1815 the Great Powers once again requested Hortense and her son to "move on." This time they indicated Switzerland as a place where her sojourn would be comparatively inoffensive. But even so, she was to remain under the closest scrutiny and restriction. She was to live in the canton of St Gall, and never to go outside of it; and she was to remain under the surveillance of the ministers of the four Powers. Even this small room was, however, denied to her by the Swiss Diet; for on hearing of the decision of the allies it hastily decreed that no member of the Bonaparte family should be suffered to dwell in Swiss territory on any conditions whatsoever. In this strait, Hortense turned to a member of her family who retained an official position of some political importance. Her cousin, Stéphanie de Beauharnais, was the wife of the Grand Duke of Baden; and in this duchy, if nowhere else, the Bonapartes might expect some measure of official protection. Accordingly, in November 1815, the queen and her remaining son set out for Constance. To reach this town it was necessary to pass through Switzerland. Twice on their journey the travellers' rooms were invaded by police officers; once Hortense was actually placed under arrest.

Early in December the refugees arrived at Constance, where they were allowed to remain in peace for something over a year. In May 1816, however,

Hortense proceeded to Berg, in Bavaria, on a visit to her brother Eugène. Here, as in Baden, the Beauharnais were connected by marriage with the existing dynasties; for Napoleon had married Prince Eugène to a daughter of the King of Bavaria. The summer months of 1816 were passed very pleasantly by Louis Napoleon in the company of Eugène's five children: in their friendships the eight-year-old boy found some compensation for the loss of his own brother. Soon after her return to Constance it became clear to Hortense that she would not be allowed to make her permanent home in Baden. Early in 1817 she was definitely requested by the court of Baden to leave Constance. This request was 'grounded it seems on her mode of living, and the apparent extent of her correspondence.'[1]

Hortense hesitated for a while whether she should seek a final home in Bavaria, or Switzerland. Although the decree against her residence in Switzerland was still in force, she had been allowed, for the good of her health, to make a short stay in one of the Swiss cantons in 1816. She now received from the canton of Thurgau a definite invitation to reside in its territory. Encouraged by these tokens of a more tolerant attitude on the part of the Swiss authorities, Hortense purchased in February 1817 an old country house at Arenenberg, in the friendly canton of Thurgau. Her previous experience at the hands of

[1] Stratford Canning to Castlereagh. Berne, 21st February 1817.

the Great Powers led her, however, to insert a clause into the deed of sale, stipulating that the transaction should not be binding on her if the government refused to sanction her residence at Arenenberg.[1]

That there would be long and vexatious opposition to her settlement in Thurgau, Hortense had every reason to expect. Apart from this, the *château* was in no state for immediate occupation: extensive alterations were necessary to turn the almost ruinous building into a comfortable country house. For her immediate use, Hortense therefore purchased a house at Augsburg, in Bavaria; and thither she proceeded in May 1817, on her departure from Baden.

Into the details of the grave debates, with which ambassadors and ministers of the five Great Powers discussed their attitude towards this act of the Duchess of St Leu, it is hardly necessary for us to enter. As an instance of the portentous gravity with which they regarded her every movement, it may suffice if we give one brief extract from the lengthy despatch of the English envoy in Switzerland, on the morrow of the purchase.

'My first step,' wrote Stratford Canning to Castlereagh, in February 1817, 'has been to consult with the other ministers concerned in the business, not omitting the French envoy. They are unanimous, and I confess that I agree with them, in the opinion that we have at present no adequate means

[1] Canning to Castlereagh, 21st Feb. 1817.

of controuling either the correspondence or the movements of Madame de St Leu. The position which she has selected on the banks of the Lake of Constance, at the very extremity of Switzerland, whether accidentally or not, is of itself calculated to render observation difficult. The police of the canton of Thurgovie, as in most parts of Switzerland, is too weak to be depended on. The employment of secret agents would be attended with expense, and from the remoteness of the situation would be exposed to continual failure. An avowed agent placed on the spot, and authorised to inspect her correspondence—by which alone it may be presumed that any mischief can be done—would doubtless be able to exercise an effectual control; but there is nothing in the protocol to justify any interference of so direct a nature.'[1]

For some time it appeared that these reasons would induce the allies to insist on the exclusion of Hortense from Thurgau. In July 1817 the ambassadors of the four Powers at Paris signed an official note, which they sent to the president of the Swiss Diet, through the Swiss chargé d'affaires in Paris.[2] This note required that the diet should enforce its decree of 1815; and the diet accordingly announced once more its intention of so doing.[3] None the less, Hortense did not abandon her purchase, and continued to alter and enlarge it, even paying

[1] Canning to Castlereagh, 21st Feb. 1817.
[2] *Ibid.*, 1st August 1817.
[3] *Ibid.*

occasional visits to Arenenberg to supervise the improvements herself. But it was not until 1821, when the death of Napoleon had somewhat allayed the anxieties of the Great Powers, that she was able finally to enter into possession of her new abode. This was to be her real home until the time of her death, sixteen years later; but a natural love of travel led her to spend almost half her life away from it. For these sixteen years, however, it was the home to which Louis returned in the intervals of his other pursuits. The exiles were fortunate in their final resting-place; for though of a rather sombre grandeur, no more lovely view could have been found, than that from the *château* looking over the Rhine as it leaves Lake Constance.

Hitherto the prince had been less fortunate in the matter of his education. The troubled years of the First Empire's close had come too early to affect his life. But the period of homeless wandering which followed rendered difficult any systematised study; and the uncertainty as to which parent was to be entrusted with the charge of his upbringing had a further unfortunate effect. Although in 1815 King Louis had only established his claim to the elder brother, yet as late as 1819 in a letter to Hortense he had written, 'in a certain time Louis also must come to me.' In the same letter he had criticised very severely the method of instruction adopted by Louis' first teacher, the Abbé Bertrand. The abbé was indeed an incompetent tutor. Cheery, courteous and good-natured, his knowledge was superficial, and his method of imparting it had the effect of rendering any subject he dealt with distasteful to his pupil, whom he still addressed by his nursery nickname of Oui-Oui. Louis was, in fact, a very docile child, but even for him the abbé proved too poor a disciplinarian. Though the father's criticism was just, the threat with which it was backed had the effect of postponing its good effects. For Hortense hesitated to engage another tutor while still uncertain whether she would be allowed to keep the younger son under her care. It was not until June 1820, when she had realised that her husband was not likely to act on his threat, that she found a new tutor in the person of Philip Lebas. The choice was a singularly happy one. Son of a republican leader who had figured in the great revolution, he had himself served with credit in the closing campaigns of the empire. Though only twenty-five years old, he was already a husband and a father, and he was glad to exchange a poorly paid civil post for the tutorship which Hortense offered him. A resolute disciplinarian, an upright and conscientious teacher, he was also a genuine scholar whose subsequent career was one of well-merited distinction. A fortnight after his arrival, in a letter to his father-in-law in Paris, Lebas thus describes his pupil. 'I cannot hide from myself the fact that my task will be anything but an easy one. My pupil is twelve years old; he has aptitude, but is not well advanced: I might even say that his knowledge on a great many points is practically nil. It would have been much more satisfactory to me, had I taken him in hand at the age of seven or eight. As it is, I find myself in the position of an architect who is bidden to make habitable an ill-built house: he has to pull down, even to lay the foundations afresh, if he would attain his object. Still I must not lose courage; though I see little love of work in my pupil, I have at least found more docility than I expected, a desire to please me, a fear of dissatisfying me, and an excellent heart. With qualities such as these one has something to build on.'

Lebas' orderly mind was much perturbed by the lack of rule which he found in the boy's life hitherto. 'When I came here,' he writes three weeks later, 'I found a child who got up at 7, or 8, or even 9' (poor Lebas is quite overcome by the bare idea of this last hour), 'according as the abbé had more or less desire for sleep.' The new tutor stops all this at once, substituting the following rather Draconian regime: up at 6; walk on the mountain-side till 7; 7 to 8.30, grammar; 8.30 to 9, recreation; 9 to 10.30, Latin; 10.30, lunch. At 12.30 they start work again with a lesson in arithmetic, followed at 1 by instruction in German or in writing. At 2 a Greek lesson—which the prince likes; from 3 to 4 he has a swimming lesson; from 4 to 6 he learns geography and history. Dinner follows at 6, and a walk afterwards; then upstairs at 8, where the boy makes fair copies of his exercises, or listens—in a state of acute mental indigestion, one would imagine—to fine passages of prose or verse read to him by his tutor. At 9 he goes to bed. Lebas is pleased, but not altogether satisfied with this prospect · next year, however, he hopes to turn to account the time spent on the two walks, by administering during them peripatetic doses of instruction in astronomy and natural history.

This routine seems to have been maintained for some little time: in October there is no change, save that the prince now gets up at half-past 6 instead of 6; he still goes to bed at 9; has one hour for meals and two for recreation—it cannot surely have been merely play—and the rest is all work. One would imagine that the prince ran a risk of becoming the proverbial dull boy; but his tutor, on the contrary, sees excellent effects resulting from this ordered life, notably a disappearance of his old dislike for work. By February 1821, Louis is reading Cornelius Nepos, has learnt the Greek declensions, and is beginning fractions : more important, he is learning to spell, an accomplishment of which he was entirely innocent when Lebas arrived. In the spring of this year Louis made his first communion, and on this occasion he received from his father, a very devout Catholic, the most friendly letter ever addressed to him by the ex-King of Holland.

'I give you my blessing,' wrote the Count de St Leu, 'with all my heart . . . and on this solemn occasion I renew the paternal benediction which every morning and evening I bestow on you.'

In the summer of 1821, Louis Napoleon's education entered upon a new stage. For when Hortense left Bavaria for Arenenberg, she was prevailed upon by Lebas to leave her son behind at Augsburg, in the charge of himself and his wife. At the same time the tutor obtained permission for his pupil to attend classes at the college or gymnasium of Augsburg. Both these concessions were highly valued by Lebas: for the two things which he considered most useful for Louis' education were the absence of his mother, and the presence and competition of other boys.

In August, the tutor describes the effect of the news of Napoleon's death both on his pupil and on Germany. The former could barely remember Napoleon's caresses, save in the way in which a child imagines itself to remember the events of its infancy which it has often heard related. But his sensitive spirit was so much moved by his uncle's death that his tutor gave him three days' whole holiday, no ordinary concession from Lebas. Germany had reason to remember Napoleon in very different fashion; but Lebas notices only an overwhelming indignation and regret, in which men of all parties join, at the manner in which the great man had as they supposed been done to death.

A year later, in July 1822, we find the prince reading the eighth book of the *Metamorphoses* and the first book of the *Odyssey*. Lebas is satisfied with his industry, but still has to complain that his pupil does not readily concentrate his attention on the matter in hand. In the same month the old abbé wrote very sensibly to Lebas on this subject, which might, he thought, be due to physical causes: time might be the best cure for it, any too drastic effort to correct the fault might have a bad effect. In November of the same year the tutor writes more hopefully; he can discern in his pupil growing powers of imagination, and the faculty of expressing his ideas with ease and almost with elegance. But the year 1823 was less fruitful. King Louis had several times allowed his elder son to visit Hortense at Arenenberg; he now insisted, naturally enough, that Louis should be sent to visit him. Lebas accompanied the boy to Marienbad, where his invalid father was taking the waters. There they stayed for a month, the tutor all the while lamenting this break in their studies. On their return things fared no better, for it had been arranged that both parents should spend the winter with their children in Rome; so, at the end of October, master and pupil had again to leave Augsburg, reaching Rome in the middle of November. Hortense found Rome a much more pleasant wintering place than Augsburg; and Louis was naturally pleased with the change. But Lebas was greatly perturbed at this long interruption of his pupil's education. 'He goes to bed late,' he wrote, 'he gets up late; works little and lazily until luncheon; rides at midday, comes in tired at three o'clock; yawns over his lessons till five, and then goes to pass the rest of the day with his father.' The visit to Rome was terminated by the death of Prince Eugène in the spring of 1824: utterly overcome with grief, Hortense hastened back in May to Bavaria, to be present at his funeral in Munich. Then followed a more quiet year; Hortense, mourning for her brother's death, even passed the whole winter of 1825 at Arenenberg. The death of the King of Bavaria in this year deprived the Bonapartes of their last royal protector. Perhaps for this reason, unusual difficulties were made before they were allowed passports in the autumn of 1826 to return to Rome. 'Soon we shall need a congress every time we wish to change our abode,' wrote Louis, on November 20 to his father. If the pupil complained of the obstacles to travel, the tutor complained even more bitterly of the necessity of travelling at all. He writes in December in sad dismay from Augsburg, while they were still awaiting their passports: 'Always journeys and rumours of journeys. When they are not travelling the prince's work is still in suspense, because they are preparing to travel: the greater part of his books are packed and inaccessible.' To a man like Lebas, who could not bear to be out of reach of a good library, a life of this sort was personally distasteful; but his chief source of regret was a genuine sorrow at what he conceived to be the reckless waste of the most critical years in the prince's period of education. 'Our life is a sadly squandered one,' he wrote in March 1826, 'and our studies suffer from it.' Lebas can hardly find one or two hours a day free for work; these he spends in reading Tacitus with his pupil. He protests; Hortense grants the truth of his protest, but no steps are taken to make good the lost time. 'And it would have made me so happy,' he continues, rather pathetically, 'to have seen that the dear boy should have been as distinguished by his knowledge as he will still be by his good qualities and fine character. But, alas, the highroads are not the places for a solid education! One must resign oneself to a superficial manhood when we turn wanderers at this time of life.'

This process continued for another year and a half—a period unsatisfactory enough to master and pupil alike. In September 1827, Hortense dismissed Lebas rather abruptly, pleading the necessity of stricter economy on her part: probably his attitude of perpetual protest had wearied her; possibly his pronounced republicanism and rather austere puritanism began to prove irksome to both mother and son.

It is of course arguable that, for a youth of Louis Napoleon's delicate physique, the travels of which Lebas complains so much were as valuable as the studies at Augsburg; that the months spent at Rome with his mother, at Marienbad and Florence with his father, or nearer home with his uncle Eugène, or his cousin the Duchess of Baden, had no small part in the development of a boy naturally shy and retiring. And it is difficult in any case to share the tutor's regret that the enormous programme of work, which he mapped out for the twelve-year-old boy, could not be carried out in its entirety. None the less the correspondence reveals the real flaw in the prince's education — the demoralising effects of a desultory and rather aimless travel, at a period when a fixed rule, even if it be a poor one, is better than no rule at all. Louis himself looked back on the long years spent at the college at Augsburg without enthusiasm, if not with regret; but it says something for the effects of Lebas' training that he not only recognised the defects of his own education, but set himself assiduously during his sojourn at Rome, after his tutor's departure, to correct them by a self-imposed course of study.

Many stories are told of Louis Napoleon's boyhood in Switzerland which illustrate traits in his character that were to be more strikingly displayed in his later life. At Constance, when he was eight years old, he succeeded in going out for a walk by himself: his mother's reader, Mlle Cochelet, discovered him coming home barefooted and in his shirt sleeves through the midwinter snow; outside the garden he had met a poor family so miserably clad, that having no money he had given one of the children his boots and another his coat.

Six years later, while staying with the Grand

Duchess of Baden, he was standing on the bridge which spans the Neckar at Mannheim, when one of his cousins chanced to drop a flower into the river; the princess laughingly lamented the days when any chivalrous squire would have recovered her flower for her. At once Louis, fully dressed as he was, dived from the bridge into midstream, and after swimming about for some minutes, came to the bank and presented the frightened princess with her draggled flower. This incident shows well the deep hold which the sentimental German romanticism had taken on the boy's mind; it serves also to explain the quixotic generosity of many of Louis Napoleon's later political ideas.

Probably the chief gain of these early years lay in the physical, rather than the mental, development of the boy. It is true that, unlike his brother, Louis Napoleon did not grow better-looking as he grew older. As a child, he had been distinctly good-looking; fragile indeed, but possessed of a certain delicate beauty of feature which accorded well with the shy grace of his manner. This regularity of feature he lost in early manhood, though a high forehead, a keen glance, and a bright smile saved his rather melancholy face from becoming altogether uninteresting. He had already a slight military moustache: the famous imperial was not adopted until some dozen years later. When it *was* added, it was probably a mistake, as it lengthened further a face which was already quite long enough, and emphasised the dissimilarity, already sufficiently pronounced, of Napoleon III and Napoleon I. Like his uncle, Louis Napoleon when full grown was of less than middle height. Unlike him, his form, though agile and muscular, lacked symmetry. His body was long, his legs were short. This disproportion in his figure had, however, one compensation of which the prince was very well aware. The length of his body gave him, when on horseback, the appearance of commanding height; and as he was careful to make himself a proficient horseman, he was able to take full advantage of this fact in later years.

Although the prince had lost something in appearance in these fifteen years, he had gained greatly in strength. When he went to Augsburg, he was a feeble child, shy, timid, and retiring. In 1829, the year in which he came of age, he had run rather to the other extreme. In Rome in this year he made the acquaintance of the third Lord Malmesbury, who describes him in his memoirs as 'a wild, harum-scarum youth, what the French call *un crâne*, riding at full gallop through the streets to the peril of the public; fencing and pistol-shooting, apparently without serious thought of any kind, although even then he was possessed with the conviction that he would one day rule France. . . . He was a very good horseman, a proficient at athletic games; although short, he was very active and muscular. His face was grave and dark, but redeemed by a singularly bright smile.'

This might not be an ideal method of behaviour, but on the whole it was a change in the right direction. Besides being, as Lord Malmesbury says, a very good horseman, Louis was a swimmer of quite remarkable excellence, a good gymnast, a fair fencer, and an excellent shot: as a young man, he is said to have swum across Lake Constance; while it is certain that he repeatedly bore off the prize in the annual shooting match of his canton.

As these accomplishments bear witness, his studies had by this time taken a definitely military turn. He was especially interested in the history and science of artillery, on which subject he wrote four years later a monograph of some distinction. In order to gain a more than theoretical knowledge of the service, he enrolled himself as a volunteer in the military camp at Thun, serving under an old officer of Napoleon's, Colonel Dufour. For several summers running he took his part in this very practical experience of the duties of a soldier, with a good-humoured alacrity which won him the esteem of his fellow-officers. It is not unusual to find, in the anti-Napoleonic literature of a later period, remarks disparaging these manœuvres at Thun as the merest pretence of military training. These strictures seem rather unfair. A Swiss volunteer artillery camp was not, of course, the equivalent of an actual campaign as a method of teaching the duties of an officer; but such experience as it could afford was attained in Louis' case by no royal road. Carrying his own baggage, feeding on the black bread of the country, marching at times some thirty or forty miles a day, and camping in the open—if this was not military training, it was a fairly adequate substitute for it. Nor was it the fault of the young prince that he was denied an opportunity of winning his spurs in an actual campaign of first-class importance. At the end of the year 1828 he was extremely anxious to serve as a volunteer in the Russian army against the Turks. So ardent were his entreaties that his mother gave a reluctant assent to the project. In January 1829 he wrote to ask his father's permission to join the Russian army as a volunteer in the spring. His mother had consented, he wrote; his aunt, the Grand Duchess of Baden, thought the step a worthy one; the Czar would almost certainly grant his request. 'At last I should be able to do something worthy of you. By making this campaign I should gain the advantage of perfecting my instruction, of proving the courage I have received from you, of attracting general interest by it.' And he concluded by begging his father, by all he held most dear, to allow him the chance of making himself worthy of his name. But King Louis met his son's request with an absolute refusal. No cause whatever, he said, could justify service under a strange flag in an alien cause. His father's reply was a cruel disappointment to the boy. But that it was wise and well grounded cannot now be disputed. Fifty years later another exiled prince who bore the name of Louis Napoleon won from his mother leave to seek glory in a quarrel which was not his own. This time there was no stern father to say him nay. And so the boy went forth and found what he sought—but at the cost of his life. Had Queen Hortense's leave not been over-ruled, there might have been no Second Empire. Had the Empress Eugénie's permission to her son been recalled, it is possible that we might ere now have seen the establishment of a third empire. A comparison, which clearly shows the wisdom of the father's prohibition, becomes more ambiguous if it be applied to the fate of the sons. For which of them was truly happier—the boy who died gloriously with all his wounds in front, or the man who lived to suffer in premature old age every inglorious back-handed stab that human ingenuity could devise or malevolence almost preterhuman could direct—this, of course, is another question, and one which might meet with a different answer. The event itself remains noteworthy, apart from the comparison we have suggested, if only because it furnishes the one example of effective intervention on the part of King Louis in the education of his younger son.

Although he was thus prevented from putting them to the test of actual war, Louis did not discontinue his military studies and exercises; he was, in fact, in the midst of the usual arduous routine at Thun when he heard the news of the July Revolution of 1830 in Paris. The fifteen years which had passed since his exile, though they had given some proof of the wonderful recuperative power of France, had not sufficed really to attach the French people to the restored Bourbon rule. Louis XVIII had shown no great interest or initiative in the foreign policy of his country, but his domestic rule had displayed real tact and skill in moderating the reactionary tendencies of a portion of his supporters.

Charles X, who had succeeded to the throne in 1824, was, on the contrary, ambitious and successful in his external policy. But in the qualities which had enabled his brother to reconcile to some extent the internal dissensions of France, he showed himself lamentably deficient. In 1830 the fruits of his foreign policy were ripe for the plucking: the capture of Algiers had laid the foundation of a great French empire south of the Mediterranean, and negotiations were on foot with Russia by which France might have secured the acquisition of Belgium, and so extended her territories once more towards the Rhine.[1]

[1] These schemes were of the most extensive and far-reaching character. Thus, at the crisis of the Turco-Russian war, in September 1829, a general plan for the redivision of Europe was discussed and *approved* by the council of Charles X. By this scheme, which was only to be presented to England as an accomplished decision, Russia was to get Wallachia, Moldavia, and a large accession of territory in Asia (this last with the avowed object of bringing Russia into contact and conflict with the British dominions in India). Austria was to have Bosnia, Servia, Herzegovina, and Turkish Dalmatia; Prussia would receive Saxony and Holland as far as the Rhine; Bavaria was to be slightly increased. France itself would get Belgium, Luxembourg, and the Prussian territories on this side of the Rhine. To England the Dutch colonies were to

Unfortunately, however, both for himself and for France, Charles X chose this very moment for a mad endeavour to make a short cut through the tangled obstacles with which his domestic misgovernment had surrounded him at home. This he attempted to do by an unprecedented extension of certain vague administrative powers granted to the sovereign under the Charter of 1814. The publication of the Ordinances was followed by vigorous opposition, for the most part constitutional in

be offered; but it was not expected that they would be accepted, and in the more probable event of war with England other disposition was to be made of them. The King of Saxony was to be compensated by a cis-Rhenane kingdom; while the King of the Netherlands would become King of Greece—a kingdom comprising the whole of the remnant of European Turkey (Bulgaria, Thrace, Macedonia, etc.).

Not only was the scheme approved, but confidential instructions to the French Ambassador at St Petersburg were made out in this sense. Owing, however, to the sudden announcement of peace these instructions were not sent.

Polignac kept the documents; when, however, on 28th July 1830 the Ministry of Foreign affairs was invaded by the mob, they were made away with, and in great part destroyed. But M. Bois-le-Comte, who was Prince Polignac's *chef du cabinet* and minister of foreign affairs, had kept in his own possession copies of all the papers.

In the autumn of 1856 some considerable ill-feeling had arisen between France and England, owing to differences as to the interpretation of clauses in the Treaty of Paris. The Comte de Bois-le-Comte took this opportunity, on 26th November 1856, of sending these papers to Napoleon III, with the suggestion that he would do well to devise some such Anglophobe scheme with Russia himself.

Napoleon III proceeded instead to show the whole of the documents in question to Cowley, the British ambassador, even allowing him to take them away and copy them. Thus they found their way belatedly to the archives of the English Foreign Office.

The story, however, does not end there; for Napoleon III characteristically utilised this opening as a preliminary of overtures of his own to England for a scheme of mutual aggrandisement. But the history of these negotiations, and of the rebuff which they encountered, must be told elsewhere.

intention; but a series of accidents delayed the announcement of concessions which the native obstinacy of the king had already rendered sufficiently tardy. Meanwhile, the clever juggling of a few astute politicians, and a successful *coup de théâtre* at the Hôtel de Ville—with Lafayette as stage-manager and Louis Philippe and a tricolor as *mise en scène*—had placed the Duke of Orleans on the throne of the Bourbons. The constitutional opposition had not desired a change of dynasty, but only the due observance of the Charter by the existing one : the armed revolutionaries who had fought in the streets of Paris desired not a new monarch, but the abolition of monarchical government. Yet, when the confusion of the July days had subsided, it was Louis Philippe who had emerged from them—for all the world like the rabbit produced from the conjurer's silk hat, a slightly scared rabbit seeming itself to share something of the general surprise which greets its appearance. It was not quite what Paris had expected, but there was a very general disposition to accept the result with alacrity. The prudent welcomed it as a compromise : the provinces accepted it as an accomplished fact. Ingenuous enthusiasts saw in Louis Philippe a saviour of the nations, a Napoleon of peace, a citizen king : ingenious apologists[1] discerned in the House of

[1] *E.g.*, Guizot, *L'Histoire de la Révolution d'Angleterre*. It was to refute this comparison that Louis Napoleon, during his imprisonment at Ham, wrote his *Fragments Historiques*, 1688 *et* 1830 ; see p. 202 below

Orleans in 1830 the counterpart of the House of Orange in 1688.

Indeed, the parallel was, at first sight, a curiously striking one. On the ruins of a premature parliamentarianism a great king had established a "new monarchy"—despotic, centralised, autocratic. A century and a half passed; the circumstances which justified the original despotism ceased to exist, smaller kings had succeeded to the great position and lowered its prestige. The reigning monarch, though personally a man of estimable character and admirable intentions, was attached to an unpopular domestic policy, and espoused to an unpopular foreign wife; he loses his crown and his head to a republican revolution. The republic falls almost at once before a military dictator; the dictator is personally successful, but his attempt to secure a dynastic succession for his son fails. The ancient dynasty is restored in the person of an astute man of the world, a king of really statesman-like instincts, though he might appear to be intent only on never again going on his travels: shrewd enough to see the necessity of humouring the parliamentary spirit, and able enough to hold in hand the more reckless of his own supporters. To him succeeds a fanatic brother, obstinate, priest-ridden, tactlessly despotic: a man whose hand of clay flaunts the mailed fist. An unwarrantable extension of a vague constitutional privilege deprives him of his throne. Such, briefly, were the antecedents alike of the English revolution of 1688, and of the French revolution of 1830. Each revolution ended in the acceptance of the vacant throne by a younger branch of the old dynasty on a professedly parliamentary basis. Surely if ever the history of the past could shed light on the prospects of the future, France, too, might now hope that she had at last found, like England, a permanent settlement of the problem of constitutional government. But here the parallel, hitherto one of the most remarkable in all history, broke down completely. Those who based on it their hopes of ultimate Orleanist success were unmindful of the thousand and one disparities which mar the nicest and most symmetrical of historical parallels. For us, it is enough to take note of the one essential cause of divergence, which, in itself, was the sum and consummation of the other thousand. In England in 1688, there did not exist the vestige of a Cromwellian legend; in France in 1830, there did exist a Napoleonic legend, whose growth alone was a disturbing factor sufficient to throw the parallel out of gear. Only slowly do the two lines show signs of parting. In either case a long period of unrest followed the revolution, during which the success of the constitutional experiment remained in doubt. But in England, throughout that period of uncertainty, this one thing was certain, that the chances of a descendant or imitator of Cromwell were nil. Conceive the uprising in England of such a man, who, 'recognising the regular though ephemeral title' of son Richard, should style himself Cromwell III !

It so happened that there did actually exist in England, during this very period of unrest, the one man in her history who was really qualified to play the part of a Napoleon. For the greatest general England ever produced was also one of the boldest, the most ambitious, and most unscrupulous of English statesmen. But even for him the anti-Cromwellian feeling was too strong. In the striking phrase of a recent historian, 'Dark across the path of Marlborough's ambition lay the sinister shadow of Cromwell.' The fact was, that as in France men who had no other political opinion in common united in their praise of the dead Napoleon, so in England they agreed in cursing Cromwell. Thiers and Victor Hugo were at one on the first point; Clarendon and Ludlow united on the second. Two centuries were to pass before Cromwell in his turn found his Thiers and his Vendôme column: but when Carlyle produced his great vindication of the Protector, and Lord Rosebery raised his statue in the precincts of St Stephen's, the time had long passed when a Cromwellian legend could be of any dynastic importance.

It would be a mistake to imagine that even in the revolution of 1830 there was no trace of Bonaparte feeling. During the July days many houses in Paris, especially in the workman's quarter, were adorned with placards on behalf of Napoleon II. But where was Napoleon II? Napoleon's son, while he lived, was the only possible claimant to that title. Any effective effort, however, on behalf of the Duc de Reichstadt was out of the question while he remained a virtual prisoner in the hands of Austria. Moreover, his days were already clearly numbered by the disease which caused his death two years later. In his enforced absence, Prince Napoleon, Louis' elder brother, was invited by certain Bonapartists in Paris to put himself at their head, but he declined to attempt a civil war against a sovereign not yet proved unworthy of the popular cause. From America, when all was over, arrived a futile manifesto from King Joseph on behalf of the Emperor's son. Louis himself did not move from the round of his military duties at Thun. Though his letters show that he was watching the course of events in Paris with consuming interest, he remained at Thun until his camp broke up in the autumn. At the end of October he started quietly with his mother on the usual winter visit to Rome, intent to all seeming on nothing more noteworthy than the ordered routine in which the preceding winters had been spent. But the year 1830 was one in which ordered routines were apt to be rudely disturbed, nor were the effects of the July days confined to France. Among the countries which felt the shock of the revolution in Paris was one which was to be almost as intimately connected as France itself with the fortunes of Louis Napoleon: one for whose sake he made larger sacrifices, and to whose cause he rendered greater services, than perhaps any other sovereign has ever done for a nation not his own. That country was Italy; and it was to Italy that Louis Napoleon was going quietly with his mother in the autumn of 1830.

CHAPTER IV

THE FIRST ATTEMPT TO DELIVER ITALY—AND
WHAT CAME OF IT

> These are the records half effaced
> Which with the hand of youth he traced
>   On history's page :
> But with fresh victories he drew
> Each fading character anew
>   In his ripe age.
>
> LONGFELLOW.

A LEISURELY journey, broken by a fortnight spent at Florence in the company of Prince Napoleon, brought Hortense and Louis to Rome about the middle of November 1830. A fortnight after their arrival, the death of Pope Pius VIII left the Papal States without a master at a very critical moment. Since 1821 the fallen cause of Italian independence had been kept alive only by secret societies, of which the Carbonari were the most powerful; and latterly these societies had made the Papal States their headquarters. Already their hopes had been kindled by the success of the July revolution in France, and by its consequences in Belgium and Poland; the interregnum at Rome which followed the Pope's death seemed therefore to afford a favourable opportunity for a fresh endeavour to win freedom for Italy.

Now, with the possible exception of Poland, there was no country in Europe in which a national cause was so intimately connected with the name of Napoleon as in Italy. Italy had not been conquered by Napoleon, but overrun by him; on her soil he had defeated not Italians, but their foreign oppressors. Italian sentiment did not resent the rule of a man himself half Italian by descent. Italian interests were not noticeably injured by a government which, if rigorous, was at least more rational than most of those which came before or after it. Under its bracing influence Italy awoke to strenuous if somewhat artificial life; under Napoleon's banners her sons showed that they had not really forgotten how to die. The Italians were alone among the peoples of Europe outside France in regarding Napoleon's victories with something like national pride; alone too in this, that they not only gained nothing, but had not expected to gain anything, by his fall. The cause of national independence, even of national unity, had been advanced by his actual rule; while from St Helena he had of course explained to them that his one purpose for their future had been the foundation, as a kingdom to be ruled from Rome by his second son, of a truly free and united Italy.

It was natural, therefore, that the Bonaparte family should be favourable and not altogether disinterested spectators of the Italian movement,

For what they were denied in France, they might find compensation in Italy. In December an informal gathering took place in Rome of some of the most prominent members of the family—including besides Louis and his mother, King Jerome and Cardinal Fesch. It is uncertain whether any plans for common action resulted from this meeting, but it is clear that it had the effect of alarming the French and the Papal governments. The elder Bonapartes retained considerable private fortunes. These, it was believed, they were ready to sink in the revolutionary cause in the hope of political aggrandisement. Louis Napoleon, as well as his elder brother, was supposed to be himself a member of the Carbonari. On this point it is still impossible to speak with absolute certainty; the old Scots verdict of 'not proven' seems to be all that history can yet arrive at on the question—a verdict which in this case certainly admits of the usual inference.[1] Probably both brothers had given verbal though not written engagements to this society, signifying their co-operation with its methods and objects. It is certain that the governors of the city regarded Louis' presence in Rome with suspicion and dislike; and when, shortly after the family conclave at his mother's palace, he proceeded to ride through the streets with the tricolor displayed on his person, thus flaunting with ostentatious indiscretion his sympathies with the national cause, they at once

[1] See Appendix, p. 362.

demanded his immediate departure from Rome. Despite the expostulations of his uncle, Cardinal Fesch, he was conducted by Papal troops to the frontier, whence he proceeded to join his brother at Florence. Hortense, who remained in Rome, was unfeignedly pleased to see him removed out of harm's way, even in so unceremonious a fashion; for she had no desire to see her sons risk their lives in Italy in a cause which she recognised as hopeless. She wrote to them at Florence, warning them in a very sensible letter of the hopelessness of any united effort on Italy's behalf at that time, and begging them to beware of the alluring suggestions of men who had nothing to lose, who saw only what their imagination wished to see. 'The man,' she continued, 'who allows himself to be carried away by the arguments of the first comer, without making use of his own judgment, will be a mediocrity all his life. There exist magical names that may exercise a great influence over coming events; but they should not appear in revolutions except to re-establish order, by giving security to nations and checking the unbalanced power of kings. Those who bear them must wait with patience; if they foment troubles, they will share the fate of adventurers who have been made use of, only to be deserted or betrayed on the first mishap.' To which the princes replied very dutifully that they had carefully read their mother's letter, and entirely recognised its wisdom. They then proceeded immediately to act in direct opposition to its advice, only to prove by bitter experience how correct had been their mother's forecast of events. Menotti, an enthusiastic patriot from Modena, visited the princes at Florence, and appealed to them to let their glorious name become a rallying point for the down-trodden patriots of Italy. His enthusiasm and eloquence gained the day; and when, on February 5, 1831, Bologna rose in revolt, the two brothers put themselves at its head. If we think the better of the mother for her wise advice, we need not perhaps think the worse of her sons for disregarding it. Their action, reckless as it was, was generous and single-minded enough. By this time, any hopes the elder members of the family had based on the Italian disturbance were already at an end. King Louis, Jerome, and Cardinal Fesch were alike opposed to the rash act. They used every possible argument to induce the young men to return from the rebels' camp; and finding that impossible, they refused to countenance their efforts or to give them financial support. After their experience of the previous year the princes had not expected to receive any encouragement from their parents; this time, however, they had avoided their probable opposition by starting without informing them of their intention. It was only when Hortense reached Florence, at the beginning of March, that she learnt of her sons' departure to the scene of the rebellion. Expecting to meet them on her arrival, she found instead a letter from Prince Louis waiting for her. 'The name they bore and the engagements they had accepted obliged them,' he wrote, 'to act as they had done.' Other letters, joyful and enthusiastic, followed from Terni. 'For the first time I know what it is to live,' wrote Louis (from Terni, 26th February); 'before I have done nothing but vegetate. A fairer or more honourable position than ours could not be imagined.'

The two princes had indeed been received at first with wild enthusiasm, and had been raised to the chief commands in the little army. 'The revolutionary forces assembled near Foligno and Viterbo are variously computed at 3000 and 5000 men,' wrote the British minister at Florence. 'They have been joined by two sons of the Duke of St Leu, the ex-King of Holland, who were received by the troops with great enthusiasm.'[1] Both brothers displayed courage and resource. Prince Napoleon succeeded in repelling a body of Papal troops who attempted to recapture Terni and Spoleto, and Louis made his preparations for the assault of Cività Castellana with a coolness and certainty of aim which won the respect of men older than himself. He rightly judged that if this assault were successful, Rome would lie open to his attack. It was in the fighting before Cività Castellana that Count Felix Orsini lost his life; Orsini,

---

[1] E. H. Seymour to Palmerston, Florence, 1st March 1831. 'Duke' is a misnomer: on his abdication in 1810 Louis assumed the modest title Comte de St Leu. Nothing in his wife's subsequent conduct caused him more annoyance than her adoption of the same territorial title with the higher rank of Duchess.

whose son, a generation later, thought he could best serve the cause for which his father died, by attempting to assassinate Louis Napoleon himself. So threatening appeared the dispositions of the rebels that the new Pope hastened to make provision for his escape from Rome, in case the insurgents should press him further.[1] Indeed, had Gregory XVI been able to oppose no more formidable forces than the Papal troops to their advance, the leaders of the insurrection would probably have carried their movement to a triumphant conclusion. But while making his preparations for retreat from Rome, the Pope lost no time in appealing for deliverance to Austria; and Austria at once prepared to come to his aid. It now became evident that unless the revolutionaries also could hope for foreign intervention in their favour, their cause was lost. France was the only country whose help they could expect. But so long as Austria could point to the presence of the two princes in the rebel ranks, as evidence of the Bonapartist character of the movement, Louis Philippe would have an admirable excuse for refusing to intervene on its behalf. Accordingly the insurgents became as eager for the princes' departure as they had been for their arrival. While on the point of following up their attack on Cività Castellana by a march on Rome itself, the brothers were recalled by the revolutionary government of Bologna, and replaced by General Sercognani. Bitterly disappointed, they

---

[1] E. H. Seymour to Palmerston, Florence, 7th March 1831.

obeyed these orders and returned to Bologna, where they were informed that their further services were not required in any capacity. Accepting with the best grace they might the humiliating situation in which they were placed, the brothers retired to Forli. They had found neither glory nor gratitude in their adventure, but dangers in plenty still awaited them. In dismissing the princes the revolutionists had deprived their movement of the chief element of its existing strength, without in any way securing the help they hoped from France. Louis Philippe did not lift a finger on their behalf. After the departure of the princes the Papal government no longer feared those who still remained in arms, and the advance of the Austrians showed by this time that the movement had no hope of success. It also had the effect of encouraging the lesser governments to refuse the princes passage through their territories. Tuscany forbade them to cross its frontier. The Austrian minister at Florence told King Louis that their return to Switzerland would not be permitted. An Austrian fleet in the Adriatic prevented escape by sea : and from the amnesty published by the Austrian general on his arrival in Papal territory their names were expressly excepted. Hortense indeed was warned that the princes would find no protection in their imperial rank if they fell into the hands of the Austrian troops, but would be liable to the death penalty which had been declared against all foreigners taking part in the movement. Realising that their position was one of extreme danger, she resolved to remain in Florence no longer, but to go herself in search of them. Before leaving the city, she obtained from an English friend a British passport, made out for an English lady travelling with her two sons through Paris to England. For she had determined on a line of retreat whose apparent risk might be its real security. If in those troubled times Switzerland was indeed not strong enough to offer a safe refuge for her sons, she might at least be sure that in England they would be safe from the molestation of Austria or France. The direct route seemed barred by the decree of exile which forbade the princes to set foot in France. But where every road seemed dangerous this might be the safest, since nowhere would their presence be less suspected.

Armed, then, with this passport for future use, Hortense set out from Florence on March 10, in search of her sons. Ignorant of their whereabouts, and imagining that they were still at the front, she had travelled as far south as Perugia before learning that they were really at Forli. Turning northwards, she was met by the news that her elder son was dangerously ill, and desired greatly to see her. Half out of her mind with grief and anxiety, she hastened forward, refusing to believe the rumour which met her that her son was not ill but dead. But at Pesaro, Prince Louis himself confirmed the tale. After a three days' illness,[1] his brother had died in his arms on March 17, fever-smitten at

[1] E. H. Seymour to Palmerston, 22nd March 1831.

Faenza. On the eve of the occupation of their city by the Austrians, the whole population of Forli had joined Louis in following his brother to the grave, mourning the death alike of their short-lived hopes and of their champion of a day. For Hortense, however, it was no time to mourn the dead, but to save the living, if by any means her younger son *could* be saved from his brother's fate. Louis himself was very ill. Yet the Austrians were marching on Pesaro, and it was impossible to remain there. At all costs they must avoid the advancing menace of the Austrian troops. A hurried drive brought mother and son to Ancona; but here the latter's condition became so much worse that further travel became out of the question for the time. In nursing his brother Louis had himself been infected with measles, the disease with which his brother's illness had begun. Hortense, who throughout the whole of this Italian episode is seen at her best, was equal to the emergency. She at once engaged a place for her son in a vessel about to start for Corfu. His passport for that island was procured from the authorities of Ancona before the arrival of the Austrians, and his luggage was ostentatiously put on board. And when next day the Austrian army entered the city they believed that the proscribed prince had made good his escape to Greece.

In reality he was lying delirious and in high fever in the palace occupied by his mother. Announcing that she herself was very ill, Hortense placed the real patient in a small inner room which opened out of her own. Every precaution was taken to conceal the fact of his presence; but when the Austrian commander proceeded to demand the palace for his own use it seemed that none could be effective. The queen, indeed, was allowed to retain a few rooms for herself; but for a week the prince lay sick in a room which was only divided from that of the Austrian commander by the thickness of a double wooden door; forbidden to speak, lest the sound of a man's voice heard through the thin barrier should betray the secret of his presence. It was no time for a lengthy convalescence. As soon as Louis was so far recovered as to be able to travel with no greater danger to himself than that involved by his continued presence in Ancona, Hortense announced her intention of leaving the city. Never dreaming that her son was going with her the Austrian commander raised no objection, but furnished her with a pass through the Austrian lines. Prince Louis was disguised as one of her footmen. In order to lessen the chance of his disguise being discovered, the queen started on her journey before daylight. Very early on the morning of Easter Sunday she passed through the Austrian lines, and as she explained that she wished to hear mass at Loreto on her way, the unusual hour of her departure created no suspicion.

Elaborate precautions such as these, though they did not prevent an occasional Italian from recognising the prince, yet saved the party from any interference on the part of the Austrian officials until the Papal States were left behind. But Tuscany was still to be traversed, and here the chances of detection were even greater; for Louis and his brother had been very familiar figures in the little kingdom. Thinking to decrease the danger, the fugitives crossed the frontier at midnight; but even so they narrowly escaped summary arrest. The most stringent orders had been given that Louis was to be prevented from entering Tuscan territory. Hortense was not to be allowed to proceed until she had been examined by a special commissioner of police; but the commissioner was at this hour in bed some miles away. He had, however, left orders that no one was to be allowed to proceed until his return. Hortense sent her passport by her own courier to the commissioner; fortunately he was sleepy, and had no mind to turn out on such an errand in the middle of the night; he therefore signed the passport, on receiving a most solemn assurance that Prince Louis was not with his mother. When the morning came it was almost certain that the man would discover his mistake, and exceedingly probable that he would endeavour to repair it; the more so as the courier, in the hope of putting him off his guard by seeming innocence, had invited him to call and inspect the party personally the next morning at Camoscia. Meanwhile a few precious hours were gained, but even this slight advantage seemed likely to be lost when the fugitives arrived at Camoscia, and found that they could obtain no relays of post-horses there. It seemed as though they might be forced to keep their engagement after all. There was nothing for it but stay awhile and rest their wearied horses: these, indeed, were more fortunate than their masters—they could be stabled without trouble. But for Hortense or her son to enter the inn would have been to court recognition, since it was full of political refugees like themselves. Hortense could at least rest in her own coach; the future Emperor of the French, very recently recovered from a dangerous illness, had to sleep on a stone bench in the open street. The man who was to become the most powerful potentate in Europe could only hope to save his life by making his bed correspond to his flunkey garb.

As soon as the horses were fit to move, the fugitives proceeded with what speed they could. Starting before daybreak, they travelled along by-roads and changed horses, and drivers, as soon and as often as they had opportunity. By this means they were enabled, after a long day's drive, to take a night's rest in a small village in comparative security; for by this time they might hope that they had shaken off any possible pursuers. It was still, however, necessary to pass through Siena. As this town was an habitual stopping-place of Hortense on her yearly visit to Rome, she could not hope to pass through it unrecognised. She therefore made no attempt at an impossible incognito, but drove boldly through the city in the daytime.

Since there was no other road than that which went through the city, Louis could not avoid passing through the town without serious risk of losing his way, and so falling into the hands of the police who occupied the whole neighbourhood. He therefore went as far as the city gate in his mother's carriage; while her passport was being examined there, he jumped out and hastened through by-streets to the Florence gate. A little way beyond the city he was to wait for his mother; but again no horses could be procured, and those they had could not go on without two hours' rest. This unexpected delay nearly led to the two missing each other; but fortunately the carriage met Louis just as he was returning in search of it to the city gate, where he would probably have been discovered and arrested.

The most hazardous part of their journey was over when the Tuscan frontier had been again crossed, and Pisa and Lucca left behind. Hortense now fell back on her original English passport: Louis no longer travelled as her servant, but as one of the two sons mentioned in the passport; the place of the other was taken by a young nobleman, also deeply implicated in the recent rebellion, who had accompanied Hortense from Florence, and had hitherto been disguised as one of her servants. At Pietra Santa they turned aside to see the home of that elder son for whom Hortense had been obliged to find a substitute; for now that the immediate danger for the living son had been largely surmounted she had time once more to feel the loss of the other. Delay was still unsafe, however, and a narrow escape from recognition caused the fugitives again to hasten onwards. They passed hurriedly through Massa and Genoa towards the French frontier, which they crossed by way of Antibes. At Cannes they halted, sleeping on French soil for the first time after fifteen years of exile. So ended Louis Napoleon's first attempt to deliver Italy. The whole episode remains one of the most obscure in his life. As we have the facts at present, it is less the impetuous ardour of the son than the courage and resource of the mother that impress our attention. But it remains clear that in this adventure Louis was under fire for the first time, and that he behaved creditably enough in his first brief tenure of military command.

From this youthful intervention of Louis Napoleon in Italy there resulted in any case two facts of first-rate importance. The death of his brother rendered all but certain his own eventual succession to the position of head of the House of Bonaparte. By an arrangement made in 1804, Napoleon had limited the succession of his empire, in default of direct issue of his own, to two of his brothers and their male descendants. These brothers were Louis of Holland, and Joseph, afterwards King of Spain. Now Napoleon's own son was by this time in ill-health, and Joseph had no sons. Hence in becoming his father's sole heir, Louis Napoleon became also the practically certain successor to the primacy of the Napoleonic house. To most men this would have seemed the emptiest of empty honours: to Louis Napoleon it carried with it the entail of a vast inheritance. To mark his sense of this fact, the prince reversed the order of his Christian names, signing himself for the next seventeen years Napoleon Louis, instead of Louis Napoleon. Henceforth his every effort must be devoted to making good the claim which this signature implied; to hastening the day when his first name might be shed entirely, and he should be able with regal simplicity to write himself 'Napoleon.'

Even more important was the other consequence which followed from this affair. It can hardly be questioned that his youthful intervention in an Italian rising served permanently to interest Louis Napoleon in what was to be the greatest achievement of his life—the liberation of Italy. There was indeed a strange difference in the fashion of his exit from Italy and of his next entrance as her champion. Now as a sorry fugitive he was being huddled in disguise from Italy where his life was forfeit, to France wherein he was forbidden to set foot by a decree of perpetual exile. Then as the most powerful sovereign in Europe he was to return from France, of which he was absolute ruler, to Italy in whose cause he had mobilised what was still the first army in the world. Yet the two events cannot be wholly disconnected. If in the winter of 1831 Louis Napoleon had not played his puerile part in the feeble rising of Bologna, Napoleon III would hardly have risked his crown for Italy in the summer of 1859.

CHAPTER V

LOUIS NAPOLEON A POLITICAL APPRENTICE

> Must I not serve a long apprenticehood
> To foreign passages, and in the end,
> Having my freedom, boast of nothing else
> But that I was a journeyman to grief?
> SHAKESPEARE.

ALTHOUGH Louis had recovered from his illness by the time he left Italy, he was still in far from good health. His brother's death, and the inglorious ending of an enterprise on which he had embarked with such high hopes, had thrown him into a condition of profound melancholy, resembling somewhat the periods of sombre silence with which his father was afflicted. This mood passed from him when he found himself once more in France. Apathy gave place to an absorbing interest in every detail of the life he saw around him; interest to an intense desire that he himself might be permitted to share in future in the civic rights of his own country. He seems to have imagined that Louis Philippe might be induced not merely to repeal the sentence of exile which hung over him, but even to allow him to serve in the French army. His mother was less hopeful. It was true that the king was to some extent under obligation to her, for in 1815 she had secured pensions for his mother and aunt, and permission for them to reside in France during the hundred days. Louis Philippe had, in fact, given her to understand that she might rely on his good offices. But when her son showed her a rather grandiose epistle which he had addressed to the king, asking his leave to serve as a simple soldier in the French army, Hortense begged that he would at least wait until they had reached Paris, when a personal appeal might be made with more chance of success.

To Paris they came after an uneventful journey, during which they were careful to conceal their identity. On her arrival, Hortense lost no time in informing the king of her presence. Louis Philippe was not particularly pleased at the appearance of these rather embarrassing visitors, but he finally consented to see the queen. He received her secretly, and with extraordinary precautions against discovery, at the Palais Royal. He was affable, almost affectionate in his manner. He could sympathise only too well with the sorrows of an exile; soon he hoped that there would be no French exiles; he was resolved that none should exist under his rule. Meanwhile could he serve her in any way? She had just claims, he knew, on the French Government. She must make him her family lawyer, and he would see that her affairs were attended to. As to her son's request, he would be glad to see the letter, and consider it; only it was essential that the prince's presence in Paris should remain a profound secret. Hortense was gratified at her reception, and returned in high spirits to her hotel. There she found her son in bed, suffering apparently from a fresh attack of the fever which had prostrated him in Italy. An obliging doctor now forbade his removal from Paris. Louis Philippe learnt of the prolongation of their visit with annoyance not unmixed with suspicion; Casimir Périer, the only one of his ministers whom he had informed of their presence, openly avowed his belief that the prince's illness was a mere fiction designed to procure him a few days in Paris, which he might spend in plotting against the new dynasty. These suspicions were natural, and possibly well grounded; it is clear that Louis did, during his short stay in Paris, enter into relations with some of the republican leaders; while in the autumn of the same year traces were found of his acquaintance with some Bonapartist plotters, who were arrested while arranging a rising in the eastern provinces. It seems probable that Louis really was unwell; but it cannot be denied that his second feverish attack was as timely as the first had been dangerous and inconvenient. A week's delay at Ancona had meant the hourly possibility of ignominious capture; a week's delay in Paris now excused his presence at a time when

F

the strong Bonaparte feeling which already existed there would be sure to find expression.

The fifth of May, the anniversary of Napoleon's death, had by this time become a day of national celebration in his honour. This year the manifestation promised to be one of unusual importance. For Louis Philippe's Government had decided to restore the Little Corporal to his original position on the Vendôme Column, and the work was now actually in progress. It was hoped that this official tribute to the memory of Napoleon would deprive the growing force of the Napoleonic Legend of any anti-dynastic aims; possibly that it would even turn it into a source of strength for the new monarchy. None the less, Louis Philippe, who had not yet been a year on the throne, could not but feel some anxiety as to the success of this rather risky experiment. And the presence of Hortense and Louis Napoleon within a stone's throw of the Vendôme Column was not calculated to lessen that anxiety. On May 4 a pressing message was sent by the hand of a king's aide-de-camp, insisting on their immediate departure from Paris. Fortunately he arrived at a moment when the doctor was actually applying leeches to his patient, and Hortense succeeded in satisfying the messenger that her son could not make the journey that day. She was thus able to watch on the following day from the window of her hotel the vast crowd which assembled round the Vendôme Column to honour Napoleon's memory. She was informed, however, that unless her son's life would actually be endangered by the journey, there must be no further delay in their departure. It was not possible to represent Prince Louis as being in any immediate danger of death, so on the 6th, Hortense and her son left Paris, and about a week later they arrived in London.[1] There the prince was at once prostrated by a severe attack of jaundice, caused apparently by a rough passage at a time when he was not very fit to travel. His illness, however, though acute, did not last long, and the warm welcome which the exiles met in London helped them both to forget a new disappointment of their hopes. For Louis Philippe had given Hortense to understand before she left Paris, that though he could secure the revocation of the act which exiled her, yet he could not promise as much for her son. And even if at some future date Louis were permitted to return to France, it would still be impossible for him to serve in the army unless he first abandoned his own name. This stipulation was not unreasonable from the king's point of view, but it sufficed to render useless to Prince Louis any concessions which were

[1] According to some accounts—*e.g.*, M. Duval, *Napoléon III, Enfance, Jeunesse*—they remained in Paris until the 12th, and did not reach Calais before the 18th of May. In any case they seem to have gone straight to London, though the first mention of their arrival occurring in the *Times* is a full month later. 'Prince Louis Napoleon Buonaparte, second son of Louis Buonaparte, has arrived in London, and is staying with his mother, Hortensia, Duchess of St Leu, formerly Queen of Holland. Also, Achilles Murat, son of Murat, is in town, and these eminent foreigners paid on Friday a visit to Earl Grey.'—The *Times*, Monday, 20th June 1831.

made to depend on it. For at the time his name was his one possession, and to abandon it would have been to abandon his claim to the inheritance which might devolve on him. The king's reply was accompanied by an offer of financial assistance; this Hortense had refused.

Louis and his mother stayed in England for nearly three months. The greater part of this time was spent in the capital, where they were visited and entertained by many persons of distinction. No official notice was taken of their presence save by Talleyrand, the French ambassador, who anxiously enquired as to their present object in visiting London, and the date and route of their return journey to Switzerland. Indeed, on the last two points he saved them the trouble of coming to a decision for themselves. They had intended to return almost immediately by way of Belgium; they were informed that they must not leave England until the beginning of August, and that even then they must avoid Belgium. The July monarchy wished to celebrate its first anniversary without the presence of its embarrassing visitors of May; and the passage of Louis Napoleon through Belgium might give rise to political disturbance in the newly constituted kingdom. It was suspected that disturbance of this sort might be not merely the result, but the object of the projected journey: Prince Leopold, the newly elected King of the Belgians, did not himself share this suspicion, but the precaution was a very natural one.

AN APPEAL FROM POLAND

It was not, therefore, until the 7th of August that Hortense and her son left England. Their return voyage through France was uneventful, and before the end of the month they found themselves once more at the quiet retreat of Arenenberg. Here Prince Louis was to spend the greater part of the next five years. Unlike the exciting months he had just passed, this was to prove the least eventful period of his life—save for that other lustrum which he spent ten years later in imprisonment. At the moment of his return, it is true, an event occurred which appeared to promise a repetition on a larger scale of all the alarms and excursions of the preceding year. At the end of August 1831 a Polish deputation reached the prince at Arenenberg, begging him to put himself at the head of the insurgents. In some ways this was a weightier appeal than that to which Louis and his brother had yielded so readily a year ago: the Polish revolutionary movement in itself was a far more serious affair than the Italian rising had been; and this appeal bore the signature of some of its most distinguished leaders and generals, entreating the prince, as 'the nephew of the greatest captain of all the ages,' to put himself at their head. None the less, he refused. His mother, who had lost one son already in a like cause, redoubled her endeavours to dissuade the survivor from another mad adventure of the same kind. This time her advice was supported by her son's own experience of its previous truth. Moreover, Louis Napoleon had never quite that sympathy with the Poles which he always had for the Italians; he did not feel himself committed to the support of their cause as he was to that of Italy; possibly, too, he recognised that he had only been invited to head the movement at the eleventh hour, when its chance of success had practically vanished. His refusal in any case was only given with reluctance; according to some accounts he actually reconsidered it, and had gone secretly as far as the Swiss frontier, on his way to Poland, when he was met with the news of the fall of its capital on September 8, and deterred from further progress by the grim announcement that 'Order reigned in Warsaw.'

Now, at any rate, he recognised that the revolutionary period of 1830-31 was at an end, and that with it had closed any present prospect of advancing his position by acting as champion with the sword of any of the distressed peoples of Europe. He therefore turned his attention to the possibilities of a literary vindication of the Napoleonic claims. Realising the great service which Thiers, Béranger, Victor Hugo, and others were, consciously or unconsciously, rendering the imperial cause by their writings, he resolved himself to embark on a series of political pamphlets; which should serve at once to attract attention to his own person as a claimant of the traditions of the empire, and also to show that the liberal and democratic tendencies which had been attributed to the Emperor, were not repudiated, but rather welcomed, by his descendants.

On the first of these pamphlets—for they hardly deserve a more dignified name—Prince Louis was engaged during the winter of 1832. It was published under the title of *Rêveries Politiques* in May 1832. As Napoleon's son the Duke of Reichstadt was still alive at this time, it is he who throughout the leaflet is spoken of as the inheritor of Napoleon's claims; and from this fact some of Louis Napoleon's apologists have striven to show that his writings were not originally inspired by any personal ambition. But since the Duke of Reichstadt was known to be in the last stages of consumption at the time of the composition of this pamphlet, and in fact died two months after its publication, the contention in any case has very little value; and it becomes altogether untenable in the light of one significant clause in the 'Sketch of a Constitution' which is appended to the *Political Reflections*. That clause, which has been rather curiously ignored, provides that in the event of the son, or nearest surviving relative of the Emperor, not being a suitable candidate, the people shall be empowered to choose for themselves a fit successor. Thus Prince Louis disposes not only of the Duke of Reichstadt, should his illness chance to prove a lingering one, but also of the two brothers of Napoleon, who, by the terms of his will, would still intervene between himself and the inheritance, even on the death of the duke. The fact was, that since the death of his brother in Italy, Louis was convinced that he himself was the only member of the Bonaparte family who could forward the imperial claims. His father was a confirmed invalid; his uncle, King Joseph, was an old man, and had no sons. The incompetence of the older members of the Napoleonic house had been sufficiently proved in 1830, for Louis believed—and many who were no well-wishers of the Napoleonic cause shared the belief—that a resolute imperialist candidate would have had a good chance of success in Paris at the time of the July revolution. The *Political Reflections*, therefore, must be regarded as the first public assertion by Louis Napoleon of his position as a possible candidate for the imperial heritage. The prince avows himself a republican by inclination, who is none the less driven to the belief that under existing conditions an empire is the only form of government in which the liberties of the French people can be preserved. If the Rhine were an ocean—if, that is, France were an insular and not a continental power—he would be in favour of a republic in practice. As it is, while giving the elective power to the people, and the deliberative power to the legislative body, he would reserve to the emperor the execution of the people's will.

The paper as a whole is slight and somewhat sentimental, fluent in expression, but not particularly striking in conception; if there is little in it to provoke criticism, there is also little to arrest attention. Another and more substantial treatise appeared in 1833, entitled *Considérations Politiques et Militaires sur la Suisse*. In so far as it concerns Switzerland it is a sympathetic and really intelligent study of the condition and prospects of the country, based on intimate knowledge of its customs and recent history. But Switzerland, of course, was not the author's sole concern. 'If in speaking of Switzerland I have been unable to prevent the frequent recurrence of my thoughts to France, I trust that my digressions may be pardoned,' he writes in the preface; and these digressions form indeed no small part of the whole. The *Considérations* met with a favourable reception in Switzerland; and their author, who had received the civic rights of the canton of Thurgau a year before, was now made an honorary citizen of the Swiss Republic. The compliment was the more remarkable as Louis had not abstained from some rather searching, though entirely friendly, criticism of the Swiss institutions; pointing out in particular the necessity of adjusting the possibly conflicting rights of the individual canton and the republic as a whole. The importance of this question was soon shown in the case of Switzerland, by the conflict between the Sonderbund and the Protestant cantons; while later—and on a larger scale—its gravity was demonstrated by the war between the Confederate and Federal States in America.

A year later the prince received another mark of local esteem which gave him even greater pleasure. In July 1834 the canton of Berne made him a captain of the artillery regiment of their canton. At this time he was already busily preparing a Manual of Artillery for the use of the Swiss Army. Here the prince had a subject which he had already studied minutely; one in which he continued to take a keen and practical interest until the end of his life. The result was a treatise which, if too technical to be of any general interest, was possessed of far more value than the rather vague political generalisations of the previous pamphlets. Unlike its predecessors, this volume was not avowedly concerned with current political events; but even more than its predecessors was it designed to forward the political ambitions of its author. The *Manuel d'Artillerie* was a book of real merit, a closely printed, closely reasoned volume of over five hundred pages, succinct in form, precise in detail, clear and lucid in expression—almost a model of what such a book should be. It may or may not have been the unaided work of the prince; in any case, it was a volume on the title-page of which Napoleon's nephew could put his name without fear of criticism.

Much industry and study must have gone to the composition of the book; industry not less untiring was now spent on its distribution. Every French officer with whom the prince had the slightest personal acquaintance, or the remotest connexion through some common friend, received a presentation copy of the work, with a friendly letter assuring its recipient of the author's personal esteem and regard. By such means Louis Napoleon endeavoured, not unsuccessfully, to make his name familiar in the French army.[1] If the favour remained unacknowledged, no harm was done; if an answer was forthcoming, it was easy for Louis to judge from its terms whether he had found a possible friend; and unless his reply had been absolutely frigid, the officer found himself the recipient of further correspondence from the prince. Officers with whom Louis had succeeded in establishing friendly relations would receive further copies, with the request that they would give them to their comrades, telling them at the same time that the prince would be glad to hear from them their opinions on his work.

Not only French officers, but also the prince's military acquaintances in Switzerland, Germany, and even England received similar communications from him : one such letter which has not hitherto seen the light, we reproduce on the following page; it was addressed to Sir Robert Wilson, a distinguished English general, and shows very well both Louis Napoleon's activity in distributing his work, and also his wide interest in the subject with which it deals.

'I send you,' writes Louis, 'a work which I have recently published : I beg you will accept

[1] 'A book called the *Manuel des Artilleurs*, which is said to have some merit, and has been widely circulated among military people, is represented to have been written by Prince Louis.'—Granville to Palmerston, Paris, 4th Nov. 1836.

it as a token of my remembrance, and shall be happy if it merit your approbation. If it would not be an abuse of your kindness, I would beg you, General, to be so good as send the second copy, which I enclose, to any distinguished officer of the English artillery, asking him on my behalf to be kind enough to give me exact particulars of the *breech-loading cannon* recently constructed in England. As I am in touch with all that goes on in France and Germany, I could in return give him all the particulars he might desire on the artillery of these two countries.'

The prince goes on to plead his great interest in the subject as the excuse for making this rather bold demand, and the letter concludes with some personal compliments to the general himself.[1]

Although Prince Louis lost no opportunity at this period of exhibiting himself publicly as a

---

[1] 'Général,

'Je vous envoye un ouvrage que j'ai publié dernièrement; je vous prie de l'accepter comme un souvenir de ma part, et je serais heureux qu'il méritât votre approbation. Si ce n'était abuser de votre complaisance, je vous prierais, Général, de vouloir bien remettre le second exemplaire que je vous envoye à quelque officier distingué de l'artillerie anglaise, en lui demandant de ma part qu'il voulût bien me donner des renseignements exacts sur les canons qu'on a construits dernièrement en Angleterre pour être *chargés par la culasse.* Comme je suis au courrant (*sic*) de tout ce qui se fait en France et en Allemagne, je pourrais en revanche lui donner tous les renseignements qu'il désirerait sur l'artillerie de ces deux pays. Je vous demande pardon, Général, de vous charger d'une telle commission, mais d'un côté l'amour de la science et de

Général

Je vous envoye un ouvrage que j'ai
publié dernièrement; je vous prie de l'accepter
comme un souvenir de ma part, et je serais
heureux qu'il méritât votre approbation.
Si ce n'était abuser de votre complaisance
je vous prierais Général de vouloir bien
remettre le second exemplaire que je vous
envoye à quelque officier distingué
de l'artillerie anglaise en lui demandant
de ma part qu'il voulût bien me donner
des renseignements exacts sur les canons
qu'on a construit dernièrement en Angleterre pour être
chargés par la culasse. Comme je suis
au courant de tout ce qui se fait en France
et en Allemagne, je pourrais en revanche
lui donner tous les renseignements qu'il
désirerait sur l'artillerie de ces deux pays.
Je vous demande pardon Général de
vous charger d'une telle commission, mais

Letter showing Louis Napoleon's method of
distributing his Manuel d'Artillerie

[OVER.

d'un côté l'amour de la sienne et
de l'autre le souvenir de l'amabilité
que vous m'avez toujours témoigné
m'ont encouragé à vous demander ce
service.

J'ai été si charmé du séjour que
j'ai fait dans votre beau pays
que je serais bien heureux de pouvoir
y retourner. Vous serez une des
personnes que j'aurai le plus de plaisir
à revoir.

Adieu Général, ma mère me
charge de la rappeler à votre
souvenir, je vous prie de croire
à ma considération et à mes sentiments
distingués.

Napoléon Louis Bonaparte

Arenenberg Canton de Thurgovie. ce 24 Mars 1830

candidate for an alternative form of government in France, yet his private correspondence shows that he had no delusions as to the true difficulties of his situation. A letter written in January 1835 to his friend M. Vieillard, his brother's former tutor, is worthy of quotation in this connexion. 'I know,' wrote the prince, 'that I count for much through my name, but nothing as yet through myself; aristocrat by birth, I am democrat by breeding and by conviction; owing all to inheritance, yet really all to election; ... taxed with personal ambition if I take one step outside my wonted track, taxed with apathy and indifference if I stay quiet in my corner; an object of fear by reason of my name to liberal and absolutist alike, I am in fact without political friends of any sort, save those whose experience of the freaks of fortune makes them regard me as one who may conceivably become a useful tool.' Yet with full knowledge of the difficulties which beset his first steps,

l'autre le souvenir de l'amabilité que vous m'avez toujours temoignée m'ont encouragé à vous demander ce service.

'J'ai été si charmé du séjour que j'ai fait dans votre beau pays que je serais bien heureux de pouvoir y retourner ; vous serez une des personnes que j'aurai le plus de plaisir à revoir.

'Adieu, Général, ma mère me charge de la rappeler à votre souvenir, je vous prie de croire à ma considération et à mes sentimens distingués.

'NAPOLÉON LOUIS BONAPARTE.

'ARENENBERG, CANTON DE THURGOVIE,
'*le* 24 *Mars* 1836.'

Correspondence of Sir Robert Wilson, Brit. Mus. Addl. MSS. 30, 116 f. 53.

the prince announces his firm intention of pushing forward, deterred by no secondary interest, debarred by no obstacles, until he has forced himself 'to an eminence high enough to catch the dying rays of the sun of St Helena.' It would be difficult to imagine a juster or more clear-sighted appreciation of his position and prospects than that contained in this letter; while its closing sentence is an epitome of his whole effort at this time. It is not perhaps unfair to see in this last picturesque phrase a recognition on Louis Napoleon's part of the need of judicious self-advertisement. Certainly he lost no opportunity of bringing himself into notice. Any reference in the French Chamber to his family, or the law which banished them, brought a letter of expostulation from his pen; any little mark of local esteem from his Swiss friends produced a note expressing his gratification—letters which generally recurred to the text of his imperial pretensions, and were always couched in a style suited to the position claimed rather than that occupied by their writer. Did any idle rumour gain currency about the prince, he would take it up, toy with it, explain it, expand it, and finally with infinite circumstance and ceremony give it the *coup de grâce* of ultimate denial. So, in 1831, he had issued an elaborate denial of the report that he was seeking the crown of Belgium; so, in 1835, he went out of his way to deny a rumour that he was a suitor for the hand of Queen Maria of Portugal.[1] Not content with giving a serious contradiction to a report which was in no danger of being taken seriously, he proceeded to give reasons for a hypothetical refusal on his part to share the throne of Portugal even if it were offered to him : he has not forgotten the noble conduct of his father, who abdicated the throne of Holland because he could not reconcile Dutch interests and French; the hope of some day serving France is worth more to him than all the thrones on earth. Any attention which utterances of this sort could provoke was, of course, rather that of ridicule than respect; but even so it was not without value to the prince at this time. Indeed, one of the elements of his success as a pretender was the fact that he was not afraid of making himself ridiculous—possibly because he was not always conscious of doing so. A sense of humour is almost as effective a deterrent as a sense of honour; and for a political pretender it may even be the more awkward possession of the two.

[1] Queen Maria's first husband was Auguste de Beauharnais, a cousin of Louis Napoleon's. This fact alone gave the rumour any semblance of truth. I can find no sign that even among the long list of candidates submitted to the queen, Louis Napoleon's name was ever seriously put forward. Queen Maria herself wished to marry the Duc de Nemours, and a considerable party in Portugal favoured a royal alliance with a son of Louis Philippe. But the energetic representations of England checked the design: ' I informed the Marquis of Saldanha that I would not make use of qualifying and diplomatic phrases, but tell him at once that the marriage of the queen with a Frenchman would play the very devil in England with the Portuguese cause.' (Lord Walden to Palmerston. 'Most Confidential.' Lisbon, 28th May 1835.) As usual, it was the house of Saxe-Coburg which eventually supplied the eligible prince.

If at the time Louis Napoleon was glad to avail himself of any rumour which linked his name with royalty, he could not complain if after his own accession to power there should be found persons willing to boast that they themselves might easily have been connected by marriage with the future Emperor of the French. For the most part these assertions, as they share the motive of Louis' hypothetical refusal of a royal consort, so they share also its emptiness of truth. In this category may probably be included the two claims which have been made to the honour of refusing offers of marriage from Louis Napoleon during his sojourn in Switzerland. Of these, one was made on behalf of a Mauritius tea-planter's widow; the other on behalf of a Mlle Bocher, afterwards the wife of one of Napoleon III's ministers. Neither claim was advanced until long after Napoleon III's death.

But to this period does belong the one attachment of Louis Napoleon in early life, which did certainly come within measurable distance of marriage. After the death of his wife, in November 1835, King Jerome with his two children came to visit Queen Hortense at Arenenberg. Neither then nor at any subsequent time was there an entire sympathy between Louis and Jerome's son, Prince Napoleon. But with the king's daughter, the Princess Mathilde, Louis Napoleon soon fell deeply in love. He was twenty-seven, she was seventeen, a gentle, accomplished, and beautiful princess,

Parents on both sides smiled on the match. There was no hurry, but there were no serious difficulties. Settlements were arranged, and everything seemed to promise a smooth course for true love.

But for Louis Napoleon smooth courses had no attraction; or such occasional attraction as they did present to him came but as a temptation to be resolutely put aside. A few slight obstacles must in any case have been forthcoming, for King Jerome was a man inclined to drive a hard bargain, and there was some haggling before the marriage settlements could be arranged. But to Louis these details must have seemed more than ordinarily trivial. For while they were in process of arrangement he was himself busied in very different fashion. Rightly convinced that he had found an admirable empress, he intended to offer her no smaller dominion than an empire. To the suggestions of his relatives, urging him with one voice to seek a life of peaceful retirement for himself and his wife, he turned a deaf ear. Dust and strife and the heat of the day must first be encountered, ere Louis Napoleon's bride could reach the palace he intended her to adorn.

That there were limits to the amount which pamphlets and correspondence could effect for his great cause was a fact of which Louis had long been acutely conscious. At the end of 1835, he was, as we have said, twenty-seven years old—an age at which his uncle had achieved his magnificent Italian campaign of 1796. The prince could not but feel that it was high time that he made some more decisive effort to challenge the opinion of France than he had hitherto done. The four years which had passed since his own Italian exploit had been monotonous enough, though they cannot be said to have been entirely wasted. The summers, save for the usual period at the artillery camp, had been spent at Arenenberg; the winters occupied in travel and study at Geneva, London, and Rome. Some useful work had been done, and some valuable friendships made. But it was only in this year, 1835, that the prince met the most important of all his early friends—M. Fialin, better known by the title he had recently assumed of Viscount de Persigny. Born in the same year as Louis Napoleon, he had entered the French army in 1825, and in three years became adjutant of the 4th Hussars. His military career, however, was cut short in 1830 by his ardent support of the extreme revolutionary movement; he was accused of insubordination, and retired. He thereupon went to Paris, and became a journalist; in 1834 his vigorous and enthusiastic advocacy of the Bonapartist cause attracted the attention of King Joseph, who gave him a letter of introduction to his nephew. If this was really the means of bringing the two young men together, it is noteworthy as being almost the only service of real value ever rendered to Louis Napoleon by any member of the imperial family in his attempt to render possible the restoration of the imperial dynasty. Indeed the prince's faith in his name and in his own future was the more remarkable—and in a sense, the more admirable—that it was shared by none of the Bonaparte family, who regarded his efforts without encouragement or support, and greeted his failures with disavowal and ridicule. His mother alone never derided his ambitions, but even she had no particular hope of their fulfilment. 'You complain of men's injustice,' he wrote to her in 1834; 'I venture to think that you have no right to complain. How can you expect the French to remember us, when by our own act we have sought oblivion for fifteen years; when, these fifteen years every action of every member of my family has been inspired by the fear of compromising himself, and by that alone; when they have avoided every occasion of displaying their persons, every means of publicly recalling their memories to the mind of the people?' It was this resolution at all costs to escape oblivion which had been the prince's ruling motive in the last four years: the time was now come when he was resolved to seek an opportunity of presenting himself personally to the French people as a candidate for the imperial throne. During the year which followed his meeting with Persigny this resolution took shape and substance, and by the summer of 1836 a definite scheme had emerged. Prince Louis was to appear with only a small body of personal adherents at some frontier town; the garrison was to be gained over, and a march on Paris was to follow, which it was hoped would prove as bloodless and triumphal as had been the return of Napoleon from Elba. It only remained to choose the starting-point, and a variety of reasons rendered the decision an easy one. The north-eastern frontier was at once the most accessible to Louis and the nearest to Paris. The most important garrison town on that frontier was known to be in a state of profound discontent towards the July government.[1] There, too, was stationed the 4th Artillery, the Emperor's own regiment, which had opened to him the gates of Grenoble in 1815; and since their colonel had undertaken to declare in his favour, the prince had more than *a priori* evidence of its readiness to play a like part in this second return from Elba. The choice of the starting-point could, therefore, be no longer doubtful. It was in the provinces of Alsace and Lorraine— their names not yet coupled by the sinister hyphen which linked them later—that the supporters of the democratic empire were most numerous and most enthusiastic. It was from the city of Strasburg— whose effigy in the Place de la Concorde was not yet shrouded for its long mourning—that Louis Napoleon hoped to win his way back to the imperial throne.

[1] 'In that city, perhaps more than in any other place in France, a republican spirit prevails.'—Granville to Palmerston, Paris, 4th November 1836.

CHAPTER VI

THE FIRST CLAIM TO THE INHERITANCE

Begin: the getting out of doors is the greatest part of the journey. . . . Stay till the waters are low, stay till some boats come by to transport you, stay till a bridge be built for you; —you had even as good stay till the river be quite past.
ABRAHAM COWLEY.

ON the evening of October 31, 1836, there reached Paris a telegraphic despatch—or rather a fragment of one—which threw the cabinet of Louis Philippe into a state bordering on consternation. It ran as follows :—

'Strasburg, Oct. 30, 1836. This morning, about six o'clock, Louis Napoleon, son of the Duchess of Saint Leu, who had in his confidence the colonel of artillery, Vaudrey, traversed the streets of Strasburg with part of . . .' Here the despatch broke off abruptly: it had been sent by the *télégraphe aérien;* a fog along the line of signals prevented the transmission of the remaining portion, which would have informed the king what had happened to this audacious young man, who had thus paraded the streets of a strong garrison town with an unknown following. Indeed, what might not have happened in the thirty hours which had passed between the sending of the message and the receiving of it? In that time the rebellion, if such it were, might have gained a formidable headway; even now the restorer of the empire might be moving in triumphant progress towards Paris. For it is hardly possible that the precedent of 1815, which had prompted the prince to his action, can have been absent from the mind of Louis Philippe in the hours which followed. Guizot in his memoirs gives a graphic description of the cabinet council hurriedly summoned to meet at the Tuileries; of the flitting to and fro of the anxious queen and princes, asking questions which could not be answered; of the wakeful night spent by the king and his advisers in preparing for eventualities which never occurred, the hours of weary waiting for news which did not come. For the despatch had stopped short, like the *feuilleton* which was just making its first appearance in French journalism, at the most exciting moment of its narrative. There was nothing for it, however, but to wait for the morning; and with the morning came the concluding instalment of the despatch. With it came also a personal report by special messenger from General Voirol, the governor of Strasburg, in which he related the whole story of the rising. After all had not telegraphy, then in its infancy, played him this rather childish prank, King Louis Philippe would have been spared a great deal of needless anxiety. For the entire affair had been over in something under three hours, and the would-be emperor was already under lock and key when the original message was despatched.

The sense of relief was overwhelming. It was possible to smile now at the fears of the previous night; it was politic to conceal the fact that one had ever felt afraid. The news of the rising was now for the first time made public in terms of contemptuous brevity and calculated unconcern. In its published, and possibly doctored, form General Voirol's despatch in no way suggested that there had been anything in the rising which could cause the Government a moment's uneasiness. Part of the 4th Artillery had indeed joined the prince, but all the other regiments had remained faithful; *ce jeune imprudent* had been arrested, and everyone concerned—except, of course, this same foolish young man and his insignificant following—deserved great credit. The French press and the foreign correspondents in Paris followed the official lead almost without exception, and for the most part in all good faith. Indeed, the belief of a young man, personally almost unknown, that he could enter France and with a body of fifteen obscure followers effect a bloodless and triumphal progress to the Tuileries, obliterating all opposition by the mere shadow of his great name—this was a thing which in the event of success would have seemed sublime, but in the light of failure could only appear ridiculous. There were, moreover, certain accidental absurdities in connexion with the affair which the Government exploited with much dexterity and success; they even contrived to give the impression that they had been completely informed of the whole circumstances of the plot for some time past, and had deliberately allowed it to go so far as it had gone in order the more effectually to demonstrate its futility. How far this was from the fact is shown by a letter written by the Duke of Orleans on the afternoon of November 1, the day on which the news of the failure of the revolt had arrived. Writing to his brother, the Duke of Nemours, he congratulated him that owing to his absence from Paris he had learnt the whole story at once, and thus escaped 'the *horrible* uncertainties we have gone through. The whole of last night we sat up without news: I had decided to set out for Strasburg, when M. de Franqueville arrived.'

Indeed it can hardly now be questioned that the July monarchy was conscious of having narrowly escaped a crisis of real gravity; and that there was far more justification for their first alarms than they would have cared to admit. For the insurrection had been neither hastily resolved on nor altogether rashly executed. As we have seen already, Louis had been steadily cultivating the acquaintance of French officers ever since the publication of his military work; and from the time of his meeting with Persigny, in 1835, had been contemplating some such enterprise as that which he had actually attempted. In that year he began to frequent Baden-Baden, a watering-place which by its nearness to the French frontier served as an admirable point for his preliminary preparations; here he could meet, without giving rise to suspicion, the discontented residents of Alsace, and interview the officers of Strasburg who were inclined to his cause. The first important military recruit was Laity, a lieutenant of an engineer battalion in the Strasburg garrison—a wholehearted adherent whose services were to prove only less valuable than Persigny's. But an acquisition of greater immediate importance was Colonel Vaudrey. His distinguished military record, his noble bearing and appearance, most of all the important position he now occupied, marked him as a man whose adherence would be a most valuable addition to the cause. For he had served with bravery and distinction in the Napoleonic campaigns; he was a soldier of fine presence and commanding physique; he was a commander of the 3rd and 4th Artillery regiments stationed at Strasburg. Certain grievances against the Government of July disposed him to listen with favour to the prince's suggestions; but it was the charms of a fair enthusiast in the Napoleonic cause, a certain Madame Gordon, to whom Persigny had introduced him, that finally overcame his last hesitations. It was late in the summer of 1836 when Prince Louis received his promise of support, and the assurance that the colonel of the most Bonapartist regiment in France would declare himself in his favour when the time for action came. It was a very great gain, but the prince looked higher still. He was convinced that General Voirol himself, the governor of Strasburg, would not refuse to aid him. In the middle of August he wrote the general a letter which was practically an open overture. Voirol did not reply, and informed his Government of what had happened. Yet no steps were taken to prevent the progress of the plot, and Louis still believed that Voirol would not oppose him when the time came. Two months before the rising he rode over to Strasburg, entered the city at nightfall, and was presented to a party of some twenty officers. His reception was enthusiastic; no particular precautions seem to have been thought necessary against the possibility of betrayal. So unguarded and so indiscriminate were the prince's advances that it is hard to avoid the conclusion that many officers who did not, as things turned out, declare themselves in favour of the rising, were yet curiously lukewarm or still more curiously short-sighted in their devotion to the monarchical cause; and that not a few were careful, without committing themselves too deeply in case of the failure of the movement, to avoid any such gratuitous excess of zeal as should prevent them from claiming a share in the advantages of its possible success.

When all but the final arrangements had been made, Louis left Baden and returned to Arenenberg on a short visit to his mother. On October 24 he told her that he was starting the next day to join a hunting-party in the Principality of Heckingen, and early in the morning of the 25th he bade her farewell. Although she may not have been fully aware of his plans Hortense seems at least to have realised that it was not quite an ordinary parting, for as he left she placed on his finger her most cherished possession, the wedding-ring with which her mother Josephine had been married to the Emperor. A year later, when next her son saw her, Queen Hortense was on her deathbed, so that the parting was practically their last.

Troubled by no gloomy reflections, the prince set forth with his one serving-man to recover his throne. They reached Freiburg on the evening of the 25th, and remained there until the morning of the 28th. During that time they were joined by Colonel Vaudrey and Mme Gordon; but other and more important officers whom the prince had expected to arrive from Paris did not appear. To wait longer seemed useless; so on the 28th they advanced on Strasburg, entering the city just before the gates were closed for the night. Persigny had preceded them, and was already in residence in lodgings which he had taken a month ago. There the prince passed the night, and spent the following day in interviewing the leaders of the revolt. On the evening of the 29th a final council of war was held. The date of the rising had originally been fixed for the 31st; but it was resolved on Persigny's advice to act on the 30th. It has been stated that the change of date had a great deal to do with the failure of the attempt, but there is no sufficient evidence to show that any important accession to the prince's forces would have resulted from a day's delay; while it is manifest that to linger in Strasburg on the brink of action was a course so dangerous that nothing short of great and apparent gain could justify it.

Another change of plan in connexion with the movement had, however, a really important effect on its chances of success. The garrison of Strasburg consisted of three regiments of the line, two artillery regiments, and a battalion of engineers. But two of the infantry regiments were stationed in remote and isolated portions of the town, and could therefore be ignored, in so far at least as the opening moves of the game were concerned. The order in which the three remaining regiments were to be approached was an important question, and one on which decision was not easily reached. The 4th Artillery, Napoleon's old regiment, and the one now under Vaudrey's immediate command, was stationed in the Austerlitz Barracks at the south of the town. The 3rd Artillery, with the engineer battalion, was in the centre of the city, near the open space of the Place d'Armes; unlike the 4th Artillery, it had its cannon close at hand and ready for immediate use. The only other regiment to be considered was the 46th Infantry, which was stationed in the

Finkmatt Barracks under the northern rampart of the city. It had been originally intended that the prince should present himself first to the 3rd Artillery, the largest and most important regiment in the town. If it were won it was practically certain that the 4th Artillery would follow its example, and the engineers would in all probability do the same. After that it would not matter whether the infantry and population did or did not follow suit; possessed of the arsenal and 150 cannon the prince could from the Place d'Armes terrorise into instant obedience the entire city, and the infantry even had it wished could have offered no effective opposition to such a display of force as this. The plan was simple, practicable, and almost assured of success if once the 3rd Artillery joined the prince. But it is characteristic of his whole nature that he finally put his veto on it. He did not wish to date his reign from a successful military revolt, or to terrorise a civilian population into silent obedience to his will. He desired to rely not on the army alone, still less on any one branch of the army, but on a spontaneous outburst of democratic enthusiasm in which soldier and citizen, infantry and artillery, should join. There must be no attempt, therefore, to over-awe the civilian population or even the line regiments; the movement must be without bloodshed, and if possible without even the threat of bloodshed. As the commanding position of the 3rd Artillery had now ceased to matter, it was resolved to appear first, not to them, but to the 4th Artillery, in the Austerlitz Barracks. So far the change was good, for in any case it would probably have been wise to begin with the regiment which was known to be the most Bonapartist in the garrison. But instead of proceeding at once to the 3rd when the 4th Artillery had been won over, it was now resolved that the prince with the main body should go right on to the 46th Infantry; detachments of the 4th Artillery would meanwhile distribute proclamations among the citizens and the troops; and all would converge together in the Place d'Armes to be joined by the 3rd Artillery and the engineers. As compared with the original plan it was complicated instead of simple, and though not altogether impracticable it left far greater room for some disastrous hitch. It was, however, eminently characteristic of the humane and visionary turn of the prince's mind to sacrifice a present concrete advantage for the future triumph of a vague but magnanimous idea.

This alteration had of course been resolved on some time before the final meeting on the evening of the 29th, which was concerned only with last details of its execution. At ten in the evening the gathering broke up. The prince and his little band of immediate followers remained in hiding for the night in a house rented by one of their number, situated at no great distance from the Austerlitz Barracks.

Louis here proceeded to write out his proclamations; he had considered it prudent to avoid having them printed in advance. Then he wrote two letters to his mother, one announcing the success of his effort, the other its failure. This epistolary exercise was probably a mere means of passing the time, for Louis had not quite his uncle's supreme gift of detachment, and sleep was beyond his summons on such an occasion. But it is wiser to leave success to announce itself than to prepare proclamation of it before it is won; and of this fact Louis was soon to be rudely apprised.

Six o'clock in the morning was the hour fixed by the conspirators for their appearance at the Austerlitz Barracks. An hour before that time a body of cavalry was heard advancing in their direction, and the conspirators thought themselves betrayed at the last moment. But they were unmolested. At last the hour struck. Turning to his followers, the prince said simply, 'Gentlemen, the time has come. Now we shall see whether France still remembers twenty years of glory.' 'Have no doubt of it,' they answered: 'France follows.'

Dressed now in the emblems of their brief authority, the little band sallied forth. The prince wore a blue artillery uniform; on his shoulders were a colonel's epaulettes, on his breast the star and broad riband of the Legion of Honour, upon his head a general's hat not unlike the famous cocked hat worn by the Little Corporal. Colonel Parquin, a veteran of the Napoleonic wars who had long been a frequent visitor at Arenenberg, was dressed as a general. De Querelles, a retired cavalry officer, bore the shrouded eagle of the empire.

The morning was dark and cold; there had been some snow, but with daybreak it gradually ceased to fall. The distance to be covered was short, and in a few minutes the party arrived at the Austerlitz Barracks. Vaudrey had gone there an hour earlier, and had already made every preparation for their reception. When the prince entered the courtyard of the barracks the regiment was already drawn up on parade, though entirely ignorant of the cause of their assembly at this unwonted hour. Directly he saw Louis, Vaudrey advanced to meet him, and led him to the centre of the square. In a few stirring words he introduced the prince, who had come to win back the people's rights—could the nephew of the Emperor count on them? The question was soon answered. Shouts of 'Vive l'Empereur!' long, loud, and almost unanimous were the reply. The prince had to make a sign with his hand to procure a hearing for himself. He had appealed to them first, he said, on account of the great memories they had in common. 'In your regiment it was that the Emperor Napoleon my uncle, served as captain; in your company, he made himself illustrious at the siege of Toulon; and yours again was the regiment that opened the gates of Grenoble to him on his return from the isle of

Elba. Soldiers, there are new destinies reserved for you. Yours is the glory of beginning a great enterprise; yours the honour of being first to salute the eagle of Austerlitz and Wagram.' From Querelles he took the eagle, and holding it aloft before their eyes, he bade them behold in it not merely the symbol of their country's glory, but the harbinger of its liberty. Renewed and enthusiastic cheers greeted the prince's address. Every sword was waved, and every voice raised; the regiment seemed resolved to outdo its own record in devotion to the imperial cause. The regimental band struck up; Prince Louis took over the command, and marched out of the barracks in triumph at the head of the regiment. In accordance with the new plan, by which everything was to be attempted at once, a number of detachments were now broken off from the main body and despatched on their several missions. Laity went off to his engineer battalion; two other lieutenants were sent to rouse the 3rd Artillery; Lombard, a military doctor of Strasburg, was sent to seize the printing offices, and print with the utmost despatch proclamations from Prince Louis to the army, the nation, and the citizens of Strasburg. An officer was sent on in advance to inform the 46th Infantry of what had happened, and to prepare them for the prince's reception; one detachment was sent to seize the telegraph office, and another, under the immediate command of Persigny himself, to arrest the prefect.

Meanwhile the main body, headed by the prince and Colonel Vaudrey, made their way towards the centre of the town. It was still early morning, and even the main streets were at first almost empty. But soon crowds gathered on the way, and many of them took up the soldiers' cry—'Vive Napoléon! Vive l'Empereur! Vive la liberté!' According to the insurgents' own account the popular enthusiasm was so great as to delay the prince's progress, since numbers of the crowd pressed closely round him or rushed out to embrace the eagle which Querelles was carrying. What is certain is that bodies of civilians hostile to the Government gathered in the streets, ready to throw in their lot with the rising in case of its further success.[1]

To the prince at the moment such success may well have seemed assured. Both at the police station and at the military headquarters the guard on duty turned out and presented arms as he passed. So escorted and so greeted, he reached the Place d'Armes. Here he halted the column while he himself with his staff went up to General Voirol's rooms, hoping by a personal appeal to win him to his cause. But the general refused. Surprised and mortified, the prince after some parley placed

[1] Granville to Palmerston :—

'PARIS, *Nov.* 4, 1836.

'I am told from good authority, that Parties of Republicans linked arm in arm appeared collectively in the streets, waiting to see whether the attempt of Louis Buonaparte and Colonel Vaudrey would occasion the defection of any considerable portion of the garrison.'

him under arrest. Parquin himself was left in charge of the prisoner; but he proved an inefficient custodian, and the general managed to make his escape shortly after the prince's departure. This was the first check, but it was far from being a fatal one. The prince returned to the square, and together with Vaudrey and the greater part of the 4th Artillery resumed the advance towards the Finkmatt Barracks.

It was now that a really serious and perfectly avoidable mistake was made. The barracks in question consisted of a long building parallel to the ramparts, from which they were only separated by a narrow enclosed court—the parade ground of the 46th Infantry. It had been arranged that the prince should advance by way of the ramparts. The courtyard was not ten yards in breadth, and a voice less clear and penetrating than Louis' would have been perfectly audible from the ramparts. The fact that the prince would have made his appearance with a whole regiment at his back would have added greatly to his chances of success, while even had he failed his unmolested retreat would have been absolutely assured; and it would still be possible for him to make his appeal to the 3rd Artillery.

Instead, however, of adopting this course the regiment now advanced by the Faubourg Pierre, a street broad enough in itself, but only communicating with the barrack square by a narrow lane. The prince was therefore obliged to leave half his troops in the Faubourg, while he himself with four hundred men marched up the lane. To secure his retreat he was forced to leave the majority even of these outside in the lane, so that on entering the barrack-yard he had with him only his staff and a small escort.

The results of this gratuitous error were now visible. It had rendered the failure of the appeal to the 46th not only more probable, but more fatal. For in entering the courtyard Louis had placed himself in a trap from which escape was hardly possible should the infantry declare against him. Another minor mishap was also revealed. The officer who had been despatched to prepare the 46th for the prince's arrival had not yet appeared. Hence the troops, instead of being already on the parade ground, were still in barracks. For a few minutes, however, it seemed as though not even this series of misfortunes were going to affect the success of the movement. Indeed it had now almost reached a stage in which it could survive a few initial mishaps. The prefect and General Voirol were under arrest: so were the colonel and brigadier-general of the 3rd Artillery—the only officers in that regiment from whom serious opposition was expected. The telegraph office and printing presses were in the hands of the prince's followers; Laity with his company of engineers was advancing to join the revolutionary forces, and portions of the 3rd Artillery were already on their way to the general rendezvous at the Place d'Armes.

Even in his straitened position in the barrack-yard of the 46th it seemed as though Louis would achieve his purpose. On seeing his entry from the barrack windows the soldiers began to flock down to the courtyard. Many of them took up the cry of the artillery; shouts of 'Vive l'Empereur!' were heard on all sides. An old sergeant who had served in the Imperial Guard ran forward and kissed the prince's hand. The soldiers were visibly impressed by the incident, which was precisely of a kind that would appeal to them most strongly. Some of the 46th were actually being formed into companies by the prince's officers. A few steadfastly refused to support the rising; a larger number seemed already to have decided in its favour, but the majority still wavered, awaiting some decisive impulse in one direction or the other. It was a moment when a word, a masterful sentence might settle the fate of the entire movement, and with it perhaps the destinies of France for a dozen years to come. That word was spoken. Suddenly, from the back of the barrack-yard an officer snapped out, 'Soldiers, they are making fools of you. This person they present to you as the Emperor's son is only a dummy in disguise.' Another officer caught up the cry, adding, 'I recognise him. It is Colonel Vaudrey's nephew.'

Instantly the whole aspect of affairs was altered. The faithful were confirmed in their resistance, the waverers rallied to the voice of authority. For the prince it was a paralysing blow. Had he so wished he might by this time have been in command of 150 pieces of cannon; instead, he had preferred to rely solely on the magic of his name. And now in a moment this weapon was struck from his hand. To some extent it was even turned against him: for of the 46th, it was just the men who had been most ready to welcome the descendant of the Emperor who were most furious that they should have been tricked by the vain use of his name. The artillery indeed remained faithful, but all chance of winning over the infantry was lost.

Vainly now the prince's partisans tried to drown all dissident voices in a great shout for the emperor. Confusion of utterance, bewilderment of spirit, had overtaken his followers. Cries and counter cries were heard. The infantry surged forward towards the prince; more artillery from the Faubourg came up to his rescue and drove them back. In doing this they unfortunately separated Louis Napoleon from his staff. From the ramparts the populace, who had not ceased to cheer the prince, hurled stones and curses on the infantry. Talandier, the colonel of the 46th, ordered the gates of the barrack-yard to be shut. Two of the prince's officers who were still with him offered to force a passage with their swords through the infantry; indeed, only by some such drastic step as this could he now hope to make good his escape. But Louis refused; he was determined that in no case should blood he shed. The infantry re-formed. The prince and his recent rescuers were driven back against the wall of the barracks. The prince defended himself without wounding his assailants; finally, they closed on him and made him prisoner. He was formally arrested by a young officer of the 46th.[1]

Vaudrey was still free, and still in command of the greater portion of his regiment. Talandier demanded his surrender, but he refused, and the artillery showed themselves eager to defend him. But another clever falsehood confidently uttered disarmed him in his turn. Talandier told him that the enthusiasm of the citizens in favour of the rising was entirely due to their belief that it was in favour of the restoration of Charles X; that they would be ready to tear Vaudrey in pieces when they discovered its true object. Staggered by this last blow, the colonel dismissed his men

[1] Probably Sub-lieutenant Pleignier. It is interesting to find that fourteen years later this same officer appealed personally to Louis Napoleon for promotion, promising to be zealous in his service. In September 1850 a great review of troops was held at Versailles; Louis Napoleon, as President of the Republic, was present. Normanby, then British ambassador, accompanied him. 'It may interest your Lordship,' he writes to Palmerston, in a despatch dated 26th September 1850, 'if I here add a word upon an incident that occurred within my own personal observation. In riding in at the great gate of the station at Versailles, an officer in the uniform of a captain came between the President and myself and presented a petition, saying, "I hope you will remember me; I was the officer who arrested you at Strasburg." The President took the petition from him, saying, with perfect calm, "Your name is—— What you did on that occasion was your duty, and certainly would not be an impediment to your advancement; but I have already made enquiries about you, and the report is not favourable." On the officer attempting to add something, as to the zeal with which he would now serve his Government, the prince stopped him, saying his case should be further inquired into.'

and yielded himself prisoner; for he now believed that resistance was hopeless, and that it might even endanger the prince's life. Persigny alone had the heart to attempt desperate measures. On hearing of the prince's capture he hurried back to the artillery barracks to get the guns out, for he at least had no scruples as to the shedding of blood. But what would have been perfectly feasible before had now become impossible. Vaudrey alone of the insurgents had access to the arsenal, and no one else could order out ammunition. And Vaudrey was now a prisoner. The last faint chance of success had therefore disappeared. Lombard destroyed the proclamations; Persigny burned the prince's private papers, and then made good his own escape. A few shots fired over their heads from the Finkmatt Barracks dispersed the crowd. The officers and men of the 3rd Artillery and of the engineers who had already set out to the general rendezvous of the revolt returned in haste to their barracks, and found to their relief that the authorities were easily satisfied as to the innocence of their morning excursion. Indeed it was soon evident that a perfect harmony of purpose existed between culprits unwilling to be caught, and a Government unwilling to find culprits. The rising was to be minimised; it might be necessary to bring to trial officers caught red-handed, but it was neither necessary nor politic to bring to light further ramifications of the plot; it was impossible to deny the revolt of the 4th Artillery, but it was easy to ignore signs of disaffection in the remaining regiments of the garrison.

By eight o'clock in the morning, in something less than three hours from its inception, the Strasburg insurrection was at an end. So unexpected had been its sudden collapse and so bright had seemed its prospect of success, that the messenger to whom Louis had entrusted his two letters to his mother had already despatched the one announcing the success of the undertaking. The queen's reply, recommending her son to display moderation and mercy in his victory, was one of the features of the affair which lent itself most readily to the ridicule of the Government. For at the moment she wrote it her son was a prisoner in rigorous and solitary confinement.

In prison at Strasburg he remained until November 9, when he was brought to Paris. He arrived there on the 11th, and was lodged for the few hours he spent in the capital at the Prefecture of Police. After long and anxious consideration, Louis Philippe's advisers had determined not to bring the prince to trial. There were many reasons which prevented them from doing so. Hitherto they had been successful beyond their hopes in their effort to cast ridicule upon the whole affair. In the Parisian press Louis Napoleon was portrayed in a series of grotesque caricatures; he was represented as having adopted in every detail the historic costume of the emperor; he was depicted as a person contemptible in appearance and lacking in ordinary intelligence. 'I was told this morning,' writes Granville in his despatch to Palmerston on November 4, 'that the young Louis Buonaparte fainted at the moment of his arrest, that he has since been continually shedding tears and writing letters[1] imploring the mercy of the Government: and that these letters are ill-written and ill-spelt.' To our ambassador this account seemed 'extraordinary'; to the French Government its circulation, like that of the other inspired comments on the affair, was abundantly satisfactory. Now to have put Louis on his trial, whatever the issue of that trial might be, would have been at once to demonstrate the absurdity of such reports as these. Moreover, even if his condemnation were assured, the prince would have increased his hold on the popular mind; as a political martyr his importance would become considerable; attempts might be made to rescue him, or petitions circulated to procure his pardon. But it was far from probable that any jury could be found in France at the time which could be relied on to condemn such a prisoner, and his acquittal could not but be a most awkward rebuff for the Government who brought him to trial. The dilemma was avoided by the course

[1] It is hardly necessary to point out that had this really been Louis Napoleon's attitude, the Government would easily have obtained from the prince the promise of a continual residence in America, a promise which, as a matter of fact, they were utterly unable to extract from him. Hortense indeed did write both 'to the king and to Count Molé, supplicating mercy for her only son (Granville to Palmerston, 11th November 1836). But Louis resented this action.

actually adopted by Louis Philippe's advisers, that of shipping the prince off unceremoniously to the United States. There was much to recommend the plan to them. Its apparent generosity would confirm the impression that they declined to take the matter seriously. Nothing could be simpler than to see that the prince was not allowed to reach land until the first interest in the affair had subsided; nothing easier than to suggest, and during his enforced silence sedulously to spread the rumour, that he had promised the king that when he had reached America he would remain there. If he did remain, the Government's object would have been attained; if he did not, at least they would have inflicted on him a stigma not easily effaced; despite his denials a vague idea would still survive that somehow he had abused the simple-hearted generosity of the affable old king.

There was, indeed, not much of simplicity in the king's conduct. At the same time it is not easy to sympathise with the rather exaggerated abuse which the majority of imperialist writers have bestowed on his conduct in refusing to have the prince tried. They have assumed that Louis had a sort of prescriptive right to a trial; and that the denying of it to him was an intolerable grievance. As a matter of fact the king had, of course, a perfect right to deal with his prisoner in any way he should deem most conducive to the stability of his own Government; in this case the course he actually adopted was clearly the wisest one open to him. But in the Government's very successful attempt to represent him as having promised to remain in America for a term of years, the prince had indeed a really legitimate grievance. His own vehement denials failed completely to convince the majority of his contemporaries that he had given no such promise; and when he returned to Europe a few months after his landing in America the renewed abuse of him in the French ministerial press was generally regarded as justified. It was only in 1840, when he was placed on trial for his attack on Boulogne, that a chance admission on the part of one of the Government prosecutors showed how groundless this charge was. 'Pardoned unconditionally,' said M. Franck-Carré, referring to Louis' treatment after his former venture, 'ought he not to have remembered that his machinations were not feared?'

This indirect and unintentional admission was the only withdrawal ever made by Louis Philippe's Government of the charge they were now deliberately preparing against Prince Louis. Although it should have been considered a sufficient vindication of the prince's action in this respect, yet it did not stop the circulation of the charge. Even at her friendliest, during the Crimean War, Queen Victoria, for example, repeated and believed it; while so kindly an observer as Disraeli made the Prince himself plead guilty to it in *Endymion*. The following extracts from the despatches of the British ambassador at this time are therefore of importance;

for they form a more conclusive refutation of the charge than any hitherto forthcoming. On November 7, Granville writes: 'It has been decided by the French Government not to bring to trial Louis Napoleon Buonaparte. The mode of dealing with him has occupied for the last three days very much the attention of the French Government. He will be removed from Europe; but it is, I believe, still uncertain whether an arrangement will be made with him and his family for his being allowed to go to the United States of America on his own parole not to return to France; or whether as a prisoner of war he shall be conveyed to some distant possession of France.' Four days later, however, he writes: 'Louis Napoleon Bonaparte will not be brought to trial: he will not be sent to any French colony; he will be permitted to go to the United States of America, not being even required to engage his parole not to return to France.' Nothing could be more explicit than this; and Granville goes on to explain the French Government's reason for an act which he describes as 'illegal, but not unprecedented.' 'There is strong reason to believe that no jury in the Eastern provinces of France would be found who would condemn a member of the Bonaparte family for a political offence; and it seems now doubtful whether his associates at Strasburg may not be acquitted.'[1] Here we have a shrewd sidelight on the motives of Louis Philippe's generosity towards his prisoner;

[1] Granville to Palmerston, 11th November 1836.

here, too, we find the most conclusive proof of the duplicity of his Government's subsequent action in accusing the prince of breaking his promise to the king.

During his short stay in Paris Louis was not allowed to see his mother, who had hastened there in case her intercessions should prove necessary or effectual to save her son's life. A few hours after his arrival he was hurried on to Lorient, the port from which he was to sail for America. Although he reached the coast on November 13, a series of contrary winds prevented the *Andromède*, the frigate which was to convey him to the United States, from leaving France until the 21st. During the interval the prince wrote a letter to his friend M. Vieillard, expressing his misery at the Government's refusal to allow him to share the fate of his friends, and denying that he had even been asked to engage himself to remain in America. At the same time it is clear that he did not contemplate an immediate return, for in a letter to his mother, written at the same time, he announced his intention of becoming a farmer and cultivating his own land in America. On the day of his departure the sub-Prefect of Lorient handed the prince a small case containing 15,000 francs in gold. This deed has been rightly praised as a kindly and considerate act on the part of the king. But it must be remembered that it was only the partial restitution of a very much larger sum which had been found in the prince's possession at the time of his arrest, when 200,000 francs were taken from him and confiscated. Moreover it was a piece of generosity which cost Louis Philippe little and paid him well, for it formed a very fitting close to the incident from his point of view.

In accordance with sealed orders which were only opened when the *Andromède* had been some days at sea, her captain proceeded to make a vast détour to Rio de Janeiro; and it was only after some weeks had been spent off the Brazilian harbour that he proceeded towards New York, the prince's final destination. Throughout the long voyage, which was an unusually rough one, the prince was treated with the utmost consideration and respect by all on board; indeed Napoleon himself on his journey to St Helena could hardly have been the object of more profound or sympathetic attention. None the less his reflections, as shown in a long budget—half letter, half diary—which he wrote on the voyage and sent to his mother on reaching America, were far from pleasant ones. He had, indeed, less to reproach himself with than has sometimes been imagined. Saving that one all-satisfying argument, success, his attempt lacked hardly any of the contentions which have been used to justify risings against constituted authority. He had not sought to suppress by force a popular government, but to overthrow by a popular movement a government which he believed to rest on force alone. He had deliberately refrained from the use of intimidation, when by availing himself of such means he might have greatly increased his prospect of success. And in spite of this self-imposed limitation he had come within measurable distance of achieving his purpose. For what must still appear rash and reckless in the movement the prince's own presence at its head must be held in some measure to atone. For it is idle to deny that in assuming this position he took his life in his hand. His conduct on the day itself had been sufficiently creditable. His calm and phlegmatic nature was not indeed one of those on which, as on Macaulay's hero, 'danger acted like wine'; when the time for action arrived he was not more—but neither was he less—courageous than in the period of preparation which preceded it. Courage of calm persistence and steadfast endurance he possessed in no ordinary degree; but owing to this dead-level characteristic it was seen at relatively less advantage in moments of crisis and action than in periods of suffering and persistent misfortune. For he was capable of none of that sudden exaltation, nothing of the Homeric joy of battle, which takes possession, for a space, of many more peaceful souls than his in times of sudden stress; yet neither was he subject to the fits of reaction and depression which come to most men when the battle has been fought—and lost.

So it is possible that in the supreme moment at the Finkmatt Barracks another and not really greater man might, by some inspiration, some sudden assertion of personal supremacy, have saved his cause from inglorious collapse. So it is certain that in the period which followed its failure, a greater man than Louis Napoleon could not have shown a worthier resignation, or faced with calmer dignity the prospect of imminent death. For this was the penalty which in the first hours of their captivity the prince and his followers seem to have believed the Government would inflict upon them.

Two personal griefs in connexion with the affair are revealed by the prince's letters written at this time. No sooner had King Jerome learnt of the Strasburg attempt and its unhappy ending than he at once, and in peremptory terms, renounced all further connexion with Louis, abruptly breaking off the negotiations for his daughter's marriage with the prince. Great as was the benefit which eventually resulted to the imperial cause even from the failure of the Strasburg insurrection, yet that benefit was dearly purchased by the rupture of this engagement. Princess Mathilde really understood Louis Napoleon, and such a marriage would have given him not only a sympathetic wife, but a gentle, wise, and loyal counsellor. Incidentally, it might have saved him from much of the annoyance to which he was subjected by the jealousy of Prince Napoleon at a later date. By what it might have promoted, and no less by what it must have precluded, this marriage would have had a great and probably a beneficent effect on the prince's future career.

Greatly as Louis was grieved by the breach

of this engagement, he was for the moment almost equally distressed by the fear that the Government might succeed in its attempt to represent him as having escaped the fate of his companions by his own act: he had not feared ridicule in the event of failure, but he did deeply resent the unjust implication of cowardice.

But greater than any personal anxiety was his concern for the fate of his companions, whom the Government had put on their trial. He feared that his absence might prejudice their case, or that the Government, after thus isolating them, might inflict on its lesser victims a punishment which it had not dared to impose on himself. As a matter of fact Louis Philippe's Government was given no opportunity of displaying either clemency or severity towards its prisoners. Its first intention had been to have them tried by court-martial;[1] but on realising that they might appeal to the Court of Cassation against the legality of such a mode of trial, and that such an appeal would certainly result in their favour, a second council of Louis Philippe's ministers decided that they should be tried by the ordinary Court of Assize.[2] This was done at Strasburg in January 1837, and after a trial which lasted for twelve days a local jury unanimously, and in the teeth of the evidence submitted to them, found the accused not guilty. The prisoners throughout displayed

---

[1] Granville to Palmerston, 4th November 1836.
[2] *Ibid.*

extraordinary spirit and audacity; so far from extenuating or apologising for their actions, they appeared to glory in what they had done. Distinguished counsel were engaged in the proceedings, which were followed with interest and reported in detail both in French and foreign journals. For the first time since the fall of the empire, a certain amount of attention was drawn to the existence of a possible Bonapartist pretender; during the time of the trial some 8000 copies were sold of a biography of Prince Louis which had been hastily printed for the occasion. On the day of the acquittal the whole city of Strasburg, not excluding the garrison, was in a state of wild rejoicing; the released prisoners were received with triumphant welcome, and on the evening of their discharge were formally entertained at a public banquet.

By the tidings of this triumphant acquittal Louis Napoleon was greeted on March 30, 1837, when he landed at Norfolk, in Virginia, at the end of his long voyage. The news was confirmed by an Italian friend, Count Arese, who, together with the prince's valet, Thélin, had hastened to America to join him in his exile. And so, in setting foot in the New World, he was able to take new hope for his chances of success in the Old. For in that acquittal he found—if not the ideal ending of his venture, at least some compensation for its failure, and a sufficient vindication of his own action in his own sight.

CHAPTER VII

LOUIS NAPOLEON A POLITICAL PRETENDER

Omnium quae dixerat feceratque arte quadam ostentator.
TACITUS.

ON his arrival in America Prince Louis did not expect to find himself altogether friendless. From the time of the downfall of the empire until 1832, King Joseph had been living in the United States; and although he had been in England for the last few years, yet he was now on the point of returning to America. As soon as he knew that he was himself bound for the same country, Louis had written to his uncle to inform him of the fact; he had hoped to obtain introductions from him to various influential persons in New York, and possibly to buy from King Joseph a little land, which he might till as a farmer. But now, as always, the prince was to find himself deprived of any help from his own family: on his arrival in New York, whither he proceeded at once on his landing, he found neither response nor greeting from his uncle, for the ex-King of Spain did not even condescend to acknowledge the receipt of the prince's letter. Louis now wrote to him again; this time the deference with which he still thought it fitting to address the nominal head of the Napoleonic house hardly conceals his scorn of the policy which the elder members of that family were pursuing.

'Had I succeeded at Strasburg,' he wrote, 'and we were very near success—had I marched forward on Paris, drawing the people after me spellbound by their memories of the empire, and had I on my arrival played the pretender and appropriated the regal power—ah, then, indeed it had shown grandeur of spirit to disavow my conduct, to cut me adrift. But now? Now I have made trial of one of those rash enterprises which alone can re-establish what twenty peaceful years have caused to be forgotten. Into that enterprise I fling myself, taking my life in my hand, convinced that even my death would help our cause: through no will of mine I escape bayonet and scaffold—only to meet despite and disdain at the hand of my own family.'

His short sojourn in America was the occasion of another injury inflicted on the prince by a different member of his family. Shortly after his own arrival there appeared in New York a certain Prince Pierre Napoleon, who proceeded to scandalise the city by a series of discreditable escapades. Some twenty years afterwards the emperor himself was charged with the actions of his rowdy, ne'er-do-weel cousin. It was left to one of the many American friends whom he made during his stay at New York, to expose the confusion.

Indeed, the prince suffered little from his uncle's refusal to give him introductions in New York. On his arrival there, he at once found his way into some of the best society in the city: during his two months residence in America he was a good deal 'lionised,' and received more invitations than it was possible for him to accept. He was entertained not only by some of the oldest and most aristocratic families of New York, but by its leading *littérateurs*, including Cooper, Halleck, General Webb, and Washington Irving. Those who made his acquaintance, found him thoughtful, reserved, and silent to the verge of dullness; and marvelled that a young man in other respects so entirely sane, should be in the habit of prefacing his statements of his future intentions with the words, 'When I am emperor.'

The fact was that the verdict of the Strasburg jury had convinced the prince that his political life was not ended after all. He at once renounced his first intention of buying land in the United States and there pursuing a pastoral existence for the rest of his days. He did not, however, contemplate any immediate return to Europe, but hoped to turn his enforced visit to America to a useful purpose. At the end of May he had determined to make a year's tour of the United States.

Doubtless this design, had it been carried out, would have resulted in the appearance of a companion volume to the *Considérations sur la Suisse*, a volume which would probably have exceeded in value his work on the smaller republic. For the prince's impressions of America, as shown by the letters he wrote during his short residence in New York, are of quite exceptional interest. 'The states of America had acted in their own interest, at a time when their only interest was commerce, in separating themselves from the mother country,' he wrote to Vieillard, in a letter dated April 30, from New York. 'But a minor who declares himself to be of age at sixteen, let his physical strength be what it may, is only a child. We are men only when we have reached the full development of our physical and moral forces. Now this country possesses immense material forces, but in moral forces it is entirely deficient. The United States believed themselves to be a nation as soon as they had a government elected by themselves, a president and chambers. They were, and are still, only an independent colony. The transition is going on daily, . . . but I do not think it will be completed without crises and convulsions.' Hitherto their problems had been simple; a few police regulations had been all that was really requisite for their government. 'But now the population has thickened. It is composed of an American type that is sharply defined, and of daily arriving immigrants who have no education, no popular traditions, and for the most part no patriotism. . . . In the midst of this world of traders, where there is not a man who is not a speculator, it has entered the heads of a few honest men that slavery, although it is highly profitable, is a bad thing; and for the first time, the heart of America has vibrated for an interest that is not financial.' Thus Louis Napoleon lights by chance upon the subject which was to be the occasion of those very convulsions which he predicted; revealing incidentally that he fully realised a fact hidden to most Frenchmen of his day—that in their war with England, the revolted states were contending in an entirely practical manner for commercial and material advantages; that though they might throw their grievances into constitutional form, and indulge after their success in high-flown aphorisms, yet the colonists were in no true sense imbued with the great ideas so soon to find expression in the French revolution. One final remark from the same letter deserves quotation, a remark which would suffice to show that the prince's impressions were based on an acquaintance with the Northern and not the Southern States. 'Here there is the right to act, but not to think,' wrote Louis; 'here there is liberty to acquire, but not liberty to enjoy.' This stricture has not lost its truth of a people to whom the pronunciation of the word leisure is a stumbling-block, and the meaning of it a mystery unto this day.

In fine, Louis Napoleon's impressions of the Northern States give evidence of so much insight, that we would gladly have more of them; but this is not the only reason why the abandonment of his American tour is to be regretted. For it is at least possible that a detailed and methodical survey of the United States at this time might have saved the prince from grave error in his subsequent policy. To have written a book on American institutions is not, perhaps, necessarily to have a complete capacity for the diplomatic handling of international relations with America; but study spent on such a work might have altered for the better, and could not have altered for the worse, Louis Napoleon's political dealings with the United States. A more intimate acquaintance with the political feeling of the North might have shown him that if he would offend that feeling he must be prepared to render it powerless; a more intimate acquaintance with the social conditions of the South might have induced him to give effective support to the Confederate forces at the crisis of the Civil War. But the journey was never made. For while he was making his final arrangements for it, the prince received a letter from his mother which caused him to abandon his design.

For many years Queen Hortense had been in ill-health, and latterly she had been suffering from a disease which only an operation could arrest. The sudden shock of learning that her son was a prisoner whose life was justly forfeit, the hurried journey to Paris, the sad return without sight of him, and finally, the long period of cruel suspense in which she waited for news of his arrival in America—for the French Government, which had insisted on hurrying her return journey to Arenenberg, had not informed her of the explanation of her son's long silence—all these had combined to hasten the progress of her illness. On her return to Switzerland it became clear that the operation could no longer be delayed. Early in April she wrote this farewell letter to Louis, believing that it would be the last she would ever send him :—

'My dear Son,

'I have to undergo a severe operation : should it not succeed, I send you by this letter my last blessing. We shall meet each other again, shall we not? in a better world, where you will rejoin me, though not I hope for many years to come; and you will remember that in leaving this one I have no one to regret but you—you whose loving kindness alone gave my life here any charm. It will be a consolation to you, dear boy, to think that you have made your mother as happy as she could be made. . . . Quite certainly there is another meeting. . . . Hold this sweet hope: it is too necessary not to be true.—Your loving mother,

'HORTENSE.'

But the specialist who had been summoned to perform the operation saw at once that he had come too late. With a kindness which it would be hard to justify and harder to condemn, he gave the queen to understand that he would not operate—not because such a course was useless, but because it was unnecessary; not because she was too ill, but because she was not ill enough. And so Hortense on hearing her death-warrant, believed that she had received a fresh lease of life: she hastened to write again to her son, in order as she said that she might be the first to tell him the good news. But Dr Conneau, her family physician, who did not know what hope Hortense might have given her son of her recovery, but did know that any hope at all was false, had written on the envelope the words, 'Venez, venez.' The letter was delayed in transmission, and only reached the prince on June 3. He at once booked a passage on the next homeward-bound packet, the *George Washington*, and sailed on the 12th. It is characteristic of him that even so he did not omit to write a formal letter to the President of the United States, informing him of his reasons for leaving; insisting that he had made no sort of promise to abstain from returning to Europe, and expressing his regret at his inability to visit the President at Washington. It was his policy to assume that his comings and goings were a matter in which the heads of nations should naturally feel concern.

On July 10 Prince Louis reached London. The French ambassador refused to give him a passport for Arenenberg; neither the Austrian embassy nor the Prussian legation would help him. Finally he procured a passport made out for an American friend; the Swiss consul made no difficulty about signing—relations between France and Switzerland were already strained—and on the 30th Louis left London in disguise. He sailed to Rotterdam, and coming up the Rhine by boat reached Arenenberg on the evening of August 4. When Louis saw his mother on the morning after his arrival, it was clear that she had not many weeks to live. Although her son summoned doctor after doctor to her bedside in the vain hope of reversing the sentence, it was his own presence there, rather than any assistance they could give, which enabled her to hold on to life for two months after his return. On the 9th of October, in the early morning, she died:—her hands extended towards the son who had done so much to comfort her later years. For, indeed, whatever his later shortcomings as a husband, it must be set down to the credit of Louis Napoleon that he was to his mother an almost ideal son; indeed, in this case, the relationship was invested with the almost pathetic tenderness which can exist between a French mother and her only son. Unfortunately, it is not possible to write of Hortense that she was an ideal mother. Courage, high spirits, large-hearted charity, and devoted attachment to her son—all these qualities she possessed; and the love he had for her, no less than the crowded throng of Swiss peasants who were present with him at her funeral, bore witness to them. Yet the immense influence which her position as her son's sole guardian, and his own singularly receptive nature, placed in her hands, might certainly have been put to better use than it was. With all the talents and almost all the virtues, Hortense was not in the ordinary sense of the term a virtuous woman. We have seen reason for the belief that the denial of Louis' right to his father's name was mere malevolent scandal; but Hortense might justly have incurred her son's reproaches for having by her later conduct rendered such scandal possible.

Her failings in this respect had a more serious result. A highly impressionable boy, in whose eyes his mother could do no wrong, was brought up in an atmosphere in which the ordinary definitions of certain offences were blurred; he was accustomed to the belief that the possession of an artistic temperament excused its owner from the exact observance of conventional morality. It would have been better, perhaps, if in an education in which so little stress was laid on moral integrity there had been less insistence on religious exercises : a spirit so naturally devout as Louis Napoleon's would almost certainly have discovered religion for itself, and might possibly have accepted with Christianity the obligations which it ordinarily imposes. As it was, he learnt to believe that the devout attachment to Catholicism which characterised both himself and his mother was compatible with frequent lapses from its precepts in these matters; he was thus for ever released from what was probably the one binding force which could have restrained a nature such as his from its peculiar weakness. We are not suggesting that that nature was in itself a peculiarly vicious one, or that a tithe of the assertions based on this supposition are actually true. But the fact remains that while other rulers of men have offended as he offended without noticeably impairing the efficiency of their government, the private faults of Louis Napoleon and the scandal occasioned by them did most seriously affect and detract from his public services to the State. And for the evils which befell her country by this cause, that eminently patriotic Frenchwoman, Hortense de Beauharnais, Queen of Holland, Duchess of St Leu, cannot escape her share of blame.

It was, of course, with thoughts very different from these that Louis followed his mother's coffin to the last impressive service at the church of Ermatingen, before it passed where he could follow it no longer, to its final resting-place in France. For a government which could afford to be more merciful to the dead than to the living had allowed the queen the last boon she asked of it—leave to be buried at Malmaison, her home during the happiest period of her life.

Towards the prince himself less indulgence was shown. The news of his return to Europe had caused considerable annoyance to the advisers of Louis Philippe. The French ministerial press gave renewed currency to the false assertion that in leaving America he had been guilty of breach of faith; at the same time a hint was given to the

Swiss Government that his continued residence in Arenenberg would be displeasing to France. When after his mother's death Louis showed no signs of immediate departure, but instead, proceeded in January 1838 to instal himself in a new house at Gottlieben, these protests took a more definite form.

The French ambassador, the Duke of Montebello, repeated his request for the prince's expulsion, grounding it on the public declaration of the Swiss Diet in 1815, forbidding any Bonaparte to live in Switzerland. The duke 'himself recently informed me,' wrote the English representative at Berne at the end of January,[1] 'that his efforts have been hitherto confined to unofficial communications with Mr Am Rhyn, late president of the Vorost, at whose suggestion in consequence the Thurgovian Government has caused an insinuation to be conveyed indirectly to the above-mentioned personage [Louis Napoleon], that he might perhaps find it convenient to take up his quarters elsewhere. . . . He does not, however, appear disposed to understand the hint, nor does the French ambassador seem to entertain hopes of succeeding by the use of such gentle and circuitous means.' 'It seems generally admitted,' adds Morier, 'that the character and talents of the personage in question are too insignificant to render him personally formidable to the French Government,' but 'some of the principal actors in the Strasburg plot are said to be at present residing with him.'

[1] Morier to Palmerston, Berne, 31st January 1838.

As he expected, Montebello achieved nothing: the president refused to act at all except on an official demand, and then he would only be willing to refer the matter to the judgment of the Cantons.[1] Here the question stood at the middle of February, and here, in all probability, it would have been allowed to rest but for an event which occurred in Paris a few months later.

Early in June 1838, Laity published his account of the Strasburg insurrection, in which he had played so prominent a part: an account designed to show that the affair was in reality a serious and almost successful revolt, and that the Government's affected disdain was neither genuine nor justified. By an act of extraordinary folly, the account was at once seized, its sale forbidden, and its author placed in prison, pending his trial by the Court of Peers. In the trial which followed, Laity adopted an attitude, not of apology or even of self-defence, but of almost defiant vindication of the Napoleonic cause and of its protagonist, Prince Louis. On the 10th of July he was sentenced to a fine of 10,000 francs, to five years' imprisonment, and to police surveillance for the rest of his life. The Orleanist Government could hardly have played more completely into the hands of their opponents had Prince Louis himself been allowed to dictate their action. In prohibiting the circulation of Laity's volume they had given it the best advertisement it could have received. Left alone,

---

[1] Morier to Palmerston, 13th February 1838.

it would have found few to read it, and hardly any to take it seriously. But when its distribution was forbidden, large numbers of curious or interested persons were at some pains to procure a copy; and when its author was condemned, those readers became convinced that the extraordinary severity with which he had been treated was the best possible proof of the truth and importance of his writings. What would have been an obscure pamphlet was thus made an object of real political importance.[1]

The excessive severity of the sentence passed on Laity gave him the rank of a political martyr; while the nature of his offence was so nearly connected with the liberty of the Press—always a burning question to the constitutional party in France at this period—that he did not fail to obtain the sympathies of all newspapers hostile to the Government, as well as of some which were ordinarily its supporters. In short, the Government had by its act accomplished what the pamphlet would have attempted in vain. It had made it clear to the world that to the advisers of Louis Philippe the Strasburg affair was in reality a matter of serious moment, and that its authors were objects of fear rather than ridicule to the Government they attacked.

Incidentally, the trial of Laity had, of course, directed a considerable amount of interest and

[1] Of sufficient importance, for example, for Granville to consider worth sending to Palmerston, 27th June 1838.

attention towards Louis Napoleon himself. As though to make sure that he should have not merely the reflected merit of a vicarious martyrdom, but the direct compliment of personal persecution, the Molé Government now proceeded to address an urgent note to the Federal Diet demanding his expulsion from Switzerland. This was, of course, exactly what the prince had desired. In this hope, as he afterwards admitted,[1] he had caused the pamphlet to be published; with this object, certainly, he had addressed to Laity, on the eve of his trial, a letter in which he assumed full responsibility for the publication and the contents of the offending document. The French Government's demand was therefore a piece of persecution most welcome to its apparent victim.

But to the Swiss Government it was for a number of reasons most unpalatable. Switzerland had always regarded with jealousy any attempt to diminish her privileged position as the refuge of political exiles; and in this case the peremptory form of the French request would have made immediate compliance seem an act of humiliating submission. Moreover, Prince Louis had shown himself a more desirable guest than many exiles. His evident appreciation of their hospitality, his sympathetic study of their institutions, the interest he displayed and the active part he took in their military training, their local shooting-matches, their

[1] Letter to M. Vieillard, 10th June 1842. See p. 324.

rural pursuits—all these had won him a considerable popularity with his Swiss hosts, and had rendered him a valued and important citizen of his own canton of Thurgau. Doubtless, too, the fact that the prince had money to spend, and spent it freely, was not altogether without its influence on a race which was already beginning to learn how profitably the foreigner may be entertained.

Instead, therefore, of at once complying with the French Government's demand, the Swiss Government proceeded to a leisurely and not over friendly examination of its terms. They did not, indeed, venture on a downright refusal; but in the manifold devices of a constitution framed to hold in elaborate equipoise the balance of local and central authority, they found ample opportunity of postponing a definite answer. The Federal Diet took note of the demand, adjourned its discussion for a week, and after a debate in which the French claims were freely criticised, appointed a commission to confer with the local authorities of Thurgau on the question. It was not until the beginning of September that this commission made its report to the diet; and when it did, the diet found an excuse for delay by referring the question to the Cantonal Grand Councils, arranging itself to meet again and to receive their report on the 1st of October. In the weeks which followed, the several councils voted on the question amid much local excitement, and as the month advanced it became evident that the majority of the cantons were opposed to yielding to the French demand.

By this time the affair had assumed really serious proportions. The Molé Government persisted in its request with a vehemence which was not lessened, but rather increased, by the fact that its action was condemned, almost without exception, by the entire French press; dimly conscious that it had blundered badly in making the demand at all, the Government was the more clearly aware that for that very reason it could not afford to have made it in vain. It sought and obtained the diplomatic support of Austria, Prussia, and several of the minor German courts; at the same time it began to concentrate troops on the Swiss frontier, openly threatening to enforce its demand by invasion. In Switzerland itself the excitement was even greater; on several former occasions the republic had been treated with scant courtesy by Louis Philippe's Government, and there now appeared to be a strong feeling in favour of resistance—if necessary armed resistance—to its peremptory demand. Louis Napoleon himself meanwhile was enjoying the situation to the full. Thanks to the strangely irrational process which governs popular opinion on such occasions, he was not looked askance at as the cause of the whole trouble; on the contrary, he was invested with an increased popularity, being regarded as a sort of personification of the stand Switzerland was making for her national rights. His own canton elected him deputy of its grand council; others conferred on him the rights of honorary citizenship. Some of these honours he accepted, others he declined; but always he made them the occasion of some public pronouncement in which he fully guarded his claim to full civil rights in France. For the moment his sayings and doings were reported in half the leading newspapers in Europe, and he was careful to avail himself of this new advantage.

It was only in the middle of September that Louis Napoleon at length began to take measures for putting an end to the situation. On the 17th, Persigny called on the British envoy at Berne, and presented him with a letter asking whether in case of necessity the prince might be granted a passport for England under a false name;[1] he also showed Morier a letter from Louis himself to the same effect. The prince desired an answer if possible before the 1st of October, when the diet would meet.

Two days later Persigny again called on Morier, this time to inform him that Louis Napoleon had definitely decided to leave Switzerland.

---

[1] 'BERNE, *le* 17 *Sep.* 1838.
'Monsieur le ministre,
  'Le Prince Napoléon-Louis me charge de demander à votre excellence si, le cas échéant, elle lui donnerait des Passeports pour l'Angleterre sous un faux nom; il vous prie de vouloir bien demander à ce sujet des instructions à votre gouvernement, en vous transmettant cette demande je saisis l'occasion, etc. etc.
      'VICTE DE PERSIGNY.'

'On my asking M. de Persigny,' says Morier, 'what was to be understood by the expression in his letter "le cas échéant," his answer was, "le cas où le Prince serait *obligé* de quitter la Suisse."'
—Morier to Palmerston, 17th Sept. 1838.

'It appears singular,' wrote Morier in his despatch announcing the fact to Palmerston, 'that this resolution should be made at the very time that so many of the executive councils are pronouncing themselves decidedly against the demand of France for the prince's expulsion. This has been remarkably the case with Berne, where an opposite decision was confidently anticipated, as also with Zurich and Lucerne.'[1]

In point of fact, it was precisely by timing the announcement of his voluntary departure from Switzerland at the very moment when both governments seemed definitely to have committed themselves to an irreconcilable attitude that Louis Napoleon secured for himself the uttermost advantage which the situation could afford. This fact has been clearly recognisable, even by the imperfect light in which Louis Napoleon's action on this occasion has hitherto been judged. For even had it been in his power, it could not have been his policy to bring about a war. War must have tested most severely his popularity with his Swiss hosts; war might even have rallied national opinion in France to the support of the Monarchy. And in any case it would ill have become a pretender to have served in arms against the country he hoped to rule. What was possible and eminently politic was to secure for himself the credit of having averted a European war. On September 22 the prince published a letter in which he announced his inten-

[1] Morier to Palmerston, 19th September 1838.

tion of leaving Switzerland of his own accord. 'Switzerland has shown,' he wrote, 'that she was ready to make great sacrifices to maintain her dignity. She has known how to do her duty as a free country; I shall know how to do mine. . . . It only remains for me to leave a country where my presence would be a pretext of great calamities. In quitting of my own will the only country in Europe where I have found refuge and protection, I hope I shall prove to the Swiss nation that I was worthy of the many marks of esteem they have shown me. . . . My one consolation for leaving Switzerland is the knowledge that by doing so I am saving her from great troubles.' Dignified in its terms, generous in its apparent self-surrender, this letter produced exactly the effect that its author desired. His popularity in Switzerland was redoubled; while from the Government of Louis Philippe he seemed to strip the last semblance of justification. His name had become known throughout Europe[1]; all France saw that his claims were clearly a matter of grave anxiety to the existing dynasty. Hereafter he was no longer an unknown adventurer, but a recognised pretender to the French throne; a pretender who would become no whit less formidable by his voluntary removal from Switzerland to England.

With such vigour and enthusiasm did Switzerland appear to rally to the prince's cause on the eve

[1] *E.g.*, I find that in 1838, 22 out of the 25 September issues of the *Times*, and 21 out of the 27 October ones, mention Louis by name *in leading articles*.

of his departure, that some of those who had most welcomed his letter as a solution to an awkward question were afraid that he might be tempted to go back on his published decision. On September 24, after a long debate, the Grand Council of Berne decided in the prince's favour. 'This result, which was hailed by acclamations of the people assembled in the streets, is not the least remarkable symptom of the hostile feeling against France roused by this question,' wrote Morier. 'A majority of the cantons for refusing the expulsion of Louis Bonaparte seems thus already secured. . . . It remains to be seen whether the above-mentioned personage will *now* continue in the resolution of retiring from Switzerland.'[1]

For reasons which we have already suggested, it could in no case have been Louis' intention to remain in Switzerland; least of all could it have been his policy to revoke a declaration which had won for him the sympathy and approval of many who had never hitherto allowed him a single redeeming quality. But as a matter of fact, even had he wished to forfeit his new-won reputation in this way, he had not the power to do so.

The extensive diplomatic correspondence in connexion with the demand for the prince's expulsion serves to confirm one fact which has until now remained a matter of conjecture, and to bring to light another which has hardly even been guessed at hitherto. On the one hand, it is

[1] Morier to Palmerston, 25th September 1838.

abundantly clear that the French Government did actually intend in case of necessity to proceed to extreme measures; it was no mere demonstration against the frontier, but an actual military occupation of Swiss territories, which Molé contemplated if Montebello's demands were refused.

But if the military preparations of France were more seriously intended than has sometimes been believed, the Swiss war party, on the other hand, or at any rate the leaders of that party, were less sincere than they appeared.[1] For we now learn that between them and Louis Napoleon there

---

[1] In proof of these two facts—the sincerity of the war preparations on the part of France, and the insincerity of the leaders of the Swiss war party—the following extracts may suffice, from much which makes for the same conclusion.

28th Sept.—Morier to Palmerston. 'The Avoyer Tscharner, who called on me yesterday, . . . did not scruple to declare his belief that this step of Louis Bonaparte's had been concerted with the leaders of the war party in the different grand councils, who had only made such a brave show of defiance to France from the persuasion that they would not, in consequence of this premeditated disappearance of their tool from Swiss territory, be called upon to testify their patriotism by more substantial proofs than their speeches.'

1st Oct.—Morier to Palmerston. 'M. de Montigny of the French Embassy called on me yesterday . . . He said that it had been known at the Embassy for the last three weeks that such a letter was in contemplation; he spoke of it as a matter concerted among the party who were for rejecting the demand of the French Government, for the purpose of furnishing them with a safe opportunity of braving the latter with impunity; and at the same time, expressed his confidence that the affair would now be settled without the necessity of having recourse to a military occupation of the country, a measure which he said, had been *irrevocably determined;* adding that he found at Strasburg a division of artillery under orders to march towards the Swiss frontier, and that the camp at St Omer was ready to break up at a moment's notice for the same destination.'

existed an understanding which amounted to a compact for the confusion of the common enemy. The patriotic burgers were by voice and vote to champion Louis' cause, to talk at large of Helvetian liberties, to hurl defiance at Louis Philippe and his demands. Louis on his part was at the last moment to relieve them from the necessity of translating their words into action, by himself of his own initiative bidding his gallant defenders a dignified and pathetic farewell. The arrangement lacked no element of neatness or dexterity. The French Government had desired to abash the insolence of Louis Napoleon's Swiss defenders no less than to humiliate Louis Napoleon himself. In open contest, neither the prince nor the war party could have effected anything against Louis Philippe: by this simple yet singularly effective manœuvre they were severally enabled to flout his threats and mock his revenge. Conscious of their overwhelming military advantage, the Molé ministry could safely threaten war; but confident that war would not really ensue, the Swiss patriots could no less safely accept the challenge. In a conflict so limited, the forces of the two combatants were not merely equalised, but reversed: in actual battle the victory must have gone to the giant; for that very reason, in the preliminary sparring men's sympathies went to the dwarf. No crumb of comfort was left to the French Government. It was denied the opportunity of proving that its military preparations were effective; it was suffered only to show that they were not feared. Wishing to ensure the ignominious expulsion of Louis Napoleon at the hands of the Swiss themselves, it had merely succeeded in evoking for him from those same Swiss an apparently overwhelming ovation, and in presenting him with an admirably effective and dignified exit from the scene of his triumph. All the honours of this rather farcical melodrama—the fine speeches and the plaudits of the crowd—these were divided between Louis and his gallant defenders; the French Government had to be content with the part of the blustering and baffled bully.

So clearly had Montebello's demand failed in its purpose, that it seemed doubtful for a moment whether the French Government would accept this ending of the incident. It was rumoured 'that no passport would be given to Louis Bonaparte except by a prescribed route, not at his own choice, and unless his removal from Switzerland were distinctly declared to be the result not of his own voluntary choice, but of a compliance for the demand made for his expulsion.'[1] But wiser councils prevailed: the good offices of the British Government were offered and accepted, and in due course the prince received his passports for England. For it was to England, now as once before, that Louis Napoleon turned when Switzerland was not strong enough to afford him shelter. It has been suggested that England

[1] Morier to Palmerston, 28th Sept. 1838.

was not sorry on this occasion to administer a slight reproof to Louis Philippe's administration by the alacrity with which it welcomed the prince. So far as the Government was concerned, this was not the case. Its attitude was scrupulously correct. For Persigny's application for a passport to England for the prince's use was not granted until Molé had been informed of it, and asked what action on the part of the English Government would be most helpful to him in the matter.[1]

But such motive may well have conduced to the extraordinarily cordial reception which was given to Prince Louis by English society on his arrival from Switzerland. The autumn of 1838 and the early months of 1839 marked the high-water mark of his apparent importance as a pretender. His departure from Switzerland had been the occasion of great demonstrations in his honour by members of his own canton; his leisurely passage through Germany and Holland on his way to England was turned, by dint of good stage management, into a semi-royal progress; was he not already, as one of the French papers had styled him, 'Emperor *in partibus*'? And during the London season which followed his arrival he was one of the most lionised men in the country. The newspapers of the time contain most frequent and detailed accounts of his social engagements: whether he is paying a round of visits to the country houses of the nobility, or

---

[1] Palmerston to Granville, 29th Sept. 1838. Morier to Palmerston, 5th Oct. 1838.

travelling in the provinces, or leading a fashionable life in London, his movements are recorded as those of a person of public importance. We know enough of his management of these matters to feel sure that he was careful himself to provide the Press with full information as to his doings; but it still remains clear that for a time after his arrival he figured largely in the public eye, and was the intimate companion of many of the nobility, and not a few of the notable men of the period. The considerable fortune which he had just inherited from his mother enabled him to live in some state; and though his expenditure was prodigal, it was not altogether purposeless. Disraeli in one of his political novels describes the method and discerns the motive of Louis Napoleon's profusion at this period. 'Prince Florestan had arrived in town, and was now settled in his mansion in Carlton Terrace. . . . The world thought that he had fitted up his fine house, and bought his fine horses, merely for the enjoyment of life. His purposes were very different. Though his acquaintances were limited they were not undistinguished, and he lived with them in intimacy. . . . The Duke of St Angelo controlled the household at Carlton Gardens with skill. The appointments were finished, and the cuisine refined. There was a dinner twice a week. . . . It was an interesting and useful house for a young man, and especially a young politician, to frequent. The prince encouraged conversation, though himself inclined to taciturnity. When he did speak, his terse remarks and condensed views were striking, and were remembered.' The author of *Endymion* became himself one of the prince's intimate acquaintances at this time, and his sketch of Louis Napoleon is of peculiar interest. For it is not only a sympathetic study in itself, but it proceeds from the one contemporary statesman in England whose character and career afford a real parallel to those of the future Emperor of the French. Bohemians both, they were both faced in youth with obstacles which seemed unsurmountable. These obstacles they encountered not decorously and apologetically, as became young men who attempted the impossible, but boastfully and with unaffected confidence of their future success; so that the incredulous generation which had laughed at them as madmen could never quite forgive them that their boast had been fulfilled. Both were dreamers whose dreams came true—yet not so true as to free them altogether from the charge of charlatanism. Each was eminently successful as ruler of a race whose national characteristics were foreign to him; yet both were in some sort adventurers until the end of their days. That the characters differed in some ways as essentially as the careers, is, of course, beyond question; but the touch of extravagance by which both were distinguished was not an accidental feature of resemblance. Nor would a modern Plutarch, desirous of compiling a parallel series of French and English 'lives,' seek any other companion picture for Louis Napoleon, Emperor of the French, than Benjamin Disraeli, Earl of Beaconsfield. Her own liberality, and her son's political expenditure in connexion with the Strasburg insurrection had already considerably diminished Queen Hortense's fortune. None the less, Louis inherited from her an income not far short of five thousand a year. While it is true, therefore, that Louis Napoleon was at this time a political adventurer, it must be remembered that he was not an adventurer who had nothing to lose. His name would have assured him a certain social standing; his fortune would have enabled him to lead for the rest of his days a life smoothed of all asperities. Doubtless Louis Napoleon was ambitious; but that ambition can hardly be condemned as sordid which leads a man to forfeit the certain possession of every material comfort which life can afford. Or, if such ambition be sordid, at least it is not vulgar: none other of Napoleon's family could be taxed with it; hardly any other pretender has incurred the reproach of preferring such dangerous and laborious efforts to win back what his ancestors have lost, to the leisurely and dignified enjoyment of what those ancestors have left—the remnant of a kingly fortune and the heritage of a name. In this case the fortune at any rate was spent in no niggardly fashion on behalf of the pretender's political designs. As the benefits of the Strasburg insurrection did not cease with the failure of the actual rising, so Louis had no reason to complain if the expenditure it entailed on him proved permanent as well; and he accepted without question the moral obligation of providing for the maintenance of all whose participation in that rising had compromised their future. Further expenditure was incurred in other ways. From the time of the Strasburg rising onwards there were published without intermission a series of laudatory accounts of Louis Napoleon; eulogistic commentaries on his life, his claims, his writings, and his latest political achievements. Every year saw the appearance of one or more of these publications: often they obtained a considerable sale, and always they were given a considerable circulation; sometimes they paid their way, but more often they must have involved expenditure on the part of the prince. In 1839 two newspapers were established in Paris; newspapers not merely Napoleonic in sentiment, but definitely Bonapartist in their propaganda. From these papers Louis hoped great things; indeed it must have seemed a definite step forward that he should have his own papers in a city where every branch of dynastic opposition finds in the possession of a distinctive journal the first sign of a political future—or the last relic of a political past. Louis Napoleon admitted a few years later that in his own case the experiment had been a complete failure, and that the money he had so spent was altogether wasted. A hundred and forty thousand francs was the sum spent on founding the *Capitole* alone; this was the more important of the two papers, but its influence was never considerable. And two Bonapartist clubs which were also founded in Paris during this year were equally ineffective; here again Louis was involved in a certain amount of useless expenditure.

Apart from the sums which the prince spent on objects avowedly political, much of his profusion in other ways was indirectly designed to further his pretensions. If he occupied in turn two of the best private houses in London—first, Lord Cardigan's mansion in Carlton Terrace, and then a house owned by the Earl of Ripon in Carlton Gardens—if his establishment included a baronial suite of retainers, and his stables contained excellent horses for every conceivable occasion, all this brave show was not without a purpose. It was not mere vanity which made Louis flaunt the imperial eagle on the panels of his carriage, or have aides-de-camp standing behind him when he entered his box at the opera. Nor is it without significance that all his English acquaintances of this time, who have left any record of their impressions of him, agree in dwelling on his invincible persuasion repeatedly expressed that he would live to be Emperor of France. Ordinarily silent and reserved, he was on this one point—where silence might have seemed most essential—utterly lacking in reticence. The conviction itself was undoubtedly absolutely sincere, but he may have considered the parade he made of it, as well as of his other imperial pretensions, in some degree helpful to its fulfilment. Not all his proceedings at this time can be so excused. Much of his expenditure was mere extravagance; to his fashionable pleasures he added some not unfashionable vices. From this time dates his acquaintance with Miss Howard, who was for many years not only a zealous supporter of his political ambitions, but his mistress. Another suitor for Miss Howard's good graces seems to have been A. W. Kinglake; Louis Napoleon's disappointed rival had afterwards the satisfaction of achieving an adequate revenge, by including in his picturesque and imaginative *Invasion of the Crimea* an exceptionally picturesque and imaginative account of the antecedents of the Second Empire.

Nor were all the prince's social activities calculated to advance the cause he had at heart. In August 1839 he took part in the Eglinton Tournament, an isolated forerunner of the 'pageant' of later years. Strangely enough, a proceeding which to a later and on the whole a more prosaic age appears to justify itself, was yet overwhelmed with ridicule in the heyday of the romantic reaction. Other and less innocent actions of the prince at this time seemed to his future defenders to have called for less excuse than his appearance as a knight in armour at this representation of mediæval chivalry. But in spite of an occasional false step of this kind, the majority of his social activities were useful means of retaining for himself a certain amount of the popular interest he had acquired on his arrival. Moreover, they did not at all diminish his interest in political affairs. Throughout his sojourn in England he was a close observer of the course of events in France, as he was himself closely observed by agents of the French Government. In May 1839 an attempt was made to connect his name with an unsuccessful rising in Paris; the letter to the *Times*, in which he denied all connexion with it, was shorter and more pointed than most of his disclaimers. 'If I were the soul of a conspiracy,' he wrote, 'I should also be its leader in the hour of danger, nor should I deny it after defeat.'

A few months later the French Government learnt that if he was not for the moment engaged in active plots against it, he had by no means given up his political designs. The *Idées Napoléoniennes*, published in Paris in 1839, was a new political manifesto from Louis Napoleon. The circulation of his earlier works had consisted almost exclusively of presentation copies. With the *Idées Napoléoniennes* this was not the case. Sold at the low price of half a franc, it had a large and genuine sale. In France four editions of it were rapidly printed; and by 1841 translations had appeared not only in English, German, and Spanish, but also in Italian, and even Russian and Portuguese. In publishing it, the prince desired to show that something larger than a personal ambition had lain behind his apparently reckless insurrection at Strasburg; that someone more than a mere political adventurer had inherited the name of Napoleon; that this name stood for a system, and in that system lay the sole salvation of France. A vindication of the Emperor was followed by a sustained and often telling comparison between the great administrative reforms he had introduced in the intervals of his wars, and the small achievement of his successors in four-and-twenty years of peace. Reading into the First Empire all manner of beneficent designs, the writer plainly hinted that only the restoration of the imperial system was wanting to secure their practical accomplishment. The Napoleonic idea was already a great vitalising force; it needed but to take corporate and concrete form to become the effective means of healing all that was amiss with France or Europe. 'The book of a very able mind; with few ideas, but those ideas bold, large and reducible to vigorous action.' This was Bulwer Lytton's comment—and a not unjust one—on the most noteworthy of all the written works of Louis Napoleon. 'Prince Louis in publishing *Les Idées Napoléoniennes* is evidently contemplating an appeal to the Bonapartism of France, if not of Europe,' wrote the *Athenæum*,[1] in the course of a four-column review of the book. 'He is perhaps the only member of his family who does not despair of its fortunes. . . .

[1] 3rd August 1839.

We are satisfied indeed that Prince Louis has taken a wrong view of that portion of history which he has undertaken to illustrate ; but we are equally satisfied that there are many " potent, grave, and reverend signors " in Parliament and out who will be surprised if they learn from its pages that there is such a thing at all as a philosophy of history.' To the grave and reverend signors of the French Parliament a few months later, the significance of the volume was pointed out by the one great Frenchman of his day who never fell a victim to the Napoleonic Legend. In a notable speech, wherein he pointed out to the Orleanist Government the folly of encouraging the worship of Napoleon, Lamartine spoke of 'editions of the *Idées Napoléoniennes* running to five hundred thousand copies,' as one sign among many of the danger of a possible Napoleonic pretender.

While in the *Idées Napoléoniennes* Louis had been able to present the restored empire as the ideal mode of government for France, decency forbade that he should himself describe himself as the person ideally fitted to restore it. It was left to his whole-hearted supporter Persigny to undertake a complete presentation of his personal qualifications for this rôle. The *Lettres de Londres*, published by him early in 1840, were designed to portray the prince in that light to the French people. Not content with describing his studious habits, his military interests, his athletic powers— in all of which he was more or less within the truth—Persigny went on to describe his hero as physically resembling the Emperor, a resemblance which only a most loyal fancy could suggest. Taken together, the *Idées* and the *Lettres* formed a complete statement of Louis Napoleon's claim to revive in his own person the imperial system.

By this time the prince was no longer, even in appearance, absorbed in the fashionable pursuits of London life. English society, which had greeted him so effusively on his arrival, concerned itself less with his doings in 1840. And he was himself as that year advanced ever more obviously engrossed with his own schemes. He continued, however, to give small dinner parties at Carlton Gardens, and to receive similar hospitality from the small circle of intimate friends which survived from the large number of his earlier English acquaintance.

It was on one of these latter occasions, at the beginning of August 1840, that he surprised several of his fellow-guests by inviting them to dine with him, that day twelvemonths, at the Tuileries.

CHAPTER VIII

THE SECOND CLAIM TO THE INHERITANCE

> Sir, in my heart there was a kind of fighting
> That would not let me sleep : methought I lay
> Worse than the mutines on the bilboes. Rashly !
> Then praised be rashness for it. Let us know
> Our indiscretion sometimes serves us well
> When our deep plots do pall.
> SHAKESPEARE.

DREAMING always of his future destiny, and pondering often on the failure of his past attempt to realise it, Louis Napoleon had by this time convinced himself that a second effort could not but have a very different issue. Ever more clearly in his ears rang the wild acclamations with which he had been hailed by the one regiment in France to whom he had appeared as the Emperor's undoubted heir; ever more significant seemed those answering cheers which had greeted the acquittal of his fellow-prisoners at Strasburg. As he looked back on the events of that October morning, the attempt took new form in his memory. It was no longer a forlorn hope which for an instant had come marvellously near to success; rather it was a practically certain triumph which by a fatality, through a series of perverse mischances, had been snatched from his very grasp. And if so much was true in 1836, what was not possible in 1840? In the former year his name, his very existence, was all but unknown in France. Now, thanks to the Strasburg affair itself, and to his own most skilful handling of its consequences, all the world knew that there existed in his person a vigorous and persistent claimant to the imperial inheritance. Then his only precedent had been the Emperor's return from Elba; now that precedent seemed not weakened but fortified by his own initial experience at Strasburg. Then he had been merely his uncle's nephew; now he might almost hope that France had taken notice of his individual existence.

But there were reasons far more weighty than these personal ones which induced Louis Napoleon to repeat in the summer of 1840 his hazardous appeal to the French people. The Government of Louis Philippe had by this time visibly forfeited the slight popularity of its early years. A reactionary administration at home was accompanied by a servile timidity in foreign affairs. Conscious of his declining popularity, Louis Philippe turned once more to the flowing stream of the Napoleonic Legend; if he could bathe again in these magical waters, he might renew his waning strength. He sought and obtained permission from the English Government to fetch home from St Helena the body of Napoleon. To a mind like Louis Napoleon's this was almost a challenge. The

Emperor's ashes were to be brought back to Paris. Very good; then the Emperor's heir should be there to receive them. The funeral baked meats should serve a double purpose;[1] the veteran soldiers of the First Empire, assembled to pay their last honours to its founder, should find themselves assisting also at the magnificent inauguration of the second. The fact that even his failure at such a moment would be peculiarly embarrassing for Louis Philippe had probably but little effect on the prince; for, though he faced the possibility of death,[2] failure was an alternative which he did not seriously contemplate.

Another event of the same year undoubtedly served to confirm him in his resolution. The French Government had allowed itself to espouse the cause of Mehemet Ali, a rebellious vassal of the Sultan, whose victories threatened to overthrow his master's throne. The French people had been deeply stirred by the brilliant successes of this Egyptian enigma, successor of the Mame-

[1] In this connexion, it is noteworthy that on the morrow of the *coup d'état*, when he was again seeking an occasion for the proclamation of a restored empire, Louis Napoleon's first attempt to prepare the way for his design was by a precisely similar expedient. Since Napoleon I had already been translated, the would-be Napoleon III applied to Austria for leave to transfer the bones of Napoleon II to Paris. See *Louis Napoleon and the Recovery of France*, pp. 191, 192.

[2] Six months later, he wrote from prison to his cousin, Prince Napoleon: 'To shew you how I care for you, let me tell you that before I set out for Boulogne, when I had to look all chances in the face, I made a will leaving you everything I had in the world.'

lukes, conqueror of Nubia, founder of Khartoum. The victories which had extended his dominions from the Nile to the Euphrates, and thrice seemed to place Constantinople itself within his grasp, had come as a vivid reminder to France of that early Eastern phase of Napoleon's career which had always appealed so powerfully to her imagination.

On July 15, 1840—exactly a week after Louis Philippe's son had set sail to St Helena in quest of Napoleon's body—France learned that a treaty had been signed behind her back by the representatives of England, Russia, Prussia, and Austria. The four Powers agreed to despatch an ultimatum to Mehemet Ali, and to proceed without consulting France to the settlement of the Eastern question. Palmerston was generally careful in his conduct of foreign affairs never to inflict an injury without conveying an insult. He now explained to the world at large that one must expect France to cry like a naughty child; but that its noise would be hushed at any time by the sight of the rod. For a moment this seemed doubtful. Even Louis Philippe was driven to warlike words by the cry of indignation which went up from France: to Louis Napoleon the cry seemed a plain invitation to make an end of a government of which Palmerston's description was the mere truth.

The preparations for the descent did not greatly differ from those which preceded the Strasburg venture. Lille was the point first chosen for the attempt—a strong garrison town, the headquarters of the army of the North. Thither, in the spring of 1840, were despatched Lombard and Parquin; they seem to have been well received by many of the officers, though they were not apparently successful in obtaining any definite pledges of support. To a more recent recruit—de Mésonan—was entrusted a more important task, that of winning over General Magnan, the commander of the army of the North. Mésonan succeeded in making himself an intimate acquaintance of the general's; but his overtures, when they were made, seem to have been clumsy in the extreme. They consisted apparently in suddenly showing to the general a letter of Louis Napoleon's instructions to himself, in which the latter spoke of Magnan as one of his future marshals, and bade Mésonan offer him 100,000 francs down, and deposit 300,000 more at his bankers, to meet the possible loss of his command.

According to the general's own account, given at the trial which followed the failure of the attempt, he repudiated the suggestion with the utmost indignation, bidding its bearer go and get himself hanged elsewhere. However vigorously repulsed he may have been, Mésonan returned to approach the general again in July on the same subject; again with the same results. Magnan informed his Government that a Bonapartist intrigue was afoot, but again omitted the obvious step of placing the emissary under arrest. The prince drew his own conclusions—dictated no doubt by his hopes, but perhaps not without some justification of reason. While recognising that Magnan would not declare for him in the first instance, he yet believed that he had only to win over a regiment, to be able to rely on his support. That regiment he believed he could find in the 42nd Infantry, whose commander had promised his support.

It was not, however, to their colonel, who was stationed at Calais, but to a subordinate officer, Lieutenant Aladenize, that he looked in the first instance. For the lieutenant with two companies of his regiment formed part of the small garrison at Boulogne; and the prince decided that this should be the starting-point of his venture. It was easily accessible from the sea; the garrison was small; and yet if it were won, its example would have great influence on the important centre of Lille.

In England preparations went briskly forward. Muskets were bought from Birmingham, French uniforms from Paris; buttons stamped with the figure 40 were sewn on them in London—this number being that of the other infantry regiment quartered in Calais. Proclamations were printed to the army and to the French people, and to the inhabitants of Pas-de-Calais.[1] A steamer—the

[1] A reduced facsimile copy of this last proclamation is given on the following page. The original from which it was made was carefully preserved and mounted on silk by a devout Bonapartist; it is now in the possession of Mr E. M. Merridew, *Times* correspondent at Boulogne, to whom I am indebted for leave to make this reproduction. It will be noticed that the day of the month is filled in in ink, a fact which shows that the exact date of the expedition was only decided at the last moment. The printing is the work of Dr Conneau, effected secretly at Carlton Gardens by means of a small hand-press.

Proclamation
DU PRINCE
NAPOLÉON - LOUIS
aux Habitans
DU
Département
DU
PAS DE CALAIS

HABITANS du Département du PAS DE CALAIS et de BOULOGNE!

Suivi d'un petit nombre de braves, j'ai débarqué sur le sol français, dont une *[illegible]* les destinées de la France, et non les ci imprometre. J'ai des amis puissans, à l'extérieur comme à l'intérieur, qui m'ont promis de me soutenir. Le signal est donné, et bientôt toute la France, et Paris la première se lèveront en masse pour fouler aux pieds dix ans de mensonge, d'usurpation et d'ignominie, car toutes les villes, comme tous les hameaux, ont à demander compte au gouvernement, des intérêts particuliers qu'il a et *[illegible]*, des intérêts généraux qu'il a trahis.

Voyez vos ports presque déserts; voyez vos barques qui languissent sur la grève; voyez votre population laborieuse, qui n'a pas de quoi nourrir ses enfans, parce que le gouvernement n'a pas su protéger son commerce, et criez-vous avec moi: Traîtres disparaissez, l'esprit Napoléonien, qui ne s'occupe que du bien du peuple s'avance pour vous consoler.

Habitans du Département du Pas de Calais! Ne craignez point que les liens qui vous attachent à vos voisins d'Outre-mer soient rompus. Les dépouilles mortelles de l'Empereur, et l'Aigle Impériale ne reviennent de l'exil, qu'avec des sentimens d'amour et de réconciliation. Deux grands peuples sont faits pour s'entendre, et la glorieuse Colonne, qui s'avance fièrement sur le rivage, comme un souvenir de guerre, deviendra un monument expiatoire de toutes nos haines passées.

Ville de Boulogne! que Napoléon aimait tant, vous allez être le premier anneau d'une chaîne, qui réunira tous les peuples civilisés; votre gloire sera impérissable, et la France votre des actions de grâces à ces hommes généreux, qui les premiers ont salué de leurs acclamations notre drapeau d'Austerlitz.

Habitans de Boulogne! Venez à moi, et ayez confiance dans la mission providentielle, que m'a légué le martyr de Sainte Hélène. Du haut de la Colonne de la Grande Armée le Génie de l'Empereur veille sur nous, et applaudit à nos efforts, parcequ' ils n'ont qu'un but, le bonheur de la France.

signé : NAPOLÉON.
Le C.l MONTHOLON C.t de Major général.
Le C.l VOISIN C.t d'Aide Major général.
Le C.l MESONAN Chef d'État Major.

Boulogne le 6 Août 1840.

Louis Napoleon's Proclamation to the Inhabitants of Pas-de-Calais

Edinburgh Castle—was hired for a month, as though for a party of pleasure-seekers. On August 3 a last council of war was held at Carlton Gardens; early next morning there were placed on board the steamer several cases of uniforms, nine horses, two carriages, and a considerable quantity of wine and spirits. At nine o'clock the steamer left London Bridge; only a few of the party, headed by Count Orsi, were then on board. At Greenwich, at Gravesend, at Margate, and at Ramsgate the remaining members of the expedition were taken on board—fifty-six in all. This piecemeal process of embarkation was thought necessary to avoid arousing the suspicion of the English authorities, but it retarded the ship's progress considerably; and as further delay was caused by a misunderstanding as to the spot at which the prince himself was to join the expedition, Ramsgate was not reached until shortly before daybreak on the 5th. This was the time originally fixed for the landing at Boulogne; but it now became necessary to postpone the descent for another twenty-four hours. Forestier, a cousin of Persigny's, was sent across the Channel at once by boat, to warn Aladenize of the change of plan—a change which was the more unfortunate as there was reason to think that the most formidable opponent of the scheme, Captain Col-Puygélier, the commander of the detachment at Boulogne, would on the day originally chosen have been absent from his troops.

Though it was impossible to attempt a landing in France until nightfall, it was considered unsafe to spend the day in an English harbour; it was therefore resolved that the *Edinburgh Castle* should at once put out to sea, and cruise about the Channel till midnight. This was accordingly done.

It was a motley crew at whose head Louis Napoleon now found himself. The captain of the steamer and most of the seamen were English: the men who were to appear in the uniform of the 40th were chiefly French, though they included a certain number of Poles. The sea was rough, and the necessity of spending the whole day upon it was profoundly unpleasant to many of the passengers. If there was no drunkenness on board, there was a good deal of drinking, especially among the subordinate members of the expedition. These had apparently only the vaguest idea when they embarked of the nature of the service required from them: it is clear, however, that they accepted their part readily enough when it was explained to them; their readiness, no doubt, was partly due to a gift of a hundred francs each with which these explanations were accompanied. The prince himself addressed them in a short speech: Boulogne, he told them, was the only obstacle that confronted them; were it once won, success was certain; powerful and devoted friends would second them; and 'as sure as there is a sun above us, in a few days we shall be in Paris, and history will tell that it was with a handful of gallant fellows like you that I have accomplished this great and glorious deed.' They were brave words; but the tale history has to tell of the Boulogne adventure is a very different one. Probably, however, they in no way exaggerated the prince's confidence of success—a confidence to which all his preparations bear witness. His proclamation spoke of powerful friends inside and outside France on whose support he relied. Among his papers were maps of Northern France with minute particulars of the situation of different regiments on the way to Paris; his principal followers bore the most detailed injunctions as to proceedings on entering the different garrison towns, the exact task to be assigned to each officer, the precise disposition of the forces as they were won over. In the ship's cabin were stowed not only the uniforms to be worn on landing at Boulogne, but gorgeous evening clothes for use at a magnificent reception to be held on the following evening. And there—that no touch of auspicious absurdity should be lacking to the scene—fastened to the mainmast was a live eagle, forlornly surveying the seasick saviours of France. Its presence there was attributed by the prince's apologists to a whim of Parquin: if this was so, Parquin's whims were uncommonly like his leader's, for the idea was quite Louis-Napoleonic. On the other hand, the story that it was with this melancholy fowl perched upon his shoulder that the prince landed at

Boulogne is a mere anti-Bonapartist fiction; like the nine horses and two carriages, the bird remained on the ship till all was over.

At about one o'clock in the morning of August 6 the *Edinburgh Castle* anchored off the port of Wimereux, a small coast town some three miles north of Boulogne. The steamer remained nearly a mile off from the land; the passengers were landed by boat. Over two hours were spent in the process: for there was only one boat, and it had to make four journeys to land the entire party. The landing was not effected without discovery. A customs-house officer challenged the first boat-load; he was informed that they were soldiers of the 40th Regiment sailing from Dunkirk to Cherbourg, but forced to land there, owing to an accident to their steamer. Only half satisfied by the explanation, backed though it was by the uniforms worn by the expeditionaries, the officer warned his superior, who with the entire body of his subordinates now demanded explanations. But by this time all the prince's followers were safely landed, and they had moreover been joined by Lieutenant Aladenize, with Forestier and M. Bataille from Boulogne. The customs-house forces were easily outnumbered. Their two officers were strongly urged to join the prince in his adventure; but they could not be won over either by offers of promotion should the enterprise prove successful, or promises of pensions should its failure lead to the loss of their positions. Against the wishes of his followers, Louis Napoleon thereupon insisted that they should be allowed to go free; only stopping to exact a promise of silence from them as to what had happened. The men, however, were forced to act as guides to the party on the road from Wimereux to Boulogne; but as they also obstinately refused to join the prince, they were dismissed at the entrance to the town. It was now close on five o'clock, and broad daylight. The little army entered the still sleeping town. Lieutenant Aladenize was at its head; next came Lombard, bearing a large silk tricolour, fringed with gold, emblazoned with the names of Napoleon's victories, and surmounted by a brazen eagle. The prince himself with his brilliantly apparelled staff followed, and the seeming soldiers of the 40th Regiment brought up the rear.

At the centre of the lower town the column passed a sentry post, where were stationed four men and a sergeant. The sentry, seeing what he took to be a body of superior officers, summoned the guard, who turned out and presented arms. Aladenize attempted to induce the sergeant to join the prince, but neither he nor any of his men would move from their post. This was a discouraging beginning, and it was at once followed by another and more serious check. Shortly after resuming their march the insurgents met Sub-lieutenant Maussion, an officer of the 42nd. One of them hailed him, asking him if he knew the prince. The officer, surprised, said that he did not.

M

'Come, then, I will present you,' said the other; and in spite of the officer's protests and excuses the presentation took place. Maussion found himself marching alongside of Louis Napoleon, who himself urged him to join his cause, explaining the objects of his landing. Maussion listened, seemed doubtful as to his course of action, and found a pretext for slipping out of the group. In spite of these rebuffs, Aladenize was still in high spirits; he had probably sounded some of his men already, and was in any case confident of his own influence over his two detachments. The procession went forward, unaugmented but unmolested, until it reached the barracks of the 42nd Regiment. Here for a moment it seemed as if Aladenize's judgment was correct. At his order, the sentry post at the entrance of the barracks turned out and presented arms; while the prince and his whole column marched into the barracks unopposed.

At once two men were stationed at the gateway with orders to allow no officer to enter, and to prevent anyone from leaving the barracks on any pretext whatsoever. Into a little crowd of curious civilians which had collected outside, one of the prince's partisans scattered pieces of silver, calling for shouts of 'Vive l'Empereur!' The crowd very contentedly took up the cry, scrambling the while for the one-franc and five-franc pieces which were being showered upon them. Inside the barracks Aladenize was presenting the prince to such of his men as were present. 'Here is an old soldier,' he said, introducing a sergeant to the prince, 'who deserves a pair of epaulettes.' Nothing simpler; Louis Napoleon created him on the spot captain of grenadiers. Two other sergeants were also presented, and were also promised commissions. It was a simple and gratifying process—this largesse of honours within the barracks and of money without. Nor was it ineffectual; the cry of 'Vive l'Empereur!' spread from the civilians outside to the troops within; from the sham soldiers of the 40th to the real ones of the 42nd.

Whether the prince would have gone on to turn all the privates into sergeants does not appear; for Aladenize had just succeeded in mustering them all to hear the prince's harangue, when that happened which brought the whole comedy to an abrupt and ignominious conclusion.

The fatal fault in the insurgents' conduct of affairs hitherto—if one fault can be singled out as fatal in an enterprise which never came within measurable distance of success—at any rate the most gratuitous blunder, was the omission to secure the silence of the various officials who had been passed on the way to the barracks. As at Strasburg, so at Boulogne, Louis Napoleon had given injunctions to his followers that there was to be no bloodshed. But without bloodshed it would have been perfectly easy to have bound and gagged the customs-house officials; hardly more difficult to have done the same with the sergeant and his four men at the Place d'Alton; and absolutely possible to have prevented Sub-lieutenant Maussion from leaving the insurgents' ranks, when he had once unwillingly become entangled in them. Owing to the lack of this elementary precaution, Louis Napoleon was not suffered quietly to annex Aladenize's two companies, as otherwise he would possibly have succeeded in doing. For Maussion had no sooner made his escape than he ran straight to his commander, the redoubtable Captain Col-Puygélier, and told him what was in progress. Leaving his superior officer hastily donning his uniform, he then hurried to the barracks himself. There Aladenize again attempted to overcome his scruples, but in vain; while they were still speaking, the captain himself appeared, angry and menacing. One of Louis Napoleon's officers stopped him at the gate. 'Prince Louis is here,' he said; 'join us, and your fortune is made.' 'I must see my soldiers,' shouted the captain, 'where are they?' Sword in hand, he brushed his way past the feeble, ineffectual opposition of those who were guarding the gateway. At all costs he ought to have been prevented from getting into the courtyard. Once inside, he had his men within hearing; and the effect on them of his few sharp words of rebuke was at once visible. Now, as at Strasburg, it was Persigny who was willing to attempt desperate measures to save a falling cause. He flung himself at Puygélier, intending to kill him. But at this point Aladenize interfered, declaring that if any harm befell his captain he would himself declare against the rising.

Louis Napoleon appealed to the captain, but his overtures were repulsed with scorn. For a few minutes Puygélier remained struggling to release himself. By this time some other officers had effected an entrance; they now rushed up with bare swords; a scuffle ensued, and the captain was rescued. Once among his own soldiers, he was completely master of the situation. Turning to Louis Napoleon, he abruptly ordered him out of his barracks. The prince raised a pistol which he was carrying and fired it aimlessly—accidentally, he afterwards maintained. The bullet slightly wounded one of the soldiers of the 42nd in the mouth. He may have hoped that the diversion might in some unforeseen manner change the aspect of affairs; possibly he really intended to shoot the colonel; it is just possible that he hoped to provoke reprisals and get himself decently killed. Whatever its intention, its effect was the immediate withdrawal of the invaders from the barracks; for the prince's followers had no desire for an encounter of this kind. They retreated in good order, leaving the barracks as they had entered them, without any opposition. It is noteworthy that Captain Col-Puygélier, whose loyalty and zeal were beyond all question, made no attempt to prevent the departure of the prince, or even at immediate pursuit; his first care was to shut the gates of the barracks behind them. Clearly he was far from certain of the temper of his men. He despatched, however, a small body of picked men headed by Maussion to seize the port, and shortly afterwards set out himself with others towards the upper town, to defend the castle and the arsenal.

Outside the barracks, Louis Napoleon insisted on leading his followers towards the upper town. It would still have been possible for them to return unmolested to the harbour and put out at once to sea. Some of his followers urged this course, but the prince refused to hear of it. On their way through the streets, the insurgents had to pass a number of civilians; for it was now six o'clock, and reports of what was in progress had run through the town. Money and proclamations were scattered among these bystanders. As the procession passed the sub-prefecture, the sub-prefect came out, and summoned the rebels in the king's name to disperse and to lay down their flag; he attempted to bar their way himself, but a blow from the eagle with which the offending flag was mounted sent him staggering backwards. The adventurers arrived at the upper town, only to find the gates of the ramparts closed. After attempting in vain to break through the Porte de Calais with axes, they again besought the prince—this time unanimously—to abandon an evidently hopeless adventure. Again he refused to retreat, and hurried his little company on to a tall monument, more than half a mile away from Boulogne—the Column of the Grand Army. The solitary sentinel was forced to give up the keys of the stairway;

PORTE DE CALAIS, BOULOGNE

LOUIS NAPOLEON'S PRISON AT BOULOGNE

Lombard ascended the column and planted the imperial flag at its summit. It may have been a mere demonstration; it was more probably a prearranged signal. Possibly it had been arranged that that flag should be hoisted there in case of success as a rallying-point for promised reinforcements; and Louis Napoleon may have had some desperate hope that such reinforcement might still arrive when they saw it. But by this time his own followers were no longer under his command. Seeing the approach of the regular troops and of bodies of the National Guard, most of them scattered in flight, and were captured in various hiding-places in the course of the day. The prince, according to all accounts, was firmly resolved that he would not himself survive the sorry ending of this his second claim. To get himself killed, with his back to the Column of the Grand Army and his flag flying above him, thus only could he now hope to save from ridicule a cause which in his own person—so for the moment he may have thought—he could no longer hope to serve. But if such was really his purpose, he was not allowed to carry it out; the few friends who remained at his side seized him by force and hurried him to the shore. There, about half a dozen in number, they plunged into the water, and swam out towards an empty lifeboat which was anchored close to the beach. They reached it, but found it hardly big enough to hold them. This mattered the less since at this moment the National Guard was carried away by a martial ardour hitherto kept under prudent control. Up to this time the citizen soldiers had abstained from firing at fugitives, who after all were still armed. But now, struggling into the boat but some twenty yards distant, they afforded an easy and tempting shot. A volley was fired with the happiest effects: one of the fugitives was shot dead, two others severely wounded, a fourth drowned, and the boat itself was capsized. Louis Napoleon was himself slightly wounded; he and four of the survivors were finally picked up by a boat and brought to land as prisoners. They were driven up to the castle in the upper town, and there imprisoned.

The French Government did not consider it advisable to allow their captive to remain at Boulogne a day longer than they could help. The reports of the British consul at Boulogne show that although the inhabitants remained absolutely quiet, the local authorities were extremely perturbed, and took every conceivable precaution on the morrow of the attempt.[1] Before the evening of the 6th their instructions arrived; the prince was to be removed, as soon as adequate arrangements could be made for his custody on the journey, to the fortress of Ham—a stronghold on the river Somme, about a hundred miles southeast of Boulogne. The most elaborate precautions were taken to prevent his release or escape on the way. Early in the morning of August

---

[1] W. Hamilton to Palmerston, 7th August 1840.

8,[1] Louis was put in a closed carriage, with an officer at his side who had orders to shoot his prisoner if he made any attempt to get away. A strong escort accompanied them, and sentries were freely stationed on the roadside. Ham was reached before daybreak on the 9th. Three days later — on August 12 — the prince was taken on to Paris, where he was lodged in the *Conciergerie*, in a cell which had been occupied some five years before by a notorious assassin, Fieschi. This indignity was the occasion of a letter of vehement protest from King Louis at Florence; a letter from him appeared in the French papers on August 26. His only remaining son had been enticed into a trap: the real culprits were those who had led him there; the real shame theirs who inflicted on him such an indignity as deliberately to associate his punishment with that of an infamous assassin. It was an utterance natural in a distressed father, and eminently characteristic of the ex-King of Holland; but it was hardly warranted by the facts. Louis Napoleon had neither been enticed to Boulogne by agents of

[1] All published accounts give the time of departure at midnight on 7th August. But the consul's report is explicit, contemporary, and almost certainly accurate :—

'BOULOGNE, 1 p.m., *Aug.* 8.

'Louis Napoleon left this a quarter before nine o'clock this morning, under a very strong escort, composed of Gardes Municipaux from Paris, lancers, and gendarmes.'—W. Hamilton to Palmerston.

Two months later—on 7th October—Hamilton reports that steps are being taken to fortify the place. This precaution was an undoubted consequence of Louis Napoleon's landing.

the French Government, nor persuaded to the attempt by rash friends; the deed, such as it was, was his own. And the fact that the cell had once been occupied by Fieschi probably troubled him far less than the present necessity of sharing it day and night with three gaolers.

To the French Government the suggestion that they had themselves had a hand in landing Louis Napoleon at Boulogne was not altogether displeasing; for it tended to make the whole episode yet more ridiculous in the eyes of the nation. Louis Philippe himself was anxious at once to magnify the loyalty of Boulogne, and to minimise the importance of the rising by which that loyalty had been tested. With the first object he proceeded in person to the town. Captain Col-Puygélier received the well-earned promotion to the rank of major; his troops were thanked, and at the first opportunity quietly removed to another station. But it was for the National Guard that the king reserved his most effusive thanks; in the presence of his queen and some half-dozen members of his royal family the citizen king reviewed his citizen soldiers, addressing them as his dear comrades, and explaining to them his desire to 'consecrate by this solemnity the glory that the city of Boulogne had acquired through the event.' For the constant necessity of reconciling a very bellicose people to a very pacific government had by this time made the king an adept in the art of making a little glory go a long way. Louis

Napoleon on the morning of the 6th was not more prodigal of honours to the 42nd than Louis Philippe a fortnight later to the National Guard. Had they succeeded in shooting the pretender, the king could hardly have been more grateful; after all, if they had failed to do so, it was their marksmanship and not their loyalty that had been at fault. And if loyalty were a commoner virtue than marksmanship in the citizen soldier, Louis Philippe was the last to wish it otherwise.

It was easy to reward those who had crushed the rising; to secure the punishment of its authors was not quite such a simple matter. In the case of the Strasburg insurgents the law had been allowed to take its ordinary course. But trial by jury had resulted in an acquittal, and the king's advisers had no mind to risk a repetition of this rebuff. They now fell back upon an expedient which they had employed in 1838 in dealing with Laity's pamphlet. By arraigning Laity before the Court of Peers, they had secured his condemnation and outrageously heavy punishment on a charge which could not have been sustained for a moment in any ordinary court. By an equally irregular, but in this case far more justifiable procedure, it was now determined to try the Boulogne prisoners directly before this supreme tribunal. The trial was fixed for September 28. The month of September was employed by the Government in rigorous private examinations of its prisoners; and by Louis Napoleon in such preparations for his trial as were possible for him. To all questions addressed to him he refused any answer, contenting himself with the statement that he alone was responsible for all that had been done.

The truth of this avowal might benefit his fellow-prisoners; but it must have been a reflection far from comforting to the prince himself. By his own act he seemed utterly to have undone whatever of success the labour of years had brought about. How should it profit him now that a French regiment had saluted his eagle, that a French jury had shown sympathy with his cause, that the French Government had betrayed its fear of his machinations—when for all future time the insurrection of Strasburg would be linked in men's memories with the fiasco of Boulogne, and both alike confounded in common derision? Of what use now to him were all his little successes, the outcome of so much patient manipulation, when the whole erection he had based on them had been brought to ignominious and ridiculous collapse? For their fabrications about Strasburg, Louis Philippe's Government would find the best of all possible support in the facts of Boulogne. If September 1838 marked the climax of his apparent importance as a pretender, September 1840 saw the most abject moments in the whole life of Louis Napoleon. Even that other September, thirty years later, can hardly have held more bitterness for his own soul. For the mighty mightily fallen share their grief with a host of sympathetic spectators; even the dishonoured end of one who has attained to honour makes by contrast its pathetic appeal to posterity. But to have fallen from high hopes which can never now be known to have been well founded, this is an agony that must be endured alone.

On September 28, at half-past twelve in the morning, the prisoners were brought for the first time before the Court of Peers. Louis Napoleon was led in first, closely followed by the famous advocate Berryer, who had undertaken his defence. A little man dressed in black, slightly built, pale-faced, with a calm manner and a dreamy eye—this was the first vision which the Court of Peers had of their future emperor. By his side, a much more noticeable figure, stood the venerable General Montholon, who after sharing Napoleon's exile at St Helena had in his old age placed his life at the disposal of his heir. In all, some twenty prisoners were present; the Government did not bring to trial the obvious underlings of the expedition.

It was to this rather insignificant young man that the chancellor, Duke Pasquier, first spoke. Addressing him abruptly as 'first accused,' he bade him stand; then he asked him his name, age, and profession. To the last question the prisoner replied slowly, 'A French prince in exile.' This rather striking answer to a very ordinary question was the first sign of intelligence he had given. The peers turned curious eyes upon him, and noted that his dark clothes were relieved by one ornament, the great star of the Legion of Honour. He was asking now for leave to make a short statement before he answered further questions. Leave was given, and Louis Napoleon proceeded to make the first of those short felicitous speeches in which he excelled. Often in after years he saved an awkward situation by this means, turning a doubtful issue into certain victory; but never again had he to make use of this gift in quite so desperate a situation.

He was happy, he said, that now at last he was able to speak at large in France to Frenchmen. No personal ambition had led him on, but the belief that France had never taken back of her free will what she had given in 1804. For a moment indeed in 1830 he had believed that France had formed a truly national government; but the sad experience of the last ten years had undeceived him. And so he had felt it his duty to appeal to the people; to recall to a France fallen from its great position, silent among the concourse of kings, that other France so peaceful within, so formidable without. Had he succeeded at Boulogne, he would have called a national congress and bidden it choose how it would have France governed; for only the free decision of the nation could put an end to the present troubles and discontents. 'As for my enterprise,' he continued, 'again I tell you I had no accomplices. Alone I made all my resolutions. None knew beforehand my plans, my resources, or my hopes. If I have sinned against any man, it is against my own friends. None the less, I trust they will not accuse me of having lightly abused courage and devotion such as theirs. They will understand the motives of honour and prudence which forbid me to reveal, even to them, how farreaching and overwhelming were my reasons for counting on success.

'One last word, gentlemen. I stand before you the representative of a principle, a cause, a defeat. The principle is the sovereignty of the people; the cause is the cause of the Empire; the defeat, Waterloo. That principle *you* have recognised, that cause *you* have served, that defeat *you* would avenge. No, there is no disagreement between you and me.' Upon his judges, now visibly moved, this strange young man turned in conclusion, closing his peculiar defence by dismissing as unworthy to judge him the tribunal before which he was arraigned. 'The representative of a political cause, I cannot accept a jurisdiction that is itself political. Your forms deceive no one. In the coming conflict there is room only for conqueror and conquered. If you are the men of the conqueror, I can expect no justice and will accept no generosity at your hands.' The peers stirred uneasily as they listened. It was not at all the kind of pleading that they had expected. The Government accounts had prepared them for an undignified appeal, a piteous request for mercy. But this was not even a defence, it was a defiance.

Functionaries many of them of the First Empire, whose allegiance had already in turn been given to three successive dynasties, they could hardly fail to recognise in their prisoner's statement an accusation of themselves. And what did he mean —this pretender whose cause was already so visibly lost—what did he mean by speaking of the conflict as a future one,—*la lutte qui s'ouvre?* Apart from that, he was plainly and hopelessly in the wrong, palpably guilty of a puerile and criminal folly. How, then, had he managed to lift his case above their jurisdiction, to place himself beyond the reach of their most just condemnation? Well, they would hear more; and they turned again to listen to their remarkable prisoner. But there was no more for them to hear. To the renewed stream of questions, questions mainly designed to elicit the acquaintance of his companions with his plans, Louis Napoleon returned monosyllabic answers, or more often refused to give any answer at all. The chancellor proceeded to examine the other accused. Their behaviour was exactly that of the prisoners at the Strasburg trial. They did indeed accept the shelter proffered to them by their chief, by denying any previous knowledge of his plans. But, save for that, they in no way attempted to extenuate their fault. They had followed Louis Napoleon blindly, and would follow him again. So spoke Mésonan, Montholon, Voisin, Desjardins, Montauban, Laborde and Galvani, veteran soldiers of the First Empire, who had served with distinction in many a hard-fought fight, under Prince Eugène, King Murat, and the Emperor Napoleon himself. So Orsi, Lombard, Persigny, Conneau and Bataille, whom in Italy, Switzerland, and England the prince had attached to his cause. Very different was the conduct of General Magnan, who vehemently repudiated all connexion with the attempt. 'Before God and men, on the head of his five children,' he swore that he had indignantly dismissed Mésonan as soon as the overtures of Louis Napoleon were disclosed to him. To many even of those present he seemed to protest too much. And upon those who can study his evidence and behaviour at the trial in the light of his subsequent conduct, the conclusion forces itself that it was well for the Government of Louis Philippe that the loyalty of General Magnan after Boulogne was subjected to no such severe test as befell General Voirol at Strasburg.

It was the procureur-général who, when all the evidence had been heard, addressed the court for the prosecution. His speech consisted of a pitiless recital of the facts of the attempt, followed by a powerful appeal for the heavy punishment which those facts so plainly demanded. For the rest, it was to prove useful to Louis Napoleon later, owing to a chance phrase to which we have already alluded—the phrase in which M. Franck-Carré spoke of him as pardoned unconditionally after Strasburg. On September 30 followed Berryer's speech for the defence—in which the great legitimist orator poured scorn upon a jurisdiction which existed only to defend all that Louis Napoleon had wished to attack, rending with biting anger the hypocrisy of those who condemned after failure what they would most certainly have condoned after success, caressing with mocking praise the consistency of Louis Philippe and of his ministers. The former was honouring in death as the 'legitimate sovereign of our country,' the man whom in his lifetime he had denounced and opposed as 'the Corsican usurper.' The latter were pressing for a death sentence or its equivalent on the heir of him to whose favours they owed it that they were peers at all. Berryer did well to avoid any attempt to deny or disprove the facts alleged against his clients; his object was to obscure these by appealing to high-sounding principles and abstract justification. In other respects it was not a politic speech, if its intention were to placate the peers. But such was not its aim. It was an appeal over their heads to the French people. Taken together with the prince's own speech and with the behaviour of the other prisoners, it was not without effect. The attempt itself had been ludicrous; the trial had been rendered a serious event. And what remained —the punishment—was most serious of all. On October 6 the peers pronounced their sentence. This at any rate was no laughing matter. Of the accused only four were acquitted. Aladenize was sentenced to transportation for life; Parquin—

who died in captivity—with Montholon, Lombard, and Persigny to twenty years of 'detention,' a severer form of imprisonment; Mésonan to fifteen, Voison and two others to ten, and three more to five years of the same punishment. Conneau was imprisoned for five years, and Laborde for two. And 'Charles Louis Napoleon Bonaparte' was sentenced to perpetual imprisonment in a fortress situated within the continental territories of France.

CHAPTER IX

LOUIS NAPOLEON A POLITICAL PRISONER

> The plain was grassy, wild and bare,
> Wide, wild and open to the air,
> Which had built up everywhere
>   An under-roof of doleful gray.
>
> . . . .
>
> The wild swan's death-hymn took the soul
> Of that waste place with joy,
> Hidden in sorrow; at first to the ear,
> The warble was low, and full and clear;
> And floating about the under sky,
> Prevailing in weakness the coronach stole.
>
>   TENNYSON.

A LITTLE back from the petty provincial town of Ham, itself a dull and decayed habitation in the sullen valley of the Somme, stood the imposing remnant of a fifteenth-century fortress. From the midst of a flat expanse of low-lying ground rose ponderously a massive tower, a hundred feet in height, with walls in places ten yards thick. No feature of feudal cruelty was lacking to it. In the thickness of its solid masonry dank steps of stone wound their way down to sunless chasms where men had forgotten the light. Under its shadow lay a great courtyard, with ramparts and corner towers. The surrounding moat was indeed empty, or become degenerate into a mere swamp. But it was still a double drawbridge which gave access to the building from the town, and the Grosse Tour itself still found its sombre reflection in the sluggish waters of a little-used canal. From the marshy bank would steal up in the evening a white mist, half-way to greet the dark low-lying clouds which generally overhung the place by day. If the building itself was picturesque, the surrounding landscape was desolate and monotonous to a degree; while an unhealthy site combined with an inhospitable climate to render it a far from desirable dwelling-place. Obsolete for centuries as a fortress, the place had long been used as a state prison. Here deputies of the Convention had been confined after the first and great revolution; here after its small parody in 1830, Polignac, the hated minister of the last King of France, had been imprisoned with his colleagues, thankful that behind these walls he was safe from the mob of Paris clamorous for his blood. Hither by the same Government was now sent Louis Napoleon, grateful that so he might escape and perhaps live down the ridicule of Europe.

On October 7 the frigate that was to bear the Emperor's body back to France cast anchor at St Helena. On the same day Louis Napoleon was conducted from Paris to the intended scene of his lifelong captivity. Before the middle of the month he was joined there by Dr Conneau and General Montholon, who had been permitted to serve their terms of imprisonment in their leader's company. In the corner of the courtyard farthest from the gateway stands a low range of two-storeyed buildings. General Montholon was given two rooms on the ground floor; from this a short stair of crumbling stone led to the upper storey. Here Louis Napoleon had a bedroom and sitting-room at his disposal;[1] a small bedroom adjacent to the prince's was occupied by Dr Conneau. To make the most of the little light that reached it, the long narrow passage which gave access to the rooms was whitewashed. A spare room at the end of the passage was turned by the prince into a laboratory. Every window was closely barred. From both storeys there was only one exit, and to

[1] According to the tradition lately prevalent at Ham, before occupying these rooms Louis Napoleon was confined for the first six months of his imprisonment in a small cell nine feet square in the Grosse Tour. Before the war the Château served as barracks for 300 troops, and the Grosse Tour was the only part of the building which was shown to the public. Although the concierge was positive on the point, and though his statement was confirmed by the numerous officials, civilian and military, to whose joint good offices I owed my final admission to the prince's rooms in the barracks, I am none the less of opinion that the difficulty of visiting these rooms formed the real ground of the tradition, which would be sufficiently explained by the necessity of showing something as the scene of Louis Napoleon's imprisonment. Possibly, indeed, he may actually have been confined in the cell in question during the two days he passed at Ham on his way from Bologne to Paris in August 1840: but the statement that he was immured there for six months after his return in October is conclusively disproved by his own silence on the point. For Louis Napoleon was the last man to leave unadvertised any picturesque persecution of this kind.

Both the illustration opposite, and that which faces p. 248, are from photographs which I obtained at Ham in 1909. They have since acquired a melancholy interest from the fact that the Château in general, and the Grosse Tour in particular, were among the architectural casualties of the First World War.

LA GROSSE TOUR, HAM

reach this it was necessary to pass through a guard-room. The entire building was on the prince's arrival in a very dilapidated condition. But if they were indifferently lodged, the prisoners had the consolation of knowing that they were adequately guarded. Of the four hundred soldiers who were stationed in the fortress, sixty were always on duty as sentries; outside his own rooms the prince was always followed by one of them; and when he was allowed to walk on the ramparts, sentinels were placed to watch his movements at every point, even including the far bank of the canal. Demarle, the officer who had actually arrested Louis Napoleon at Boulogne, was made governor of the fortress; four times a day he was supposed personally to satisfy himself of his prisoners' presence. All letters addressed to the prince or written by him were liable to his inspection; often they were intercepted altogether; if they were in English they might be sent to Paris for examination. Permission for the prisoners to receive visitors was at first only granted very sparingly; while the soldiers of the garrison received the strictest injunctions to hold no converse with the prince.

Almost the first visitor who was allowed to see Louis brought him news of the one fact which seemed wanting to complete his desolation. In spite of King Jerome's action after Strasburg, Louis had never wholly abandoned the hope of marrying the Princess Mathilde; the father's anger might be appeased, or even ignored, if the princess herself still cared for him. But what must have been extremely difficult after Strasburg, became impossible after Boulogne; it was not to be expected that Mathilde should cleave to a lover condemned to perpetual imprisonment. In November 1840 she was married to Anatole Demidoff. The prince broke down utterly when the news reached him. 'This is the last and heaviest blow that fortune had in store for me,' he said to Ferdinand Barrot, the friend who told him what had happened; and indeed he may well have felt for the moment that he had completely sacrificed his personal happiness, without in any way advancing his political cause.

But it was just in such circumstances as these that the real strength of Louis Napoleon's character was most conspicuous. It was no great merit in him that he accepted his fate without a murmur, that he comported himself with dignity and cheerfulness in a far from agreeable situation. For that situation was, as he recognised, entirely of his own making. But truly praiseworthy was his refusal to recognise as final a defeat which to everyone but himself seemed utterly decisive. As though Boulogne had not made him the laughing-stock of Europe, as though 'perpetual imprisonment' were the merest episode in a man's life, the most natural preliminary imaginable to eventual success, he at once set to work to repair the seemingly irreparable ruin of his fortunes. The many and various schemes in which he was engaged during these years were valuable to him as distractions from the monotonous routine of his prison life; but they were all inspired directly or indirectly by the desire to forward the cause in which he still believed. In December 1840 he busied himself with a pamphlet, in which he addressed the shade of the Emperor, translated now to his triumphal resting-place in Paris:—'Sire, you return to your capital, and the people go out in crowds to greet your return. The people throng your passage as of old; the people salute your presence as though you lived still. But the great ones of to-day, the while they do you homage, mutter beneath their breath, "God grant he be dead indeed." . . . These men who were so little till you made them so great, they have denied your gospel and your glory: when I spoke to them of your cause, they answered me "We understand it not" . . . Vainly they say that you are but a meteor that passes and leaves no trace; they shall not disinherit you . . . From the midst of your funeral pomp you have cast a glance on my sombre prison; and you who caressed me when I was a child, have said to me, "Friend, I am content with thee; thou sufferest for me."' So, sentimental and grandiloquent, Louis Napoleon apostrophised the Emperor; seeking to contrast the fate which buried his uncle's body in the Invalides, while it buried himself alive at Ham. Napoleon's funeral was indeed a great show; but of popular enthusiasm there was no great demonstration; and few indeed of the myriads who went to see the spectacle had a thought to spare for Louis Napoleon. And Louis Napoleon himself was not really in any hurry to leave his 'sombre prison.' To an English friend at the beginning of 1841 he wrote: 'I have no wish to be elsewhere, for here I am in my right place. Bearing the name I do, mine must either be the gloom of a dungeon or the glare of power.' So passed December. January found the prisoner engaged in very different manner. His chief occupation in that month was a series of experiments with the percussion caps used for priming the guns then used in the French army; seeking to find a new method for the more rapid adjustment of the cap. He wrote a brief treatise on his experiments, with the intention of sending it to the Minister of War.

With February the sword was beaten into the ploughshare. The prince obtained permission to dig up a few square yards of ground on a sloping mound at one end of his walk on the ramparts within the confines of the fortress. Here he planted seeds and shrubs whose stunted growth afforded him a mild interest for the next five years to come.

During the three months which followed, he again betook himself to serious work. In May 1841 he published a small book, entitled *Fragments Historiques*. It was a refutation of M. Guizot's elaborate parallel between the events of 1830 in France and those of 1688 in England. The prince's correspondence of this date shows that he had read widely on the subject before writing; but under a thin historical guise the book is a plainly political pamphlet. As such it is rather ingenious. It is never difficult to demonstrate the weakness of a political parallel; and it was by this time easy enough to show that Louis Philippe would hardly bear comparison with William of Orange. But Louis Napoleon attempted more than this. He endeavoured not merely to destroy the parallel but to reverse it; not merely to wipe it out, but to turn it upside down. Those who sought precedents for the Orleanist policy would find them, not in the statesmanship of William III, but in the shiftiness and subservience of the Stuarts. And the fate which befell the Stuarts might be the fate which awaited Louis Philippe.

'The Stuarts had affable manners to win people's hearts: William was dry, cold, and reserved. The reigns of the Stuarts began always under the happiest auspices. . . . William on the contrary, was from the first surrounded with innumerable dangers and difficulties. Why did the former fail with so many chances of success, while the latter was triumphant against so many risks of death? . . . The Stuarts perpetually found themselves in a false position. The official representatives of Protestantism, they were at the bottom of their hearts Catholics. Compelled to be the representatives of a system of liberty and toleration, they were absolutists by instinct. The custodians of English interests, they were devoted or sold to France. They resisted where they should have yielded, and yielded where it was their duty to resist. . . . Protestantism had become in England since the sixteenth century the emblem of every national interest. In order to be powerful within and without, the Stuarts had only to place themselves frankly at its head: instead they betrayed it abroad, and endeavoured to defeat it at home.

'William, on the contrary, was truly by nature and by conviction all he represented on the throne. He was the founder of a new order of things, the establishment of which his own skill and courage had hastened. . . . The Stuarts went to war to support their tottering power with a little glory; William went to war to increase the influence of England.'

Reverse the words Protestant and Catholic, England and France; substitute Louis Philippe for the Stuarts, and—more curious—for William III read Louis Napoleon—and the parable is explained. Louis Philippe was not mentioned by name, but even so it is strange that his government allowed the publication of so palpable an attack. Stranger still, however, is the momentary choice of William of Orange by Louis Napoleon for his own model. Silent both, phlegmatic, taciturn, there were superficially some points of resemblance in their characters. But two more different careers it would be difficult to select. Granting the connexion in their author's mind, these two sentences become rather ominous. Of the Stuarts, he says they had forgotten 'that among nations there has never been a government strong enough to suppress liberty at home for any length of time unless it gives glory abroad.' And contrasting William's advent to power with the circumstances of the Stuart restoration, he makes this really significant remark: 'In general, revolutions brought about by one leader turn altogether to the profit of the masses; because to succeed, the man is obliged to throw himself entirely on the national sentiments, and to maintain his success must remain faithful to those interests: revolutions made by the masses, on the contrary, often profit the leaders only; because the people think that their work is done on the morrow of victory, and it is natural to them to rest for a long time after the efforts that were necessary for success.' The book was rather well received, and had a respectable sale, though not, of course, approaching that of the *Idées Napoléoniennes*.

The prince had now been in prison for six months. In spite of his various occupations the winter had passed slowly enough. Moreover it had perceptibly told on his health. Accustomed to vigorous exercise, he had now none, save for his short walk on the ramparts with a warder at his heels. A more serious grievance was the utterly dilapidated condition in which he found his rooms. The paper was peeling off the walls, the doors and windows were ill fitted; and the brick floor was damp and uneven. From the first Dr Conneau expostulated vigorously against this state of things, and not without cause. For the first time in his life the prince was afflicted with rheumatism; during the whole period of his imprisonment he was subject to attacks of it, often in acute form. Poor old General Montholon wished himself back at St Helena; the tactlessness of an English governor, the vaunted indignities to which the Emperor had been subjected, began to seem endurable enough when compared with the ordered discomfort of a French political imprisonment. 'The Emperor was not so badly treated by the English in an English prison as his nephew is by the French in a French prison.' So wrote Montholon, intent doubtless on magnifying the sufferings of nephew and uncle alike, but probably quite sincere in his relative estimation of their several hardships. As a result of the persistent complaints of Dr Conneau, the Minister of the Interior made a grant of 600 francs for the renovation of the rooms. The sum was barely sufficient for the most obvious repairs; it sufficed, however, to place a proper floor in the room. Louis Napoleon was informed that he might make further alterations at his own expense; but he refused 'to put a state prison in repair.' He did, however, make certain additions to the furniture of the rooms; and in the end they were quite presentable. In May he himself addressed a letter to the Government, protesting against certain of the more pointless and gratuitous of the indignities of his treatment. 'The sovereignty of the people made my uncle an emperor, my father a king, and myself a prince by birth.' Even as a prisoner, therefore, he had a right to somewhat different treatment from that which he was receiving. Probably the letter was inspired more by a desire of calling the attention of France to his treatment than by any great hope of obtaining an improvement in it. But it seems to have occurred to Louis Philippe's Government that it was hardly politic to allow their prisoner such advertisement as a repetition of the protest would give him. Several concessions were accordingly granted to him. He was permitted to exercise himself on horseback; a privilege of which he availed himself but sparingly. For to ride solemnly round the courtyard—and this was all that was permitted him—while the walls were lined with a doubled post of sentries and the governor himself stood in the middle, this was a form of amusement which soon became wearisome. Another concession made at the same time was of more value. Louis Napoleon's valet, Charles Thélin, had recently been permitted to join him, but hitherto he had not been allowed to come in and out of the prison at his pleasure. Now the restrictions were withdrawn. The most important result of this concession was to reduce to a dead letter the inspection of the prince's correspondence. From this time too the prince was allowed to receive occasional visits from a few residents in Ham, or, more rarely, from his friends at a distance.

From June 1841 to January 1842, Louis Napoleon was engrossed with the idea of writing a book on the life of Charlemagne. The project was never realised, but the prince's correspondence shows clearly enough the form it would have taken. Of Charlemagne, as of Napoleon, it had been said that his work was brilliant in appearance, but transitory in its results; both had been compared to meteors whose brilliant careers left no permanent traces behind them. Louis Napoleon desired to refute this verdict in both cases. He purchased numerous works on the subject, both English, French, and German; he corresponded on the subject with the historian Sismondi; he devoted, indeed, more time to this unfulfilled project than he had given to his published pamphlet on the two revolutions. It need not be said that history is no loser by the abandonment of this design; it is doubtful whether the subject would even have served as a good framework for the loose generalisations of a political pretender. Towards the close of 1841 the prince returned to his chemical experiments, and in February 1842 he had indefinitely postponed the design, busying himself instead with preparing a new edition to his *Manuel d'Artillerie.*

A few months later he had a new interest. After about five months' work on the subject he published in August 1842 a pamphlet on a question then much to the fore in France—the claims of beetroot sugar to protection. One of the articles of common consumption of which Napoleon's Berlin decrees had prohibited the import was cane sugar. For at that time the traffic in this sugar was wholly in English hands. To meet the deficiency he had encouraged the manufacture in France of sugar extracted from beetroot. Other expedients designed to replace other necessities of life, whose importation Napoleon had prohibited, proved worthless enough, and had at once collapsed when the prohibition was swept away. But the beet sugar trade on the contrary acclimatised itself and became the basis of a flourishing industry. It survived the fall of the empire, and even a limited amount of competition from the cane sugar for which it had become a substitute. But now it was proposed, in the interest of the French colonies in the Indies— and indirectly in the interest of the French fleet— to sacrifice the home industry in beet sugar to the colonial cane sugar. It was, of course, the origin of the French manufacture which interested Louis Napoleon in the question. Doubtless too it was this which caused him to decide in its favour; though he avowed that he approached the question without bias, since any predilection for the beet industry due to its Napoleonic origin was balanced by the fact that his grandmother, the Empress Josephine, had been born in the French Indies. His pamphlet was frankly Protectionist. It was absurd, he said, to sacrifice the prosperity of seven departments, the habitation of four million men, to the interest of some 30,000 colonists dwelling in two small islands. It was possible in any case to protect the consumer at too heavy a price. Cheapness of goods might mean cheapness of labour, and cheapness of labour meant the misery of the people. Even England might find this to her cost. The prince's great argument in favour of beet sugar was that, unlike most manufactures, it scattered centres of labour in the country instead of conglomerating them into towns, thus rearing a vigorous and healthy population, free from the physical and moral evils which ensued from the crowding of men into small houses in great cities. In matters of tariff, he continued, 'honour often shows the right road, generally involving also palpable and positive advantages.' As an instance of his meaning he pointed to the success of the Prussian Zollverein. The treatise shared the fate of the great majority of such writings; without winning converts from those opposed to its principles, it was welcomed and quoted by men who already held its views. This party was, however, a powerful one. The beet growers regarded it as the best vindication of their position which had yet appeared; within a few months of its publication, in November 1842, a second and enlarged edition was produced.

This early essay in Protection is rather noticeable in one who was to become the greatest continental promoter of the principles of Free Trade. Its general attitude is rather like that of Ruskin's revolt from the Manchester school of political economy, twenty years later. A similar attitude is shown in many of the writings which follow during the next two years. Always an indefatigable correspondent —where correspondence could serve his aim—Louis Napoleon from the beginning of his imprisonment sought by this means to make the acquaintance of the editors of provincial newspapers in the North of France. By the end of 1842 he had so far succeeded that the columns of some half-dozen local papers were open to his writings. Of these papers, all possessed a considerable sale and influence in their own neighbourhood, while some had a more than local importance; the Parisian press occasionally quoted articles from their columns. Naturally the editors with whom Louis Napoleon would correspond were men opposed to the existing government. But it was less natural that the opposition party with which he joined hands should be almost entirely republican. For during the later years of the prince's imprisonment there was a curious approach to an understanding between him and the republican opposition. His writings at this time bear witness to this. He did not really recede from any of his pretensions. The utmost concession he ever made was drawn from him by a direct enquiry by the editor of a republican journal in 1843, as to what his pretensions would be if he were a free citizen. 'I have never thought,' he replied, 'and never shall think, that France is the appanage of a family; I have never claimed any rights save those of a French citizen; I shall never have any other desire than that of serving the entire people, when they have chosen in full freedom the form of government they desire. Born of a family which owes its elevation to the national will, I should be untrue to my origin, to my nature, to my common sense, if I did not recognise the national sovereignty of the people as the basis of my political organisation.' But in the same letter he continued, 'True I have pursued a lofty ambition, but I have sought it openly. It was my ambition to re-unite around my popular name all the partisans of the sovereignty of the people, all who aspired to glory and liberty.' Louis Napoleon never doubted, or pretended to doubt, what the result of a free choice by the entire people would be; the republicans of course were equally confident that a republic would emerge from it; both were certain that it would destroy what both wished to see destroyed—the Orleanist dynasty. Here then was the basis of a working alliance. Each party was to some extent making use of the other; the prince willing to appeal to a wider audience, the republicans glad to annex the glamour of his name. The series of articles which Louis Napoleon published in this way during the years 1843 and 1844 deal with almost every aspect of French political life. Though published at first anonymously, their authorship was soon avowed, and they attracted so much attention that in the latter year the Government intervened to prevent the continuance of the series. Their literary merit is not much more than their method of publication would suggest—that of the better class of provincial journalism. But their political views are always thoughtful, often interesting, sometimes statesmanlike. A few brief quotations must suffice to illustrate their tenor.

Dealing with a comparison then much in vogue between the English and French parliamentary methods, Louis showed clearly and well the various points which divided the French imitation from the English natural growth in its methods and results. Especially he drew attention to the profound influence of the 'tribune' in French parliamentary debates: the English member addressed the house from his place, and discussion was business-like; the French member harangued his audience from the tribune, and the result was a series of set speeches.

On another question, destined unfortunately to be a matter of more than passing controversy—on the part proper to clergy in the education of children—the prince wrote sensibly and well. The clergy reasonably claimed the right of teaching children Christianity. The State as reasonably maintained its duty of keeping public instruction under its own direction. Unfortunately, as things stood, their claims were conflicting, for the clergy were undemocratic in their sympathies, and it was impossible to allow them liberty to teach the people hatred of liberty. Atheism and ultramontanism were the enemies. Yet the worst possible remedy was disestablishment, which would force the clergy to traffic in sacred things. The education of the clergy themselves was the vital point. Here Southern Germany could give them an ideal example. There was a Catholic clergy liberal and tolerant, learned and patriotic; for there candidates for the priesthood were not isolated from childhood, and embued in seminaries with a spirit hostile to the society in which they were to live, but studied theology in universities attended by students for other professions. Let this be their model in France. Only by making your priest a citizen can you hope to make your citizen religious. 'Then, but then only,' concluded Louis Napoleon, 'shall we rejoice to see, as in Germany, ministers of religion at the head of national education, teaching our children the doctrine of Christ.'

Perhaps the most noteworthy of all these essays is one on the problem of national defence, in which the prince singles out the military organisation of Prussia as that which in the most economical, democratic, and efficient manner furnished its country with a formidable army. He urged France then, as he urged it twenty-five years later, to make Prussia its model in this respect, and to lose no time in introducing the Prussian system in France. It must, of course, be remembered, that the man who in 1843 discovered this fact was proclaiming a truth which had not yet become a truism.

The essay which most attracted attention at the time was one which least deserved it—a paper entitled *Extinction du Paupérisme*, published in the spring of 1844. It was a proposal to colonise the large tracts of land then untilled in France with the large number of men who were always lacking the proper means of subsistence. Not more practicable, it was possibly not less sincere than other schemes of the kind propounded by St Simon, Fourier, or Louis Blanc. The general sentiments were admirable, its illustrations often telling, its attacks on many existing grievances only too pointed. But as a constructive scheme it was devoid of merit. This, however, did not prevent it from having a large circulation; and as there are always many to whom clarity of utterance implies clarity of thought, to whom any reasoned scheme will appear reasonable, any Utopia practicable if plentifully empaled by statistics, the *Extinction du Paupérisme* was of all the writings of his imprisonment that which most benefited its author. Béranger and George Sand wrote to him expressing their appreciation; while in the autumn of 1844 he received an address, largely signed by working men, thanking him for his interest in their fate.

From his prison at Ham, as from his exile in Switzerland and London, Louis Napoleon maintained a close watch on the course of political affairs in France, allowing no occasion to pass unnoticed which might serve him as an opportunity for drawing attention to his own existence. In the summer of 1843, a former French deputy conceived the project of a sort of popular French Dictionary of National Biography; he proposed to begin with the life of Napoleon. But Lamartine, to whom he submitted his scheme, replied by a letter in which he pointed out that Napoleon's life was not ideally fitted for the people's instruction; and proceeded to demonstrate that France would have stood that day in a far happier position had Napoleon never been born. At once Louis Napoleon is to the fore; in a long open letter he replied in detail to the points of Lamartine's attack on his hero.

A year later, on July 28, 1844, Joseph, the ex-King of Spain, died at Florence. This event was not without its importance to Louis, for Joseph until his death remained the nominal head of his house. As such the prince had alluded to him in his speech to the Peers, after the failure of the Boulogne expedition; whether he would have remembered his claims if this expedition had succeeded, is more than doubtful. Now he was dead, and to be praised: Louis Napoleon wrote a short memoir of him, which was published in the *Revue de l'Empire*.

A young chemist who lived in Ham, M. Acar, was a frequent visitor of the prince during the later years of his imprisonment. Together they spent many hours in his extemporised laboratory, indulging in mild experiments with electricity and explosives. The prince found this occupation a pleasant change from his literary work, often turning to it after a morning spent on the pamphlet or essay on which he was for the time engaged. But even these experiments were made to play their part in the great work. In May 1843 a letter of Louis Napoleon's, on his latest electrical experiments, was read by M. Arago before the French Academy of Sciences, and was printed in the *Bulletin de l'Académie*, in the report of the society's proceedings. It was the prince's consistent policy to leave unattempted no method in his power by which he might bring his name before a fresh section of the French people.

M. Acar, the republican chemist, was not, however, his only visitor; nor were the prince's dabblings in chemistry his sole recreations from his more serious labours. Other and less edifying amusements were not wanting. The visitor to Ham was long shown the doorway by which 'La Belle Sabotière' and others of her kind came and went; the clogmaker's daughter herself became the mother of two sons by the prince. Incidents of this kind even Louis Napoleon's genius for advertisement could not hope to turn to the profit of his cause; but if he was at no particular pains to excuse his conduct in this respect, this was doubtless because he was satisfied that in France at any rate his political future would not be seriously compromised by it.

During the later years of his imprisonment, Louis was allowed to receive visits from a number of friends outside Ham. Towards the end of the year 1844 Louis Blanc came to see the prince, and spent three days at Ham in his company. That he should have done so is significant of the intimate relations which had by this time grown up between the prince and the republican party. Together they discussed the prince's own position and the entire political situation of France. Fifteen years later, when the prisoner had become Emperor of the French, and his distinguished visitor an exile from his country, Louis Blanc published an account of their conversation. This account is not without interest, though it bears signs of the circumstances of its publication. The republican seems for the nonce to have been possessed with an unwonted and almost prophetic insight into the future, and to have administered to Louis Napoleon many admirable cautions, which were signally justified by events which happened between the giving of the advice and the publication of it. Pity that in such case the truth of a prophecy in fulfilment should so often be the measure of its falsity in fact. *Non credo quia credibile.*

'Among the various circumstances still present to my memory, one,' wrote Louis Blanc, 'remains worthy of mention, on account of the strange aspect it gives to the hardness which Louis Bonaparte showed afterwards. One afternoon he was describing to me the details of his Boulogne expedition, when his voice suddenly failed; he stopped, tried in vain to master his emotion, and burst into tears. Nor shall I ever forget our stroll on the narrow rampart assigned to his melancholy walks, and overlooked on all sides by sentinels. I think I see him yet, walking with slow steps, his head bent; I think I still hear his voice, speaking low, lest the wind should carry his words to the gaoler. The conversation turned on a history of the Roman emperors, by an author whom Louis Bonaparte was praising for having defended these tyrants, branded on the shoulders for ever by Tacitus. According to Louis Bonaparte, Tacitus was in the wrong. I had not read the book which the prisoner admired so much, but the motives of his admiration were not far to seek. I combated it, and with a vivacity that led him to say, "Speak low"; and turning, he pointed out to me a man wrapped in a cloak, who was following us at a short distance and never for an instant losing sight of us.' The credibility of Tacitus as an historian has been often debated since then, but never surely under quite such curious circumstances.

That in after years Louis Blanc should give a sinister turn to his recollections of him, mattered little enough to Louis Napoleon. What was of real importance and utility to him was the favourable impression he made upon his visitor at the time itself. For at this time Louis Blanc was publishing a widely read history of France during the first ten years of the Orleanist regime. This history would in any case have been marked by a hostility to Louis Philippe and his Government;

but to his intimacy with its author Louis Napoleon owed a singularly sympathetic account of his own first attempt to overthrow that Government. He was described as 'generous, enterprising, an adept in military exercise, elegant and haughty in his uniform. There was not a braver officer or a bolder rider. Although his features were mild rather than energetic or commanding, although there was a habitual languor in his look, full of reverie, yet soldiers would doubtless have loved him for his frank manners, for the candour of his speech, for his size—diminutive, like that of his uncle—and for the imperial light which the passion of the moment would kindle in his blue eye.' Such praise from such a source, even with the qualifications which were added to it, was worth more to Louis Napoleon than all Persigny's whole-hearted eulogy.

Louis Blanc was not the only visitor who published an account of his experience. Towards the end of 1845, an American friend, Henry Wikoff, obtained with some difficulty permission to spend four hours with Louis at Ham. He described himself as much shocked at the sad change which had taken place in his appearance since he last met him in London, five years ago or more. 'He had grown much thinner, was very pale and sickly looking, and his manner, how different from the gay martial air he had worn in London! . . . From his person my glance wandered over the room, which surprised me by its extreme rudeness. It was very small, the walls bare, and the floor without covering. . . . The whole had very much the appearance of a common kitchen in some unpretending private house.'[1] The prince himself was violently affected with rheumatism, but took his visitor out for the little walk allotted him on the ramparts. 'All was flat, monotonous, and cheerless. . . . I never saw a landscape so dreary and repulsive. . . . The gloom of the surrounding objects was enhanced by the humid air and cold shade which dwelt on all around.' They returned to the prince's room before his departure. At the end of the four hours Wikoff took his leave. 'As I reached the head of the staircase,' he writes, 'I turned round instinctively for a last look at the spot I had just quitted, when to my surprise I found the prince had followed me to the door, and was looking after me. Nothing could have conveyed to my mind a keener sense of the desolation into which he was relapsing than this single act. His face and attitude both bespoke the dreariness and melancholy which surrounded him.' This picture may be a little too

[1] Of this same room, Louis Blanc wrote that it was spacious, well furnished, and provided with every domestic comfort. The contradiction is perhaps just worth mentioning as typical of many, even in points of fact, which face the biographer at every turn in the evidence for Louis Napoleon's early life. Wikoff's account was designed to discredit the Orleanist regime and to win sympathy for his friend; Louis Blanc in 1859 would have been willing even to praise Louis Philippe, so that he could thereby discredit Louis Napoleon. Through the courtesy of Commandant Répaloski I was enabled in 1909 to visit the room which then served as an officer's bedroom. It was of respectable size, neither 'spacious' nor 'very small,' some $16\frac{1}{2}$ feet in length by 15 feet broad

highly coloured, but its main features seem true enough. That his rooms were small and his life monotonous, did not greatly trouble Louis. 'My life passes here monotonously enough,' he wrote to a friend in 1841, 'because the rigour of authority is unbounded. Nevertheless I can not say that I find myself bored, because I can create for myself occupations which interest me.' As the years passed on, this attitude changed a little; he was growing weary of confinement, but still patient under it. 'It is no personal ambition,' he wrote to Vieillard in September 1843, 'which has made me risk twice over what I prized more than life, my reputation; it is not the ambition to rule which has prompted me to sacrifice once and again my private affections, my fortune, my repose. It is a loftier and more mysterious sentiment that has always led me on and held me up. To have dared what I have dared, to have endured what I have suffered, there was need that I should feel in myself something of the martyr's faith which nothing can destroy.' Later again, he half admits despondency. 'There are in me two persons; the man of politics, and the private man. The political half of me is and will remain absolutely unshaken; but the private man is very unhappy. Abandoned by all the world, by old friends, by his family, by his very father, he often lets himself give way to memories, to regrets.' Once only, in the very considerable amount of his correspondence during these years which has by this time been made public, do we find symptoms of despair. Of some suggested step at the end of 1845 he wrote: 'Better a hundred times death. Life holds no more attractions for me. I had dreamed a great dream; I thought I could be useful to France, to humanity at large. I saw outstretched before me a vast horizon, glowing with that glory which leaves no regrets behind it. I thought I should be able to ripen all that the Emperor had sown on every side. And twice over I have awoken behind bars.' More frequent in his private letters are allusions to ill-health. In July 1843 he complains of headache every day for the last four or five months. This, with rheumatism, was his chief affliction. In May 1846 he writes of pain in his eyes, which makes work impossible for the time. Dilation of one pupil is the trouble, but nothing very serious, he hopes. In the same letter he adds: 'I have had bad news about my father. Things go none too well with me either in mind or body.'

The increasing ill-health of the prisoner was in part owing to lack of regular exercise, a habit to which he had long been addicted; in part perhaps it was due to the not very salubrious surroundings of his prison. That the air was unwholesome seems probable; for former prisoners at Ham had complained of it bitterly.[1] Perhaps, too, the extreme

[1] *E.g.*, M. de Peyronnet, ex-minister of Charles X, in a letter, dated 28th Aug. 1831, published in *La Quotidienne*, speaks of Ham as 'unhealthy and very badly situated. Half the day it is enveloped in mist. The promenade consists of one end of the rampart, some sixty yards in length, and just broad enough for two men to walk abreast. From the foot of this rampart noisome vapours rise continually.'

vigour with which he threw himself into his literary work may have injured the prince's health. Generally rising very early, he at times stayed up all night at his work. During the last three years of his imprisonment he was busily engaged on a history of artillery. On this book he spent more time and trouble than on all the rest of the writings of his imprisonment put together. The work was begun without design, almost by accident. At the beginning of 1842 he took up his old *Manuel d'Artillerie*, to revise it for a new edition; but it was not until the spring of 1843 that he really began seriously to work on it. In December he is still engaged on the introduction, which he finds a work in itself. In January 1844 he had decided to publish the introduction as a separate work; he believes it will be a far more interesting one than the *Manuel* itself. 'I believe that this work will make my military reputation,' he added with *naive* simplicity. By this time the design had expanded until it comprised a complete history of the science of artillery from the fourteenth century. During the next eighteen months he continued to work on this subject with extraordinary zeal and industry, almost without intermission. Many hundreds of works on the subject, by authors French, German, English and Italian, were sent to him at Ham; from the earliest printed books to the latest pamphlet or periodical. Tracings of drawings and copies of manuscripts whose originals could not be sent were made for him by an old friend of his childhood—Mme

Cornu. He corresponded also with many military men on the subject; but his published correspondence with Mme Cornu alone for these two years is most conclusive evidence of the extraordinary assiduity with which he worked on this subject. In December 1844, Leneveu, then a leading military publisher in France, arranged to produce the book. It was printed at the publisher's expense, and the author was to receive half the profits. These terms from such a publisher show that by this time Louis Napoleon's writings commanded at any rate a respectable sale. Leneveu also agreed to place his entire military library and all his publications at the prince's disposal. This concession was of importance to Louis, who had already spent on military works sums larger than his diminished fortune warranted.

Whether his ill-health was due to hard work, long confinement, lack of exercise, or unhealthy surroundings, it is clear that in the winter of 1845 Louis Napoleon began to wonder whether his imprisonment had not continued long enough. 'Nobody writes to me; I am being forgotten,' he wrote in February to one of his friends. Now to be forgotten was the one fate he could not contemplate with resignation; if his imprisonment were really to have this effect it would cease to serve his cause. So soon as he had come to this conclusion, he set to work to raise the question of his release. He sent a messenger to ask his friend Lord Malmesbury to obtain leave to visit him.

P

Malmesbury accordingly visited Louis Napoleon in April, and it seems clear that he undertook to do what he could in the matter. The prisoner himself abstained from all appearance of interest in the question. In the summer the Orleanist Government sent to him an informal messenger in the person of the Duke of Istria. The prince was given to understand that a direct renunciation of his rights to the throne, with a formal undertaking to abstain from any hostile action against the present dynasty, would suffice to procure his liberation. Louis' reply, though conciliatory, was in effect a refusal, and negotiations were dropped. In the autumn Louis Philippe paid a visit to England, and on his return all the Boulogne conspirators who were still in captivity were released, with the exception of Louis and his companions. It now became evident that either Lord Malmesbury had failed to influence the English Government, or the English Government had failed to influence Louis Philippe. Louis Napoleon turned elsewhere.

Since his ill-advised letter of protest in the autumn of 1840 against the Government's treatment of its prisoner, the ex-King of Holland had shown little sign of interest in his son's existence. During this time he had been living in retirement in Florence, in gradually failing health. Towards the end of 1845 it became clear that he had not long to live. Suddenly in August he despatched a messenger—M. Poggioli—to Louis Philippe's ministers, asking that his son might be allowed to visit him before he died. The request was refused; but the messenger was allowed to visit the prince and inform him of his father's efforts in his behalf. Now it is possible that this was really a sudden whim on the part of King Louis, for the action would be quite in character with the spasmodic interventions to which he was from time to time prompted by his occasional fits of interest in his son's affairs. But it is more probable that the initiative in this instance came from the son; that M. Poggioli was originally commissioned by Louis Napoleon to sound his father on the subject, and that the knowledge of his approaching death made the latter readily acquiesce in any steps which might render possible a last meeting. Louis Napoleon, now as ever, neglected no possible circumstance which could be made to serve his political purpose. By putting the plea for his release into his father's mouth, he himself retained complete freedom of action. More than that, by grounding the request on a father's desire to see his only son before he died, he rendered refusal on the part of Louis Philippe difficult, ungracious, almost inhuman in appearance.

Cleverly contrived, the situation was also cleverly handled. Louis Napoleon wrote to his father, thanking him heartily for this proof of his attachment; hitherto he said he had had nothing for which he should even desire to leave his prison; now he would do all that in honour he might do to render possible the fulfilment of his father's wishes. This was in the middle of September. Louis now waited for three months, wishing to take no step in his own name until it was quite clear that his father's efforts unaided would prove ineffectual. In the interval, in letters to his friends, he declared himself quite passive in the matter. On Christmas Day, a date not chosen accidentally, he at last wrote himself to the Minister of the Interior. In a short letter, in which no word was wasted, he stated his case. His father's request had been refused; the Government insisted on a formal undertaking from himself. His duty to his father demanded that he should go as far as his honour would allow him in the matter. 'I therefore declare to you, *M. le Ministre*, that if the French Government will consent to permit me to go to Florence to fulfil a sacred duty, I engage on my honour to return and constitute myself a prisoner as soon as the Government may require me to do so.' The Government's position was thus deftly turned. The negotiations for the prince's release had been unwelcome to them, but they realised the unpopularity of a direct refusal. In seeking for an engagement from Louis they had intended to throw upon him the onus of that refusal. But the engagement they intended was one by which he should disclaim all dynastic rights or pretensions. The one he offered, while it seemed more ample, was really useless to them. For to claim its fulfilment would have made a hero of the reconstituted prisoner, and would load the Government with unpopularity. The Government after some delay replied indirectly that they could not take the prince's demand into consideration; for to grant it would be in effect to confer a free pardon, for which the king would get no credit. At the same time it was hinted to Louis that a direct appeal to the king might have the desired effect. On January 14, 1846, Louis accordingly wrote to the king. Though substantially the same as its predecessor this letter was a little less curtly worded. Without actually enlarging his engagement, Louis added words which showed that he should regard himself under an obligation if his request were granted. 'I am convinced,' he wrote, 'that your Majesty will appreciate as it deserves a step which engages my gratitude beforehand, and that touched by the isolation in a foreign land of a man who on a throne won the esteem of Europe, you will hear my father's prayer and mine.'

Under cover of a scheme for the supervision by him of a canal to be cut through Nicaragua, Louis Napoleon even offered a further concession. Indirectly, through Lord Londonderry, he undertook, after spending a year with his father, to proceed to America for this purpose. Apparently the king's first impulse was to grant the request, but his ministers persuaded him to hold out for more. Pardon must be deserved, they said, and frankly acknowledged. A letter was drawn up by the Minister of the Interior for Louis Napoleon's signature; by signing this, he could go free, but he would have plainly signed away his position as a pretender. Now here Louis Philippe's instinct was wiser than his ministers' wisdom. Louis Napoleon was in fact playing with the ministers of Louis Philippe, in exactly the same way that Bismarck played with Louis Napoleon's ministers some five-and-twenty years later. In order that refusal might place his enemy the more hopelessly in the wrong, he had gone already to the very limit of honourable concession; he now abruptly refused to go a step farther. His object had been attained. For Louis Philippe's refusal lessened his own popularity, and increased that of his prisoner. Opposition deputies took up the prince's cause in the Chamber; thirty-one members formed a deputation to ask the king for his release; this failing, they urged the prince to sign the ministers' letter, and be free. To M. Barrot, his principal friend among them, Louis wrote on February 2, thanking them for their efforts on his behalf. 'But,' he continued, 'I do not consider it consistent with my duty to attach my name to the letter of which you have sent me a copy. . . . If I signed, I should, in fact, really be asking for pardon without avowing the fact; I should take shelter behind the request of my father . . . I consider such a course unworthy of me. If I thought it consistent with my condition and honour merely and simply to invoke the royal clemency, I would write to the king, "Sire, I ask pardon."' His private letters show that Louis was disappointed that M. Barrot should have played into the hands of the Government by advising him to sign. But with the position as a whole he had no reason to be dissatisfied. His name was once more in men's mouths; his cause had been pleaded by deputies of the French Chamber; members of the English House of Lords had interceded on his behalf. The journals of Paris and the provinces busied themselves again with the discussion of his fate. Even if that fate were to be imprisonment indefinitely continued, Louis need have no immediate fear of being forgotten. As a matter of fact he had no intention of allowing his imprisonment to continue indefinitely.

Nothing now remains to be told of Louis Napoleon's life in prison save his preparations for the leaving of it. Here, then, we well may pause for a moment to review the effects of this long imprisonment on his future career and character.

It is in the first place impossible to study in any detail this period of his life without emerging from that study with a greatly increased respect for the prince's character. His untiring industry, his unbroken confidence, his aptitude in making the utmost use of every passing event, most of all his unquenchable faith in his own future—these must impress even those to whom Strasburg seemed a reckless adventure, and Boulogne a very sorry fiasco indeed. In so far as the five and a half years spent at Ham were beneficial to the prince's reputation, they were beneficial also to his future career. It has, we think, been too readily assumed that the election of Louis Napoleon to the presidency in 1848 was an absolute leap in the dark, the mere surrender of a people in blind obedience to a name. The motives of that election were complicated enough, and we shall have to examine them in their place But here it may be noted that by the spring of 1846 Louis Napoleon's existence, his claims, and something of his fortunes and his writings were known to all save the absolutely illiterate of his fellow-countrymen. Moreover it is clear that during the years of his imprisonment Louis Napoleon was by some curious subterranean process drawing to himself a real following from among the lowest of the people. Strasburg and Boulogne had attracted men's attention to him, but it was Ham that won him their sympathy.

For all this there was a price to be paid. Never robust, the prince at the end of his imprisonment found himself with sadly impaired health. A few months in English watering-places served to efface the immediate ill effects of his sufferings. But some of the physical consequences of his imprisonment proved lifelong; among them a permanent tendency to acute rheumatism, which predisposed him to that other dread disease by which the last ten years of his life were so fatally marred.

Another and not less unfortunate consequence must be noted. Naturally meditative — almost ruminative — in his process of thought, Louis Napoleon emerged from Ham a confirmed visionary. If in his later life we find at times a certain aloofness from the actual, an indefinable remoteness from the realities of political life, we may confidently assign as cause the long period of enforced seclusion at Ham. A habit of mind to which he was naturally prone was there fostered and encouraged. For it was good for him then that he should be able to subject the sordid present to a glorious future, to blot out his prison walls by visions of his kingly palace. But it was not good that when the great future had become the actual present, when the hermitage had really been exchanged for the palace, then its master's mind should still be groping forwards into a yet further futurity. Yet this was to become a mental obliquity with Louis Napoleon. A well-balanced mind, that would hold in just equipoise the past and future, must preserve its centre of gravity at the present. With Louis Napoleon this centre of gravity was permanently shifted towards the future, to the prejudice at times of that present on which the future depends. In the end the result was disastrous. At Ham it had been the prince's consolation that he could project his vision to the Tuileries; at the Tuileries it was his undoing that he should still be reaching forward to schemes as far beyond his grasp as the palace of the Tuileries itself had been distant from the prisoner of Ham.

CHAPTER X

LOUIS NAPOLEON REGAINS HIS LIBERTY

> Nec tu . . . 'Rupi jam vincula,' dicas:
> Nam luctata canis nodum arripit, attamen illi
> Cum fugit a collo trahitur pars longa catenæ.
> PERSIUS.

THERE are in the life of Louis Napoleon certain incidents so grotesque in themselves, so fantastic in their circumstances, that his biographer cannot but feel some sort of apology to be due for their narration in the sober history of a nineteenth-century sovereign. Indeed, the reader who should be confronted with the narrative in some detail while still unfamiliar with its outline, might well rub his eyes and wonder whether he had stumbled unawares on some peculiarly impudent example of pseudo-historical fiction. He need be under no such apprehension. Few novelists would perpetrate such wanton outrage on the probabilities; fewer still could with impunity make such gratuitous demands upon the credulity of their readers. It is the privilege of the historian that he may at times tell a tale which would by its extravagance destroy the reputation of the veriest master of romance. Only truth can afford utterly to disregard verisimilitude. With this much of extenuation for not a little of what has gone before, and much that is to come, we proceed to recount the manner in which Louis Napoleon took his departure from Ham.

So soon as he has begun seriously to contemplate an early recovery of his liberty, Louis found himself faced directly by what was probably the only difficulty hitherto unknown to him—lack of funds. The large fortune he had inherited from his mother had by this time disappeared. His life in London had been an extravagant one, the preparations for Boulogne had been costly, and its consequences had been financially disastrous. For Louis had felt himself bound in honour to provide for all his followers whose fortunes he had compromised : Strasburg and Boulogne together had thus saddled him with a large number of pensioners. Immediately after Boulogne he had actually settled on many of them sums which would assure them from want; his natural generosity was stimulated in this instance by a vague fear that his property, if not disposed of, might be within the reach of the law. He had retained for his personal use a sum which did not greatly exceed his own private expenditure, and the balance was quickly mortgaged for further pensions. Not only was the Swiss property sold, but certain claims of his upon the French Government were turned into money for Montholon and others of his friends. Sums borrowed in this way had naturally to be heavily paid for in interest.

If, then, at the end of 1845 the prince had money enough for his immediate necessities in prison, he was without such funds as would enable him to live at large in a style befitting a pretender. One of the advantages of his position at Ham had been the fact that while there his personal expenditure could be comparatively trifling. Indeed, as the impoverished magnate when driven to retrenchment conveniently cloaks his enforced frugality under the guise of foreign travel, so a needy pretender, seeking to economise without loss of caste, might do worse than indulge in a term of political imprisonment. Better for him a dungeon than an attic.

Of this last fact Louis Napoleon was fully aware. His first step, therefore, towards the termination of his imprisonment, was to make adequate preparation for his expenses as a free man. A hundred and fifty thousand francs would, he thought, enable him to emerge gracefully. He at once took steps to procure this sum. Among the friends who had recently been released was Count Orsi. To him Louis now wrote, explaining his necessity. Orsi appealed unsuccessfully to several of the prince's English friends, and finally turned to one who like Louis was 'a prince in exile.' One of the few German princes who had been driven from their thrones in 1830 was Charles d'Este, the Duke of Brunswick. Although deprived of his political position, this eccentric exile retained a vast private fortune. Orsi sought an audience from him, though without any great hope of success.

But Brunswick was probably not altogether unprepared for some such appeal. For in the summer of 1845 Louis Napoleon had already conceived the idea of some scheme of co-operation between himself and the duke: among his visitors at Ham at this time was a Mr G. T. Smith, an agent of Brunswick's. In June he had gravely drawn up in Smith's presence the rough draft[1] of a treaty of alliance between himself and this other dispossessed prince: by its terms, whichever of them should first return to power in his own land was to assist to the best of his ability the restoration of the other. After some hesitation, Brunswick now agreed to Orsi's request, undertaking to provide the sum required at five per cent., on condition that, with the bond, Louis should also sign this political treaty. Immediately after the interview, which took place at Brunswick House in London on December 1, Orsi set out with Smith for Ham. As a recently released prisoner himself, he had some difficulty in obtaining permission to visit the

[1] The opening sentences of this rough draft, with the Duke of Brunswick's autograph corrections, are reproduced on the opposite page. The duke's alterations are significant; notably his deletion of Louis Napoleon's characteristic proposal for the union of all Germany into one nation, to be governed under a sympathetic and progressive constitution. Since Brunswick made no alterations in the later clauses, I reproduce them, for greater clearness, not in Louis' original draft, but in G. T. Smith's signed and attested copy of it (p. 368 below). Both documents are now in the municipal archives of Geneva.

Traité d'alliance offensive et défensive entre
S.A.R Charles Fredrigs - Auguste Guillaume
Duc Souverain Brunswick à Lunebourg, et Altesse
Prince Napoleon Louis Bonaparte. —

Moi à grande viet ?Louis Charles Fredrics Guillaume
Auguste Guillaume Duc de Brunswick à
Lunebourg, Wolfenbüttel et Nous Prince Napoléon
prince Imperial de France
Louis Bonaparte, Convenons et arrêtons
à qui suit —

Art 1. Nous promettons et jurons sur notre honneur
et sur le Saint Evangile de nous aider l'un
l'autre, Nous Charles Duc de Brunswick à
Souverain
prendre possession du Duché de Brunswick,
d'Allemagne et à faire tôt ou tard de tout l'Allemagne
une seule patrie unie et à lui donner
une Constitution adaptée à ses besoins
ses besoins et au progrès de l'esprit.
Et Nous Prince Napoléon Louis Bonaparte
à faire entrer la France dans le plein
Souveraineté
exercise de la Souveraineté Nationale
dont elle a été privée en 1830 et à
la mettre à même de se prononcer
librement sur la forme de Gouvernement
qui lui convient de se donner.

Art 2.

prince; when after some delay the permission was given, it was only for an interview in the presence of the governor. Orsi introduced the secretary as a collector anxious to purchase some pictures belonging to the prince; under cover of this little fiction, the bargain was accepted by Louis Napoleon. In shaking hands with him at the beginning of the interview, Orsi had smuggled into his palm the bonds and the treaty itself, written on satin. In the afternoon when the visitors took their leave, the prince returned them to Orsi in the same way, signed. Two days later they were in London; and the money was placed in the hands of Louis Napoleon's bankers without delay.

If the end of January found the prince once more in possession of means which would enable him to live when he had regained his liberty, the end of February saw the close of all prospects of his immediate release. But Louis Napoleon had now accustomed himself to the idea of an early recovery of his freedom, and was convinced that further imprisonment was not essential to his cause.

Many stories exist of opportunities of escape proferred to Louis Napoleon during the course of the first five years of his imprisonment: tales are current of visitors who begged the prince to escape in their clothes; even of soldiers stationed at the fortress, who, when the greater part of the garrison were engaged on parade, offered to connive at his escape. Severally, these stories rest on but indifferent authority; collectively, they amount to a presumption that had he so wished, the prince might have attempted an escape long before he did, with every prospect of success. In whatever form the opportunity was offered to him, all accounts agree that such offers were invariably met by prompt and decisive refusal.

The fact was, that before the autumn of 1845 any attempt at evasion was morally impossible for Louis Napoleon. As long as his co-mates of Boulogne were his brothers in imprisonment, as long as his own escape would have left his political followers still undergoing punishment in his cause, so long was all thought of individual evasion out of the question. For escape under such circumstances would have meant that he had achieved by his own act after Boulogne the fate which was inflicted on him despite his vehement protest after Strasburg—the fate of being separated and exempted from the misfortunes in which his followers were involved.

But after November 1845 this barrier to Louis Napoleon's escape ceased to exist. With the exception of his own personal attendants, Conneau and Montholon, all his fellow-prisoners were free. And of the two who remained with him at Ham, Conneau had already served his appointed term of imprisonment, and now remained in confinement at his own request, as a companion for the prince. Montholon indeed had still three-quarters of his nominal sentence in front of him; but it was certain that any step which gave Louis his liberty would also set the general free. Hence to Louis, compunction for the fate of his fellow-prisoners was now no longer a deterrent to his escape, but an incentive to it.

Though the prince seems to have set on foot negotiations for his own release as soon as ever it was clear that by doing so he would not be deserting his companions, yet it was some time later before he turned his attention to the possibility of escape. He evidently regarded this step as a last resource, only to be attempted if no release should prove possible without the loss of personal dignity or the abandonment of his political designs. It was not until the beginning of May 1846 that he informed Dr Conneau of his intention to adopt this extreme measure. The doctor used every argument at his command—and they were strong ones—to induce Louis to forgo his intention. It was impossible to escape by night, for the governor invariably called every evening; generally he stayed for a game of whist with his prisoners, but always as he left he locked their doors upon them, after personally satisfying himself that the prince was in the building. It was inconceivable that he should escape by day: the walls could not be scaled; the sentries could not be passed; his gaoler could not be shaken off; the watchwords which would enable him to pass the successive doors were unknown to him. Even if he reached the open he would be recaptured; as for gaining the frontier it was out of the question: if he did, he had no passport. Louis listened, but refused to be persuaded. And it was left for Dr Conneau, since he had failed to dissuade him from making the attempt, to do his utmost to render the attempt successful.

In the middle of May 1846 the Government authorised in somewhat belated fashion the repair of the staircase and other more dilapidated portions of the prisoners' dwelling. On these repairs a gang of workmen was employed for about ten days. Louis determined to attempt an escape, disguised as one of them.[1] For some days the prince and the doctor watched the workmen, carefully studying their costumes, their behaviour, and most of

[1] It has been contended that the escape of Louis Napoleon from Ham was connived at by the prison authorities, and deliberately sanctioned by the French Government. No evidence is forthcoming in support of a theory which by its inherent improbability demands the most unimpeachable testimony to render it credible. The French Government had just refused to liberate Louis Napoleon, although by releasing him they would have performed an act of graceful and most politic clemency; although by such an act they would have placed Louis under an obvious obligation; although by this means they might actually have obtained from him an undertaking to depart from Europe. It is hardly credible that immediately afterwards this same Government should have liberated Louis in the one way of all others which denied their action all appearance of grace, and relieved their prisoner from all semblance of obligation; in the one way of all others which would advertise not the generosity of Louis Philippe, but the hardihood and ingenuity of Louis Napoleon. And it is almost inconceivable that with the sole object of keeping up an illusion ideally advantageous to the pretender and ideally disparaging to themselves, the French Government should afterwards have solemnly tried and condemned to terms of imprisonment men who were in effect their own accomplices.

The nearest approach to evidence in favour of this rather preposterous contention occurs in Fraser's *Napoleon III. My Recollections.* Sir William Fraser states that Louis Napoleon once told a friend of his, that Louis Philippe had given him ten days in which to escape

all the manner in which they entered and left the fortress. The result was not encouraging. The men were made to pass in single file before the two sentinels at the gateway, and closely examined as they passed both morning and evening. Then the prisoners noticed that occasionally in the course of a day, a single workman would leave the castle carrying away old timber; in this case he seemed to undergo no such methodical scrutiny. This, then, must be the manner in which the prince should attempt his own departure. The time was easily chosen. It must be after the arrival of the workmen, and before the hour of the governor's rising; in other words, between six and eight in the

from Ham; whence the author deduces that the escape was sanctioned by the king. This fragment of second-hand gossip could in no case rank as good evidence. As a matter of fact, in this instance there is no necessity to assume a misquotation; a misunderstanding will suffice. Louis Philippe's Government had sent a body of workmen to the prison for ten days; during those ten days only was escape possible for the prisoner. Alluding to these notorious facts—probably after having himself made mention of them—Louis Napoleon may easily, in a conversational account of his escape, have so far over-rated his companion's intelligence as to make use of the elliptical expression, 'Louis Philippe had given me ten days in which to make good my escape.'

Against the contention must be set all published evidence, and every recorded utterance of every person who had anything to do with the flight. It is perhaps just worth while to add, that in the contemporary correspondence of the English diplomatic agents in France I find no hint of doubt as to the *bonâ fide* character of the escape; nor could I discover at Ham itself any tradition questioning its genuineness.

The editors of *The Letters of Queen Victoria* are responsible for the statement that Louis Napoleon's escape from Ham was 'undoubtedly connived at by the authorities'; had it not thus received the sanction of a wide publicity in a work deservedly regarded as authoritative, there would have been no necessity to allude to a theory so entirely destitute of proof or probability.

morning. That there was any interval at all between the two events was due to the fact that Demarle himself was suffering from an attack of the rheumatism, so prevalent at Ham. Usually he rose at dawn. It only remained to choose the day. Here again the prince's choice was based on close observation of the habits of his gaolers. Two warders were always posted as sentinels at the doorway of the prisoner's building. But Louis had noticed that on Saturday morning one of them was regularly sent to fetch the weekly newspapers, and that the errand involved his absence from his post for about a quarter of an hour; during that quarter of an hour the risk of detection on the very threshold of his prison would be halved for the prince. The day and the hour no less than the manner of his attempted escape were thus clearly indicated. All was arranged for the morning of Saturday, May 23. Louis now proceeded to inform Thélin, his valet, of his design, and sent him to buy workman's clothes for his disguise. The clothes arrived looking impossibly new; but after having been soaked in water, dried, and carefully soiled, they seemed to promise an effective means of escape.

But Louis' designs did not altogether escape the perverse miscarriage to which the best laid plans of prisoners and princes are liable. On the eve of his projected escape, the governor told him that he would be glad to hear that two English friends, whose visit he had long been expecting, had at last obtained permission to come and see him;

they would visit him on Saturday, the 23rd. Never had host been more anxious to reply, 'Not at home,' and never would that reply have been more absolutely sincere. But what would in fact have been a particularly honest answer must from a prisoner have seemed a peculiarly impudent fiction. No excuse was possible which would not have aroused the governor's suspicions, so Louis had perforce to postpone his other engagement.

The prince succeeded in turning the unwelcome visit to some slight advantage, for he obtained from his English friends the passport of one of their servants, on the plea that he wished to despatch Thélin on an errand to Belgium. But this seemed but a small compensation for the delay, for the work was rapidly drawing to a conclusion; indeed, in order to insure that something should be left to be done on the Monday, the prince gave orders for some special repairs to be done at his own expense.

Sunday passed slowly enough. On that day Louis wrote a letter for General Montholon. The general was confined to his bed, also by rheumatism. Louis explained that he had told him nothing, wishing to screen him from punishment at the Government's hands: as it was, he hoped that his own escape would lead to the general's immediate release. It did; but the general was little pleased that he had not been consulted in the matter; the letter was only given to him after the prince's escape was known. Another letter was also written. A small room on the ground floor of the building was used as a chapel; on the morning of the 25th the *curé* from Ham was coming to say Mass there for the prisoners; and following his usual custom he would breakfast with them afterwards. Louis had grown greatly attached to this simple parish priest. 'When I am emperor,' he told him shortly before the end of his imprisonment, 'I will make you a bishop.' And bishop he made him a few years later, as well as High Almoner to his court at the Tuileries. Now, instead of cancelling his engagement in advance, Louis wrote a letter which was only to be given him on his arrival. In it he pleaded sudden indisposition, and asked him to come instead on the following morning. With this, all preparations were complete.

On the 25th, Conneau, Thélin, and Louis Napoleon arose at daybreak. Listening anxiously, and peering stealthily into the courtyard, they heard the drawbridge let down and saw the workmen enter between two files of soldiers a little after five o'clock. It was a glorious morning, but for a moment it seemed that the attempt might have to be again postponed. For the conspirators noticed that the one soldier who of all others had been remarkable for the close scrutiny to which he subjected all passers-by was now stationed at the gate. To their great relief, he was taken off duty at six o'clock. Louis Napoleon now hurried into his disguise—a coarse shirt, blue trousers, a blue blouse, and a workman's apron. It was at once evident that the soiling process had been slightly overdone. As the escape had been planned for Saturday, a week's accumulation of dirt had been allowed for; actually it was Monday morning, and the workmen's clothes were in consequence comparatively clean. But though the disguise was not quite successful in simulating the workman, it was completely successful in dissimulating the prince. Thick wooden clogs added a couple of inches to his height; a dash of rouge lent colour to his pale cheeks; a long, flowing wig fell over his ears; a peasant's hat covered his head. In his pocket he carried his mother's farewell letter to him, as well as the one written to her by the Emperor on his birth. These were talismans which had been soaked in the salt water of Boulogne while the National Guard were firing at him into the sea: they should go with him now on this yet more risky adventure, even if they added somewhat to the risk of detection on the frontier. A little after seven the decisive step was taken: the prince shaved off his thick moustache and whiskers. Now he had burned his boats. After this there could be no turning back. And as he gazed on his altered appearance in the glass, Louis Napoleon may have fingered that other talisman which he had slipped into his blouse—a short dagger, with which he could make an end in case of need. He had made up his mind that he would regard a third failure as final; and he had decided to make sure that if failure it were, final it should be. It was by this time nearly a quarter past seven. Thélin strolled out of the room into the passage, where the workmen were busy on the stairway. It was a fine morning, and—would they like a drink? It was a grand morning, and they would be delighted to drink with him. All trooped downstairs to a room on the ground floor. Here Thélin produced liquor enough for his purpose. Then he slipped out, hastened up to his master, and told him that the moment was come. Louis shouldered a short plank which he had in readiness—it had been one of the rough shelves on which he kept his books—and putting a clay pipe in his mouth stepped out into the passage. He was hardly out of the door when a stray workman accosted him, taking him for a companion. Without answering, he walked down the passage. Thélin kept just in front of him, carrying 'Ham,' his master's pet dog. Together they went down the stairs; then Thélin hurried forward to the doorway, where the two warders were posted. The valet at once engaged one of them in conversation, telling him that his master was ill: he contrived that in speaking to him the sentinel should turn his back to the door. Louis then marched out, his face screened by the plank from the other warder. Through nervousness or clumsiness—for he was a mere cigarette-smoker—he let fall his pipe as he was walking across the square; he had presence of mind enough, however, to stop ruefully in the article of his flight, and carefully collect the broken pieces. He passed the officer on guard, who was

LOUIS NAPOLEON'S PRISON AT HAM

reading a letter. On the opposite side of the square was standing the director of the works, who knew all the workmen by sight; but Louis passed him also unmolested. Reaching the doorway, he gruffly asked leave to pass. The soldiers at the wicket — especially a certain drummer — looked curiously at this peculiar workman, who wore clogs on a fine day; then they turned to look at the yet more peculiar antics of Thélin and the dog Ham. Meanwhile the wicket-keeper opened the gate. On the drawbridge Louis passed another official; the sentinel on the other side let him pass without hesitation. The prince was no longer a prisoner; but he was not yet out of danger. He had hardly passed the gate when he saw two workmen coming towards him. He held his plank before his face as he passed them, and heard them say, 'Oh, it's Bertron.' After that all went well. Louis walked slowly on; Thélin hurried forward, passed him without seeming to recognise him, and then ran towards the town. There he took a cab which he had engaged the night before, arranging to drive it himself. Without himself passing through the town, Louis now hastened as fast as plank and clogs would allow him along the main road towards St Quentin. A cemetery on the outskirts of the town, about a mile and a half from the fortress, was the point arranged for his meeting with Thélin. On reaching it, Louis fell on his knees before a cross in the graveyard and thanked God for his deliverance.

He had cause, for liberty that day meant to him no less than life. 'Ah, do not laugh,' he wrote to an agnostic friend a fortnight later, 'There are instincts stronger than all philosophies: but God save you from ever feeling them under like circumstances.'

Thélin did not keep his master waiting long. Leaving his plank and clogs in a field, Louis jumped into the cab; and together they drove off at full speed to St Quentin. On the way he got out and hid part of his disguise in a ditch. At the entrance of the town Thélin left him; Louis walked through the town and followed the road to Valenciennes. His servant meanwhile hired a post-chaise, and after a short delay overtook the prince. By hard driving, and obtaining fresh horses on the way, they reached Valenciennes at two o'clock in the afternoon. At the station an official demanded passports, but a glance at the one which Louis had borrowed served to satisfy him. The train to Brussels did not leave till four. For two anxious hours the fugitives had to wait at the station, doing nothing. If their flight had been observed, an express from Ham might yet prove fatal. Their serving-man that morning had chanced to be late in bringing their coffee and rolls; would he not think it strange that Thélin should have gone out without waiting for him? These anxieties were not lessened by the fact that Thélin was recognised by one of the railway officials, who had formerly been a policeman at Ham. The man would not be shaken off, and Louis had to listen to a long conversation, in which

Thélin was asked for news about his master. At last the train came in. The two fugitives entered it, crossed the frontier without mishap, and so reached Brussels. Louis did not even have to show his passport at the frontier. Without delay they took train again for Ostend, and sailed for England.

The fugitives owed it to Dr Conneau that their flight had remained undisturbed; for inside the fortress of Ham, while postilion and railway carriage were speeding them out of danger, the doctor was playing with extraordinary zest a comedy which might have strayed straight out of the Middle Ages. As soon as he had seen from his window that the prince was safely out of the courtyard, Conneau returned at once to the prince's rooms. Shutting the bedroom door, he lit a huge fire in the sitting-room, set a kettle to boil on it, and littered the room with sickroom paraphernalia. A little after eight the servant announced that the priest had arrived. Ah, yes; Conneau had forgotten; but in any case he feared the prince was not well enough to come down this morning. Still he would ask him. He went into the bedroom, and after a short interval returned with the letter. He bade the servant take it to the governor, who sent it on to the priest. After breakfast the governor sent to ask if he might see the prince. Conneau went himself with the invalid's excuses, explaining the nature of his illness. The governor had only wished to tell his prisoner that permission had arrived for another visitor to come and see him shortly. Conneau undertook to deliver the message. He had sent the warder already for castor oil. Someone had to be ill, so on his return the devoted doctor swallowed the remedy himself. This heroic measure failing, he proceeded to make some very realistic arrangements, by the admixture of some chemicals from the laboratory with those uneaten breakfasts about which the fugitives were so needlessly perturbed. At noon, when the room was in a sufficiently unsavoury condition, Conneau summoned Laplace, the warder who acted as servant to the prisoners, and bade him tidy it and make the prince's bed; he must make as much haste and as little noise as he could, for the prince needed rest, and must not be kept up a moment longer than was absolutely necessary. While Laplace was thus engaged, the doctor went to and fro into the prince's sitting-room, conversing with his patient in sickroom tones for the warder's edification. Laplace was duly impressed, and conveyed his impressions to the governor when the latter shortly afterwards asked him how he found the prisoner. Meanwhile, as soon as the warder had done his work and was gone, Conneau dressed up a dummy which he had ready, and placed it in the bed with its face to the wall. Then he covered its head with a handkerchief which the prince used to wear when he slept. At one Demarle returned. Conneau met him on the stairs. The prince was easier, but extremely tired; still he would go and ask him if he would like to see the governor. He went in and asked the dummy, and returned with the prince's apologies; he was afraid he was still too unwell to see anyone. The governor retired, and did not return until a quarter past seven. Ill or well, he must see the prince now, he said, as he had his report to make. Conneau opened the door into the bedroom, and called to the prince, but the figure did not answer. Then he tiptoed out mysteriously, saying, 'Hush, he's asleep.' The governor went in and glanced at the figure, and came out into the sitting-room. He would wait; the prince could not sleep for ever. And he sat down. After waiting a while, and asking where Thélin was, he began to grow impatient. The evening drum beat. Demarle started up, saying he was sure the prince was awake, he had heard him move. Regardless of the doctor's protest, he stole towards the bed, listened for a moment, and said, 'Why, he is not breathing?' Then he took hold of the dummy and shook it. 'The prince has escaped!' '*Mais oui*,' smiled the doctor. And the farce was over. Realising at last that his prisoner was not asleep, but on a journey, Demarle rushed out and had the drawbridge raised, thus locking the stable door very securely. Conneau was handcuffed, taken to Peronne, tried, and condemned in July to three months' imprisonment, amid signs of popular sympathy. Thélin too was condemned in his absence to six months' imprisonment. It would have been an equally harmless and gratifying proceeding to have sentenced Louis himself to be shot for his own share in the escape.

For on the day after that escape, master and man alike had arrived safely in London. Here they were received with unmistakable friendliness. A certain amount of sympathy had been expressed for the prince in England, when the French Government refused to allow him to visit his father. Now everyone was pleased at the cleverly contrived escape. 'The testimonies of interest I receive here are quite touching,' Louis wrote to a friend, a few weeks after his landing. But public interest in his doings soon subsided; indeed his popularity in 1846 was an even more short-lived affair than that with which he had been welcomed in 1838.

He did not greatly concern himself with the nature of his reception in England; for his first step on arriving there was to attempt to proceed to his father at Florence. Two days after his arrival he wrote to the French ambassador, volunteering the statement that his intentions were pacific; he wrote also in the same sense to the English minister of Foreign Affairs. In part, this statement was, no doubt, intended to mitigate Conneau's punishment and to ensure Montholon's release. But probably it was also connected with the prince's renewed efforts to visit his father. Either it would facilitate that visit, or it would render more ungracious any intervention on the part of the French Government to prevent it.

That Government did, in fact, intervene; the Grand Duke of Tuscany refused to allow Louis to spend even a day in his territories, stating that his refusal was necessitated by a proper deference to the wishes of France. The Austrian ambassador declined to use his good offices. The prince even wrote to Metternich, but he obtained no answer. Under similar circumstances, nine years before, he had employed false passports and travelled in disguise to his mother's deathbed. But then he had been sure of a safe retreat at his journey's end. And his affection for his mother was naturally a stronger incentive than any filial feeling towards the father who had interested himself so little in his son's affairs. None the less, Louis' private letters seem to show that the desire to visit his father before he died was a genuine one. It remained unfulfilled. For, on July 23, King Louis of Holland followed King Joseph of Spain; and from a world which had long ceased to remember their existence passed silently another of those curious and rather pathetic relics of the Napoleonic regime—the Emperor's brothers.

On his arrival in England, the prince had flung himself with some zest into the unwonted pleasures of social life; dining with his old friends, and visiting the opera, though he no longer retained a box for his own use. But after his father's death he affected for a while to live in retirement. In the beginning of August, the book on which he had laboured so hard for the last three years was published in Paris—the first volume of his *History of Artillery*. The prince was well pleased with it and its reception; but as a matter of fact, it did not render him any service at all proportionate to the time he had spent upon it. His slight essay on the *Extinction of Pauperism*, written in about a twentieth of the time, and with perhaps a hundredth part of its acquaintance with its subject, was infinitely more useful to its author from a political point of view. Louis intended at the time to work on a further volume of the history in the following winter, though he admitted that his health might unfit him for hard work for some time to come. For some little time after his escape his eye troubled him a good deal, and had to be subjected to medical treatment. His general health was also far from good. In the middle of August he went to Bath, with which he was much pleased. The surrounding country he pronounced the finest in England, and it was not until the autumn that he returned to London, greatly refreshed by his visit. At Bath, Louis was joined by his cousin, Prince Napoleon, son of the Emperor's sole surviving brother, King Jerome. Resembling the Emperor in a marked degree in feature and expression, this prince had, like the rest of his family, refrained from giving any help or encouragement to Louis in his efforts on behalf of the imperial cause. Unlike them, he was to live to reap the full benefit of his cousin's achievement.

In a letter to his friend Vieillard, three months later, Louis describes his impression of his cousin, whom he had thus met for the first time since 1835. 'The chief fault I find with him—if a natural defect may be called a fault—is the unintelligible nature of his character, sometimes frank, loyal, and open, at other times constrained and dissimulating. At one moment his heart seems to speak of glory, to suffer and sympathise with you for all that is great and generous; at another it is empty, arid, deceitful. As long as I have no positive proof of evil, I make it my practice to believe good of a man; so, while I remain on my guard, I allow free play to my impulses of friendliness or affection.' Louis Napoleon was very slow indeed in this case to accept positive proofs of disloyalty, intrigue, and ingratitude; to the end of his reign he remained a singularly generous friend to his rather ungracious cousin.

The first public act of the prince upon his return to London was the result of a revival of the old libel that he had promised the French Government after Strasburg that he would remain in perpetual exile in America. Hitherto this story had served its purpose in French ministerial journals; now it had been incorporated by M. Capefigue into a *History of Europe since the Accession of Louis Philippe.* Louis Napoleon at once published a letter to the author, indignantly repudiating the assertion. He referred his correspondent to the admission of the public prosecutor in the course of his trial in 1840; he reminded him that had his promise been such a fragile thing, the Government would have been less anxious to secure it while he was at Ham, and he himself would have been more ready to give it. 'Condemn my policy, distort my actions, falsify my motives, if you will. I shall not complain; you do but use your right of judgment. But I allow no one to impugn my good faith, which, thank God, I have known how to keep intact amid so many cruel trials.' If this seem a proud boast from the lips of Louis Napoleon, it must be remembered that when it was uttered it was unquestionably true.

The winter of 1846 did not, after all, witness a return on the part of Louis to his military studies; perhaps he realised that he had undertaken in his *History of Artillery* a task too heavy for him. In any case he could place to the credit of his first volume his election in December 1846 as an honorary member to the Army and Navy Club, a compliment which he highly appreciated. At the beginning of February 1847 the prince moved into a small house, newly built, in King Street, off St James's Square, where he remained until he left England. Though conveniently situated, it was a much more modest abode than his residence in Carlton Terrace, his home during his last sojourn in England. Indeed, the rent of three hundred pounds a year which he paid for it seems to have been excessive. In this house he collected his books, his family portraits—all his valuables which, to use his own phrase, had escaped the shipwreck. Although in that shipwreck the whole of his mother's fortune had been swallowed up, yet the death of his father left Louis in possession of a respectable estate, which with prudent management would have placed him again beyond the reach of financial difficulties. But Louis was never prudent in the matter of expenditure, and not all the watchfulness of his foster-brother Bure, who managed his estate, could keep his affairs free from financial entanglements.

The year 1847 was the last year of the prince's life as an exiled pretender. Yet at no time since his first appearance in that rôle did he evince so little interest in his own political prospects. Although he did not abandon his designs, he seems, on the eve of their fulfilment, for the first time to have postponed his hopes of putting them into effect. Perhaps he felt that it would be wise to allow some years to elapse before his next *coup*; possibly he thought that even a political pretender deserves an occasional holiday. Whatever his motive, there is no doubt about his course of action. Six months of liberty had restored him to good health; while a decent interval had by this time elapsed since his father's death. With the beginning of the year, therefore, Louis flung himself joyously into a round of pleasures; as though eager in one London season to avenge himself for the enforced seclusion of six years' imprisonment. Hardly a hermit at Ham, he was altogether a Lothario in London. One result of these amusements was a great increase in his personal expenditure. His political expenses did not decrease; if there were no publications to support now, there were still pensioners in plenty; thus Conneau on his arrival in London was presented with a practice which had cost nine hundred pounds. But to these necessary expenses were now added large sums spent by the prince on his amusements; his hunting expenses were considerable, while his losses on the turf alone in this year were out of all proportion to his means. Finding himself short of ready money, he borrowed recklessly; though it was only in 1848, and then for political reasons, that he finally mortgaged his paternal estate. Indeed, an apologist who wished at all cost to vindicate Louis Napoleon's prophetic instinct, even in the light of his conduct in 1847, would have to ground his defence on the very extravagance of that conduct. As though aware that this was the last year in which he would be dependent on his private means, as though conscious that never again could his amusements be those of an irresponsible ἰδιώτης, he proceeded gaily to exhaust the one in giving full rein to the other.

Among other tokens of comparative indifference to his political prospects at this period must be set a marked propensity to matrimony. During these two years Louis Napoleon is credited with more than one attempt to find an English bride. He is reported to have wooed successfully a Miss Rowles, whose parents lived at Chislehurst; at the last moment the engagement was broken off, owing to her discovery of the nature of his relations with Miss Howard. The prince is also said to have proposed to a Miss Seymour, who subsequently married an English nobleman. More interesting is the report which makes him a suitor for the hand of Miss Burdett, the future Baroness Burdett-Coutts. Such an alliance would have been eminently in keeping with the Orleanist regime; but nothing more incongruous with the actual tradition of the Second Empire could well be imagined.

There is a touch of extravagance even in the political ideas of the prince during this year. In the later years of his captivity at Ham, he had interested himself in a fantastic project for the junction under his auspices of the Atlantic and Pacific oceans by means of a canal cut through the Nicaraguan lakes. Certain informal negotiations on the subject had passed between him and the Nicaraguan minister for the Netherlands. At the time the scheme had its value to the prince, since it might serve as a pretext for facilitating his release. Under cover of it he was even able to justify to his followers the undertaking which he offered to the French Government, that he would if released proceed to America after a year spent in Florence with his father. But now in the summer of 1847 Louis returned to the scheme. He published a pamphlet on the subject, the greater part of which had been written at Ham. In the pamphlet he strongly advocated the claims of Nicaragua, as opposed to the Isthmus of Panama, to be the route of an inter-oceanic canal. He even proposed to form a company in England, and to attempt to raise capital to the amount of four million pounds. The canal was to be called the *Canale Napoleone de Nicaragua*. In Nicaragua itself, where there was nothing to be lost and possibly much to be gained by the scheme, there was naturally some feeling in its favour. But the English business men and capitalists whom Louis consulted were less enthusiastic. As the year 1847 advanced his own interest in it declined; with the events of 1848 the whole scheme was thrown to the winds. Among the remoter might-have-beens of history we may conceive Louis Napoleon President of a Central American Republic, leader of a latter-day Darien scheme, foretaster of the unhappy fate which befell M. de Lesseps in a similar undertaking.

But this Nicaraguan scheme possesses also an actual historical significance; for it unquestionably served to predispose its author in favour of his own disastrous intervention in American affairs. The Mexican project, as we shall show hereafter, was an earlier and more fundamental feature in the diplomacy of the Second Empire than has hitherto been supposed. In this connexion it may suffice here to point out that if for the two years which immediately preceded his return to France Louis Napoleon's mind was largely occupied with a possible millennium in Central America, within two and a half years of his assumption of the imperial title we find the Mexican scheme completely formulated and definitely advocated by the foreign ministers of Napoleon III.

A smaller and more fortunate consequence of his interest in this project may be seen in the continuous support which Louis Napoleon gave to the authors of the Suez Canal, support which was of real value in the face of international jealousies which threatened indefinitely to postpone the undertaking.

It has been suggested that the prince's continued attempts to obtain permission to visit his father after his escape from Ham were merely made for the sake of appearances; that he thought it politic to maintain a decent show of interest in an event on which he had grounded negotiations for his release. By an extension of the same argument it would be possible to discover the same motive, and no other, in his recurrence to the Nicaraguan scheme in 1847. Either conjecture would appear to be an over-subtle gloss upon the facts. In history, if not elsewhere, the simpler reading is often to be preferred; and we shall probably be safe in seeing in the Nicaraguan idea merely another sign that in the year 1847 Louis Napoleon had no great expectation of an immediate return to his own country.

Amid much that was fantastic in his policy and

impolitic in his action during this year, it is quite a relief to discover a stray letter of the prince's to the editor of the *Times*, secretly communicating to him some item of news from France, the publication of which in England might benefit his political position.[1] The letter is of interest as showing that, in spite of appearances to the contrary, Louis had not really lost sight in 1847 of his interests as a pretender to the French throne. For this is a case where generalisation is permissible; this single letter shows pretty clearly that Louis was paying attention to the English Press and watching the course of events in France. It has a more particular significance in connexion with Louis Napoleon's relations with the English press, since it shows that he had already as an exiled pretender formed the habit of sending secret communications to the *Times*—a practice which he was to continue on a more important scale as Emperor of the French.

In the autumn of 1847 occurred the last event under the Orleanist regime which gave Louis Napoleon occasion to advertise his rights and his wrongs. In his will the Count de St Leu had desired that his body might rest in the village near

---

[1] ' 3A King Street,
' St James's Square, 1847.

' J'envoie à M. le Rédacteur du *Times* un extrait d'une lettre assez intéressante que j'ai reçue de Paris. Il peut la publier si elle lui convient, mais je le prie de laisser toujours ignorer la source de cette communication.—NAPOLÉON LOUIS BONAPARTE.'

Brit. Mus. Addl. MSS. 22,723, f. 31.

Paris, whose name he had borne for forty years, the place he 'liked better than any other in the world.' His eldest son, who had died in infancy, was already buried there. The king's last request was that the body of his second son, the boy who had died in Italy, should be brought back with his own to the same resting-place. After a year's delay the Orleanist Government gave its consent.

On September 29, 1847, father and son returned together to St Leu: a guard of honour composed of veteran soldiers of the imperial army attended the ceremony. In October Louis Napoleon wrote to thank the officer who had commanded them for this 'act of homage and of reparation,' an act which had 'softened his own bitter grief at his inability to kneel before the family tomb, and for a moment had even made him forget that he was condemned to be separated, apparently for ever, from the men he loved best and the objects he most cherished.'

It was characteristic of Louis Napoleon that he should thus turn the last rites of his nearest relatives into an occasion for calling attention to his own existence. For, throughout his career as pretender he had held nothing too sacred, as he had held nothing too trivial, to be pressed into the service of his cause. The death of his mother had excused his reappearance in Europe, when Louis Philippe's clemency after Strasburg might otherwise have seemed to impose on him a moral obligation to remain in America. The translation of his uncle's body to Paris was the signal for his landing at Boulogne. The death of his father furnished him with an occasion for justifying his escape from Ham. There can be little doubt that on all these occasions Louis Napoleon was perfectly sincere in the emotions which he expressed, but it would be pressing coincidence a little far to contend that the several services which resulted from them to his cause were altogether accidental.

The funeral ceremony at St Leu and Louis' comment upon it form then a not unfitting close to one stage of his career. The curtain falls on Louis Napoleon gazing forlornly towards France, where the dust of all his dead is now foregathered; on Louis Napoleon characteristically careful to utilize the event by making it the occasion of a discourse on his own position. Even the wording of his comment on this occasion is appropriate in its perversity. In 1840, on the eve of his most abject failure, the pretender had been prodigal of his invitations to the Tuileries. It was not therefore altogether unfitting that the same dramatic irony should rule his last utterance in 1847; that on the threshold of his amazing success he should be engaged in bewailing a fate which condemned him to be separated, 'apparently for ever,' from all he held most dear.

CHAPTER XI

LOUIS NAPOLEON REGAINS HIS CITIZENSHIP

'Se tu segui tua stella
Non puoi fallire a glorioso porto.'
DANTE.

IF Louis Napoleon had never been less confident of success than in the year 1847, it is probable that at no time since the beginning of his reign had Louis Philippe felt more secure in the possession of his throne. For the first ten years of that reign he had maintained his position visibly on sufferance, at the mercy of the first fortuitous combination of the perils by which he was daily assailed. Perpetual embarrassments abroad, universal unrest at home, risings in the capital, riots in the provincial towns, insurrections in the army, tumults in the Chambers, sedition in the Press—all these to the accompaniment of plots without end for the assassination of his own person—such were the difficulties which, albeit by many an unkingly shift, Louis Philippe had managed for ten years to suppress, or at any rate to survive. His ministers had been less fortunate. Although his government was ever more clearly becoming a personal rule, the king fully realised the value of ministers, as lightning-conductors. In this capacity they served him well, but had frequently to be replaced: some twenty changes of ministry were necessitated by the storms of these early years. The crisis of the reign was reached in the year 1840. A more than usually gross affront had been placed upon France by a combination of the Great Powers. The country was on the very verge of war: Thiers as prime minister declared that no other solution was possible. The intervention of the king led to his dismissal and the preservation of peace. And now Louis Philippe found the minister who was to give him comparative peace in the later years of his reign. From 1840 to 1848, under the administration of Guizot, France experienced—it would be too much to say, enjoyed—a period of stable government. Hitherto Louis Philippe had alternately sacrificed popular ministers to the resentment of foreign powers, and peaceable ministers to their unpopularity with the Parisian mob. Now the compromise was over. Henceforth the monarchy of July was frankly reactionary at home, frankly pacific abroad. Guizot's foreign policy compared favourably with that of his numerous predecessors. Realising always, as some of them had not, that in the last resort Louis Philippe would insist on submission, he at least saved France from the humiliation of retreating at the last moment under compulsion from untenable positions. For he was generally careful to avoid the beginnings of strife. One exception he made, in the case of the Spanish marriages. He has been accused in this instance of sacrificing a national alliance to a dynastic intrigue, and certainly the incident was not very creditable to French diplomacy. But English writers have exaggerated its importance as a contributory cause to the overthrow of the monarchy. As a matter of fact, France as a whole was heartily tired of an alliance in which she played so very secondary a part, for which she paid so much and received so little in return. Even the comparative failure of the intrigue was largely outweighed by the pleasure of having for once 'scored off' England, after so many submissions to Palmerston's rather dictatorial direction.

It was no question of foreign policy which caused the fall of the July monarchy. Nor was it even the tardy outbreak of internal discontent which directly brought about its overthrow. An accident had set Louis Philippe on the throne, and another accident was to remove him from it. In saying this we do not mean to imply that the revolution of February, in ridding France of the July monarchy, did violence to the country's will. If it was an accident which led to Louis Philippe's fall at that moment, it was an essential weakness which made him hold his throne at the mercy of an accident. Only, it was this weakness of his own hold on the country, rather than the strength of the country in withstanding him, that brought about his sudden collapse. The agitations of the first part of his reign had apparently subsided. Epigram and caricature had taken the place of mutiny and insurrection. Socialist propaganda spread itself abroad, but bread riots were a thing of the past. Superficially the calm was unbroken: Guizot and his rather mechanical majority proceeded quietly on their way. Guizot was indeed a parliamentarian rather than a statesman. To the country at large he made no appeal, but he was careful to retain the suffrages of the wealthier bourgeois, the '*pays légal.*' By methods and with results not wholly unlike those attending Walpole's administration of affairs in England, he saw to it that his hold on the parliamentary majority was maintained. He availed himself to the full of those subtler forms of bribery and intimidation, by which to this day, in countries without genuine and instinctive capacity for representative government, an existing administration, by the mere fact that it is in power when it goes to the polls, can render certain its return to power. In a period of considerable material prosperity, when there were canals to be dug and railways to be laid in every direction, each constituency knew well that it must return a supporter of the existing Government, if it would secure for itself its share of the Government's favours. Once elected, the management of the deputies was an even simpler matter; for over one-third of them were paid functionaries of the crown. In fine, Guizot was a past-master of that art which in all ages has enabled political rulers to secure a calm while they prepare a storm — the art of rendering legally impregnable a morally indefensible position.

Despairing of any reform from a Chamber which stood itself in such sore need of reform, the constitutional opposition in the summer vacation of 1847 began to air their grievances at a series of 'Reform Banquets' held in the provincial towns. The substance of their demands was the extension of the franchise and the exclusion from the Chamber of paid officials. Whether these demands were really backed by an effective popular opinion may perhaps be doubted; but in any case, the method of drawing attention to them proved unexpectedly successful. For the political banquet, destined to become the tamest of public functions, was in its origin a formidable method of agitation.

As the autumn of 1847 wore on, the antidynastic opposition proceeded to adopt, for their own more drastic purpose, a device by which the constitutional opposition had only sought a tardy return to office. Still the Government remained unmoved. But when, after the Chamber had reassembled, a great Reform Banquet was announced to take place in Paris itself, Guizot at length intervened and forbade it to be held. The opposition deputies protested, but decided to comply with the Government's order. The 22nd of February, the day appointed for the banquet, dawned quietly enough. But in the morning, curious or hostile crowds began to gather in the streets; some scuffling with the police ensued; only the appearance of troops served by nightfall to restore the semblance of order. As the morning of the 23rd found the rising still smouldering, the Government called out the National Guard. To their dismay they found that it joined in the anti-ministerial outcry. Alarmed at last, the king dismissed Guizot. Paris seemed satisfied; illuminations appeared in the boulevards. Only in the lower quarters of the town did the announcement fail in its effect. From the east end a hostile mob marched to Guizot's residence, intent at any rate on breaking his windows for him. A guard had been set; upon provocation it fired. Some thirty persons were killed, and all chance of conciliation was at an end. The victims of the massacre were carted round Paris; by the morning of the 24th the rising was a budding revolution. Still the regulars were loyal, and might if resolutely employed have saved the situation. But their efforts were paralysed by the hesitation of those in authority; a futile alternation between force and concession irritated without alarming the populace of Paris.

Easily discouraged, anxious for his great estates, incapable by this time of resolute action or of quick decision, Louis Philippe was not the man to deal with such a situation as this. He abdicated in favour of his grandson, and sought safety in flight. The grandson's claims were brushed aside; a mob invaded the Chambers; a provisional government was proposed; the nominees of an opposition newspaper were installed, to the acclamation of the mob. Meanwhile at the Hôtel de Ville the staff of another and more violently republican newspaper had by a similar process instituted another provisional government, composed of more extreme men. After looking askance at each other for a moment, the two governments coalesced; and from this fortuitous conjunction of a couple of newspaper-staffs was born the Provisional Government of the Second Republic. On February 25 this Government of orators and journalists proclaimed the principle of the 'right to work'; on the 26th they decreed the immediate establishment of national workshops, laying up for themselves a rich store of troubles for the future. On the 27th, Louis Napoleon arrived in Paris.

The prince was in London when the tidings of the revolution reached England. If he had little foreseen so sudden a ripening of all his hopes, he had, at least, no hesitation in attempting to pluck the fruit. In 1830 a great chance had in his opinion been lost to the imperial cause, by the failure of any single member of his family to present himself boldly in the capital. This mistake should not be repeated. Before Louis Philippe, a fugitive in disguise, had succeeded in setting foot on English soil, Louis Napoleon, an expectant pretender, was already on his way to Paris. On February 28 the Provisional Government received a short letter from him, announcing that he had hastened from his exile to place himself under the flag of the newly proclaimed republic. The Government at once requested him to leave the country—thus acknowledging that the flag in question was not yet very firmly planted. Louis replied in another little letter (February 29): 'I thought, gentlemen,' he wrote, 'that after thirty-three years of exile and persecution, I had at length the right to find a home in my native land. You think that my presence in Paris at this time would be an embarrassment; I therefore retire for the moment. You will see in this sacrifice the purity of my intentions and of my patriotism.' And within the week he was back in London again, far from dissatisfied with the result of his excursion. In requesting his departure from France the Provisional Government had recognised and enhanced his personal importance; in his ready compliance with their wishes he had accepted with good grace a part which became him well; in his phrase declaring his departure to be but for the moment he safeguarded his freedom of action for the future, and hinted alike to friend and foe that they had not done with him yet.

He was well out of Paris for the time. Many reputations were to perish there in the mad miscellany of the next few months. The Provisional Government had ordained that a National Convention, elected by universal suffrage, should be assembled on March 5. Much would depend on the result of that election. The liberals dreaded the republic they had unintentionally created; the republicans dreaded still more the socialist mob which was for the moment all powerful in Paris. The socialists themselves dreaded most of all the verdict of the people whose champions they professed to be. For this reason they forced the Provisional Government to postpone the elections until April 23, in order, as they frankly confessed, to give them a chance of converting the electors. Although by this means they prolonged their immediate dictatorship in Paris, they only enhanced the magnitude of their electoral defeat. For every day which passed rendered it more certain that the majority would be opposed to socialism, more doubtful whether it would even be tolerant of a republic. The majority of the Assembly which met in April was, in fact, mildly republican; but while the socialists were an insignificant minority the representatives of reaction were collectively a powerful body, though for the moment they were divided as to the form of reaction which they would favour. .

Louis Napoleon was urged by many of his well-wishers to stand as a candidate at this general election, but after some consideration he decided to remain in the background a little longer. On March 12 he sent Persigny over to Paris to consult Odilon Barrot, his parliamentary champion while he was at Ham, as to the course he should pursue in the matter. Apparently the advice was for abstention, for, a week later, Louis made known in very characteristic fashion the fact that he was not standing. He sent another of his confidential communications to the Editor of the *Times*:—

'KING STREET,
'*March* 20*th*, 1848.

'Sir,[1]

'Will you be kind enough to contradict the report of my intention to become a candidate for a seat in the National Assembly of France. Believe me, yours,

'NAPOLEON LOUIS BONAPARTE.

'I wish you would contradict the report without publishing this letter.'

The postscript is typical of the care taken by Louis during these months to conceal his tracks. In this effort he was very successful; to this day many of his movements at this time remain obscure. It was during these months and for his political designs that he realised the remnant of his paternal estate; but there is no doubt that he added to the amount available for his purpose by borrowing from his English friends. He endeavoured, but without success, to obtain a further loan from the Duke of Brunswick; with strange short-sightedness the duke refused to advance any more money to

[1] Brit. Mus. Addl. MSS. 22,723, f. 32. Endorsed by the Editor, 'Not to be soiled or defaced.'

the prince. Louis Napoleon angrily declared that he should regard this refusal as being in effect a breach of the understanding between them; nor was he ever afterwards reconciled to his eccentric ally. Indeed the duke was almost the only one of Louis Napoleon's early benefactors who had reason to complain of being shabbily treated by him after his accession to power. The debt itself was repaid without doubt, and it is not perhaps to be wondered at that Louis never found himself in a position to restore such a very impossible potentate to his German dominions. But there was no sufficient reason for his refusal in after years to receive the duke at the imperial court, or to make such slight show of interest in his political prospects as might have served to satisfy his client.

The prince's one public act at this time—his last public act as an exile—was one of great boldness and discernment. In general, if there is one thing more than another which pleases a Parisian revolutionary, it is that the inhabitants of surrounding states should pay *la grande nation* the compliment of imitation whenever in its greater enlightenment it sees that the time has come for the final destruction of monarchical tyranny. In 1848 that compliment had been largely rendered; even in England a perceptible reflection of the French revolution was seen in the revival of the Chartist movement. Though not really formidable, this movement was greatly feared at the time; in London large numbers of private citizens were enrolled as special constables to assist in the preservation of order. Louis Napoleon enrolled himself in this force, and acted as special constable on April 10, the day on which the great Chartist petition was presented to Parliament.[1] A man with an eye only for the obvious would never in his position have acted as he did then. Apparently dependent on the good-will of the Parisian populace, he had gone out of his way to display his hostility to one of those sympathetic movements so dear to the heart of the revolutionary propagandists.

In reality his act was only the first of many which showed his singular insight into the desires of the mute mass of the French people, as opposed to the noisy Parisian mob. For though they had not yet shown their desire, the French people were

[1] M. Lebey (*Strasbourg et Boulogne*, p. 265), following several other French authorities, throws doubt on this fact, suggesting that while he enrolled himself as a special constable, the prince never actually served in this capacity. The fact is really beyond dispute: I have been assured of it by several persons who had their information from different eye-witnesses of Louis Napoleon on the occasion of the great Chartist demonstration. One such reminiscence may suffice, in proof of a fact which has been needlessly called in question. Among Louis Napoleon's acquaintances in London was Mr Putnam, the American publisher, father of the present head of the house, from whom I had the story. Strolling out on to London Bridge to see what was going forward on the critical 10th of April, Mr Putnam was surprised to meet Louis, armed and accoutred as a special constable. 'Et que diable fait Monsieur Napoléon dans cette galère?' laughed his friend. 'Sir,' said Louis Napoleon impressively, 'the peace of London must be preserved.' At this time, of course, almost every capital on the Continent was in the hands of the mob. M. Lebey is evidently a little at sea on the whole question, for he explains that it was habitual in London for men of the highest social position to act as a kind of amateur detectives, 'a sort of secret national guard ; a habit which the author very naturally characterises as 'one of the most singular customs of London life.'

by this time more anxious to restrain the antics of their revolutionaries at home than to encourage the hopes of their imitators abroad.

As in February Louis had been careful to show the Provisional Government that his return to exile was to be regarded as a concession and not a surrender, so now he made it known in more unmistakable terms that his refusal to come forward at the general election did not in any way imply a permanent withdrawal from political affairs. Had he stood, he wrote on May 11, in an open letter to one of his friends, his antecedents would have made him against his will the man to whom all the dissatisfied would turn as leader. But 'if France had need of me,' he continued, 'if my part were clearly traced, I should not hesitate to override all secondary considerations in order to fulfil my duty. . . . Meanwhile voluntary exile is pleasant, just because I know it is voluntary.' Louis had, in fact, during these months, two scarcely reconcilable objects in view. It was necessary that he should give the people an occasional lead, and allow them clearly to understand that there was no height which he was not prepared to venture, if they would follow him. But it was also necessary that the Assembly should be propitiated, the Assembly which might consign him again to exile, or at any rate exclude him from political life. On May 24 he wrote another letter, this time to the president of the Assembly, protesting against the maintenance of the law of banishment against him.

How had he deserved it? By declaring that France was not the appanage of any man, family, or party? By his sufferings at the hands of the Government which the Republic had overthrown? By his deference to the Provisional Government in February? By his disinterested refusal to come forward in April? It was in championship of universal suffrage that he had attacked Louis Philippe; the same cause would ensure his services to the Assembly should they be required. 'In the presence of a king elected by two hundred deputies, I could remember that I was the heir of an empire founded by four million Frenchmen. In the presence of the national sovereignty, I can and will claim only my rights as a French citizen.' These two letters are typical of Louis Napoleon's cleverness in dealing with the situation; it is noteworthy that even the letter intended for the people contained a phrase which would soothe the Assembly, while even the letter intended to propitiate the Assembly contained an allusion designed to appeal to the people.

So far, the people had not expressed their approbation, and the Assembly for that reason did not as yet take the prince's utterances very seriously. For the time it was still the socialists who were the most formidable opponents of the Government. Bitterly disappointed by the results of the general election, the party of disorder declared that they would not recognise the Assembly. On the 15th of May they attempted to dissolve it by force, and to create a new provisional government at the

Hôtel de Ville. By the aid of the National Guard the Convention triumphed : but though some of the most dangerous of its opponents were arrested, the Assembly itself lost prestige by its feeble action on this occasion. Everyone knew that a much more formidable situation remained to be dealt with—the dissolution of the national workshops—and everyone feared that a government which had faced so feebly the smaller crisis would be utterly helpless before the gigantic problem which still remained unsolved.

Early in March the national workshops devised by the Provisional Government had been opened in Paris. Some 6000 men were employed, and paid two francs a day. At first there was some attempt at supervision and restriction; and the work done was not altogether useless, though utterly unprofitable at the price paid for it. But the numbers grew fast; restrictions became unworkable; even the semblance of productive labour could not be found. By the middle of March there were 14,000 men employed; at the end of the month, 40,000; by the middle of April, 66,000. All pretence of finding useful employment for this vast host was now dropped. They were set to work to dig out the Champ de Mars, and when they had dug it out they had the satisfaction of filling it up again. Even so, they could not all be occupied; they were employed first every other day, then twice a week, and at last at still rarer intervals. That they might not starve in the streets, a pension of a franc a day was allowed on the days in which they were unemployed. And now from all France, every day and by every road, there poured into Paris a stream of vagabonds, and worse. Already, as the supervision grew lax, the proportion of genuine workmen honestly working had become an infinitesimal minority. But if two francs a day for doing useless work badly had been an attraction, a franc a day for doing nothing at all was an entirely irresistible allurement. By the end of May an army of over 100,000 malcontents was in the heart of Paris, armed, angry, menacing. The Government hesitated to take a step which must lead to civil war; yet every day that passed aggravated the evil, while it increased the ruinous waste of public money.

In helpless impotence the Executive Commission regarded its own monstrous handiwork, appalled like Frankenstein before the enormity he had himself created. Although in the face of this crisis all other dangers paled to comparative insignificance, yet the Republicans realised that neither the Legitimist nor the Orleanist parties were foes to be despised. Alone among their possible antagonists they deemed unworthy of serious notice the man and the name under whose power they were so soon to fall. Although Louis himself was not an original member of the Assembly, two of his cousins, as well as a son of Murat, had taken their seats in it without opposition. The Bourbons had passed, and the Orleanists in 1832 had reaffirmed, a law under which all members of the House of Bonaparte were banished from France. That law remained unrepealed. But so harmless and incapable of mischief did these three representatives appear, that no one had protested against their election. With a view to making regular their position, the repeal of the law of exile was tentatively discussed within a few days of the first meeting of the Assembly; on the 2nd of June its abrogation was formally proposed by M. Piétri. The proposal was favourably considered, and the discussion of it was adjourned for a week. But before that week had passed events had occurred which turned the subject of an academic debate into a question of vital importance. Louis Napoleon had broken cover.

It was while Paris was endeavouring to summon up courage to deal with the terrible monster in its midst, that the first supplementary elections were held, to fill the numerous vacancies which expulsion, resignation, or double election had already created in the new Assembly. At the last moment, Louis withdrew the veto which he had previously placed on the putting forward of his name. The result was startling to those who had but a superficial acquaintance with his past career, and no understanding of the real hold which that career had taken on the popular imagination. On June 4 in spite, it would seem, of considerable official pressure, four of the twenty-three departments vacant elected as their representative Louis Napoleon. After this, events happened quickly. Portraits of Louis, labelled '*Lui*,' spread themselves abroad with strange rapidity; from this time the prince became '*the* man' to myriads of French voters. On the 10th of June two Bonapartist newspapers appeared; another followed on the 11th, another on the 12th, and two more before the end of the week. Selling themselves for a sou to any who would buy them, giving themselves away to those who would not, often changing their names, but always flaunting the portrait and praising the character of Louis Napoleon, these irresponsible auxiliaries were of no small service to him. On the same 10th of June, a report reached the Assembly that a regiment at Troyes had refused to cheer the Republic, and had instead raised the cry, 'Vive Napoléon!' Answering a question on the subject in the Assembly, Gen. Cavaignac, the Minister of War, hinted at steps against Louis Napoleon. On the 11th, it was reported that other regiments had shown the same spirit; on the 12th, despatches from Boulogne announced that Laity and Persigny had arrived from London and were making for Paris.

The National Assembly now realised that they were faced by a fresh danger of unknown dimensions. Had any of its members been inclined to doubt the reports of Bonapartist feeling, the evidence of their own senses must have convinced them of its reality. For some days past cries for Louis Napoleon had been heard on the boulevards; and on the 12th, the day appointed for consideration of his fate, large crowds gathered to give voice to their feeling in his favour; it was thought necessary to surround the Chambers with a strong force of the National Guard.

Within the House a curious scene was enacted. The Government announced that, on the strength of the still unrepealed law, they had issued instructions to the prefects of every department to arrest Louis Bonaparte should he set foot on French soil. A small vote of supplies required for current expenses became in effect a repudiation or a confirmation of this course of action. Lamartine was put up by the Government to defend its deed. Generally he held the House spell-bound with his eloquence. To-day his magnificent rhetoric fell flat; his speech seemed to miss fire; its conclusion was marked by an unaccustomed absence of applause. But in an interval after he had spoken, reports reached the House that the Bonapartist crowd without was still swelling; that three shots had been fired on officers of the Guard, to the sound of cries of 'Vive l'Empereur!' Lamartine strode back to the tribune: under his handling the incident became a portent, the Assembly was swept away, the orator received a great ovation. The vote of credit was passed by an overwhelming majority; and on the strength of it the Government issued warrants for the arrest of Laity and Persigny, as well as of their leader.

But the warrants were never put into force. For, by an action typical of its time and of its character, the Assembly was to reverse on the 13th its decision of the 12th. Before any newly elected member could take his seat, his right to do so had to be confirmed by an examining body. It had fallen to the republican Jules Favre to report on Louis Napoleon's election. At the opening of the debate on the 13th he rose to maintain that the election ought to hold good. He quoted against the Government's present action, a statement made by one of its members on June 2, that the retention of the law of exile against Napoleon's house would be a national disgrace. Since they had taken no steps against Louis Napoleon as a candidate, the Government could not now consistently deny him his rights as an elected member. Admitted to the Assembly, he would be a simple citizen; debarred from it, he would by this act of ostracism be forced to reassume his position as a pretender—a pretendership on which the votes of some hundreds of thousands of his fellow-countrymen would have conferred a sort of legitimacy. In vain the Government attempted by reasoned argument to maintain the ground which it had won the day before. It was forced to confess that the incident which had enabled Lamartine to secure his triumph had never really taken place; only one shot had been fired at all, and that apparently by accident. A natural revulsion of feeling followed; the alarms of yesterday seemed rather ridiculous. In the end, Louis Napoleon's admission to the Assembly was voted by those who twenty-four hours before had consented to his exile from

France; and the Government, instead of resigning, calmly rescinded its orders of the day before.

If the 13th reversed the action of the 12th, the 15th just failed to treat the 13th in the same way. Closely following in London every debate in the Chamber, Louis thought this moment opportune for a hint at higher things. On June 14 in a letter to the president of the Assembly, he wrote: 'I was leaving for my post when I learnt that my election would be the pretext for deplorable troubles and fatal misunderstandings. . . . Should the people impose duties on me, I should know how to fulfil them. But I disavow all who ascribe to me ambitions which are not mine. My name is the symbol of order, nationality, and glory, and it would be a great grief to me to see it used to increase the troubles which are rending our country. To avoid such a misfortune I should be ready to remain in exile. I am willing to make any sacrifices for the good of France. Be so good, Mr President, as to acquaint the Assembly with this letter.'

The worst possible impression was made upon the Assembly by the haughty tone of this communication, by the absence of any mention of the republic, most of all by the ambiguous and sinister phrase, 'should the people impose duties upon me.' A scene of great excitement followed the reading of the letter on the 15th. Member after member rose and denounced the writer in terms of almost hysterical indignation. Luckily for Louis, none of his enemies had the presence of mind to bring forward a new law of banishment. But the danger was only postponed; it was evidently necessary that steps should at once be taken to allay the feeling in the Assembly. A messenger was sent post-haste to London; he arrived at King Street in the evening, and informed the prince of the effect of his letter on the Assembly. Louis at once sat down and wrote another letter to the president; as the first messenger was tired out, he gave it to a friend who at once started for Paris. Travelling all night, this second messenger was able to deliver this missive to the president by noon on the 16th. Though proud of his fourfold election, Louis wrote, he felt that the unjust suspicions to which it had given rise, the troubles of which it had been the cause, and the hostile attitude of the Government itself, forced him to refuse the honour. 'I desire order, and the maintenance of a wise, great, and intelligent republic; and since involuntarily I am the excuse for disorder, I place with deep regret my resignation in your hands.'

So ended the attempt to exclude Louis from the Assembly; an attempt of which Normanby, the English ambassador at Paris, wrote on the morrow of its failure that it was 'generally felt to be unjust if it had been expedient, and most inexpedient even if it had been just.'[1] Indeed, the

---

[1] Normanby to Palmerston, June 14th, 1848. Here as elsewhere, I quote from Normanby's contemporary despatches to the Foreign Office. But the substance of many of Normanby's despatches during this year, 1848, is given in his published journal, entitled *A Year of Revolution in Paris*, which appeared in 1856.

Assembly had twice over been made to appear a little foolish in this its first encounter with Louis Napoleon; and the Bonapartist journals were able to contrast very effectively the petulance, the indecision, the intolerance of the one, with the calm, the reserve, the moderation of the other. In reality the suspicions of the republicans were only too well grounded; while the apparent self-sacrifice of Louis Napoleon's action was in truth a very politic piece of foresight and good judgment. But Louis had not lost the art of putting his opponent in the wrong; and the Executive Commission in 1848 found itself in the same unenviable position as Louis Philippe after the Swiss affair in 1838. They seemed to have essayed a petty piece of persecution; while their apparent victim, in putting an end to the difficulty by a voluntary concession, retired with all the honours of the day.

But more than by the zeal of his followers, more even than by his own masterly inactivity, was Louis to be aided throughout this struggle by the pitiful incompetence of his opponents. 'The real strength of the cry for him,' if we may again quote from Normanby's despatches, 'is the odium with which the present men are regarded. . . . I do not know that they possess as a body of public men any one redeeming quality: nor if they remain in office could I foresee any other check or limit to the mischief they are capable of doing, except their personal incapacity or their parliamentary weakness.'[1]

[1] Normanby to Palmerston, 16th June 1848.

This is strong language, but it hardly exaggerates the prevalent opinion of reflecting witnesses; it must be remembered that it was held on the eve of the June days of 1848.

Daily, at a cost of 170,000 francs a day, the Republican Government was adding to the numbers and to the armaments of the force which sooner or later it must suppress or disperse. Openly the men spent part of their unearned wage on the purchase of ammunition. With clear purpose, their newspapers published lists of banks or houses where wealth was likely to be stored. Even the existing Government realised that this scandal must end. On June 21 it decreed the return of workmen to the provinces, or their enrolment in the army. The Government had chosen its own time for dealing the blow; it had waited long enough in all conscience; yet its tardy action had every accompaniment of precipitancy. No attempt was made to do gradually a deed that was bound to lead to bloodshed if done suddenly. No preparations were made beforehand for the suppression of the inevitable revolt; no armed reinforcements were summoned from the provinces, no strategic disposition was made even of the troops already stationed in the capital. By a piece of good fortune on which the Government had no right to count, and of which it made no use, the whole of the 22nd was allowed to pass without bloodshed. This day's grace was employed by the authorities in the insertion of provocative comments on the situation in the official newspapers, and the placarding of its intentions throughout Paris, in language which could not have been less conciliatory if the opposition to be encountered had been unarmed, unwarlike, incapable of resistance. On the 23rd, 24th, 25th, and 26th was fought one of the bloodiest civil wars which even Paris has witnessed. It was not until the 24th that the Executive Commission—in whose feeble hands the government had been vested for the past two months — was forced to make over its powers in dictatorial form to General Cavaignac. Only on the evening of that day did reinforcements for the party of order begin to arrive from the provinces. Even then three hundred barricades had been erected and destroyed, eight thousand prisoners had been taken, over ten thousand persons had been killed or wounded, and untold material damage done, before order was restored in the streets. Under a decree passed by the Assembly on the morrow of the war, some six thousand men were ordered to be transported without trial, not to Algeria, but to some less desirable colony of France. On June 25, Cavaignac surrendered his temporary powers to the Assembly, but was by the Assembly at once reinvested with them. He had used his dictatorship so well in time of war, that the deputies could imagine no better hands than his for the hardly less difficult task of ensuring the maintenance of order now that peace had been restored. Unfortunately there are still men to whom the gods have given to win the victory, but not to use it; men who can act with vigour in moments of crisis, but cannot maintain their mastery of events in periods of difficulty. Such a man was Cavaignac. Emerging from the June days with the immense prestige of one who had saved society, he was in a few months by his indecision, his tactlessness, his incalculable alternation of ill-timed clemency with more ill-judged severities, to fritter away the reputation he had gained.

During the whole of July and August, Paris remained in a state of siege. Measures of repression were passed by the Assembly; throughout the country a strong reaction was manifest against the extravagances of the preceding months. Cavaignac by the origin of his power was a champion of order; and in this capacity he was forced to oppose radical and socialist sedition. But by descent, by education, and conviction he was passionately, fanatically devoted to a republican form of government. And for this reason he was careful, by a sort of unfortunate impartiality, to administer on every possible occasion rebuffs to that monarchical party which had done such good service to the cause of order in and after June. 'Whoever does not want the republic,' he said in the Assembly on September 2, 'is our enemy, our everlasting enemy . . . In this struggle we are ready to abandon everything, our responsibility, our repose, even our honour, should the republic ever demand such a sacrifice.' But — again we quote Normanby — 'everyone, including the Government themselves, has been convinced within the last two months that . . . the republic has in fact no considerable party in the country, except those who would make it synonymous with anarchy.'[1] Hence Cavaignac's position was an impossible one; and in wavering between his lingering reputation as champion of order, and his desperate endeavour to maintain the republic at all costs, his action had the appearance of feebleness and irresolution. His own reputation collapsed, and with it the one chance of the combination to which he stood pledged—an orderly republic.

Louis Napoleon was still in London. Owing to some technicality, his election by Corsica, one of the departments which had rallied to him in June, did not take effect absolutely until July. This gave Louis the chance of writing another letter to the president of the Assembly, and again resigning the seat. Some entirely futile attempts had been made to connect his name with the June war; attempts equally groundless and unsuccessful were also made with regard to the monarchical leaders. The commission which was appointed to investigate the affair failed, with all the goodwill in the world, to discover any trace of external assistance given to the rebels. But until his entire innocence of this particular form

[1] Normanby to Palmerston, 7th September 1848.

of intrigue had been conclusively proved, Louis declined to make his entry into the Assembly.

At last, however, at the end of August, he declared his intention of presenting himself as a candidate at the next supplementary elections. In the letter announcing his intention, he wrote: 'Now that it has been demonstrated that my election in four departments was not the result of intrigue, and that I have remained a stranger to every kind of manifestation and political manœuvre, I should consider myself as avoiding my duty if I did not respond to the appeal of my fellow-citizens.' The elections in question took place on September 17. Thirteen seats were vacant. The result amply justified the opinion Normanby had reached ten days before. In every case the moderate Republican—Cavaignac's candidate—was beaten. There were two victories for the Red Republicans; three or four for the monarchical Conservatives. But these results paled before the triumph of Louis Napoleon. For of the thirteen departments vacant, five had elected him; three hundred thousand votes had been cast in his favour, in addition to those which he had received in June.

Called back in such imperious fashion to his country and his civic rights, encompassed already by the suffrages of half-a-million electors, Louis Napoleon now took final leave of his little lodging in King Street. On September 24 he arrived in Paris, and drove to a hotel in the Place Vendôme.

Thrice banished from his country; six years a captive; deported once to America; tried once for his life; imprisoned at Strasburg, at the Conciergerie, at Ham; escaped from the bullets of Papal troops in Italy, and of the National Guard at Boulogne; passed in disguise through French gaolers and Austrian soldiery; Louis Napoleon, in the fortieth year of his age and the thirty-third of his exile, had returned to his birthplace in peace. And as the September evening fell, and the marvellous lights of Paris twinkled out in the gathering gloom, from the window of his hotel he could look full upon the towering column, whence the Emperor with folded arms surveyed his capital—and his heir.

CHAPTER XII

AFTER MANY DAYS

> To Mecca thou hast turned in prayer
> With aching heart and eyes that burn:
> Ah, Hajji, whither wilt thou turn
> When thou art there, when thou art there?
>
> JAMES ELROY FLECKER.

IF Louis Napoleon's fourfold election in June had nearly occasioned his banishment from France, his fivefold election in September almost resulted in his exclusion from political power. Both events caused the republican authorities a momentary fit of terror; but while the first had found them actually engaged in discussing Louis' future fate, the second came upon them as they were framing the constitution under which they themselves were to govern or be governed.

In May a commission had been appointed to draw up a republican constitution. At the end of August the constitution thus prepared was submitted to the Assembly. The legislative power was placed in the hands of a single chamber of seven hundred and fifty paid members, elected by universal suffrage for three years; a chamber which could not be dissolved; which might indeed adjourn itself, but even so was forced to leave a committee with power to reassemble it at any moment in case of need. The executive power was given to a president, elected for four years by universal suffrage; unlike the deputies, he could not be re-elected; he could dispose the army, but could not command in person; he could not suspend existing law or retard new law. Theoretically his powers were far less than those of a constitutional king. This constitution was examined in detail by the Assembly in September, and accepted in the end, practically without alteration. A clause implying the recognition of the 'right to work' was struck out; an unsuccessful attempt was made to substitute a double for a single chamber. But the really critical debates were those which dealt with the manner of electing the president. At first the supporters of the republic had welcomed universal suffrage as the proper and democratic method of election. But the return of Louis Napoleon by five departments in September convinced the more clear-sighted republicans that universal suffrage would not give them what they wanted. Various amendments were proposed with the object of reducing the president to impotency, or making him a servant of the Assembly, not merely appointed by it, but liable to be dismissed by it at will. But the only proposal which had any real chance of being adopted was one which, while it left intact the president's powers, made him owe his office not to universal suffrage, but to the vote of the Assembly. This proposal, although in flat contradiction to their previous utterances, was now supported by Cavaignac and his ministers. It was supported by republicans who, like him, had discernment enough to perceive that the country did not want a republic, and devotion enough to desire in spite of that knowledge to impose a republican government on the country. It was opposed by some extreme radicals; by the whole body of the monarchical opposition; by the large number of republicans who were still confident that the country was republican; by a small section of them who maintained, that even a republic was not worth the having unless the country desired it, that it better became a republic to die by the will of the people of which it professed to be the expression, than to live by means which did violence to that will; better for it an honoured memory than an existence prolonged by means which would dishonour the name it bore. This last section was numerically the smallest in the Assembly; yet it was the section whose influence was to decide the issue. For among its members was that poet and prince of orators, Lamartine. The debate—one of the most critical in the annals of parliamentary discussion—was brought to its conclusion on the 9th of October. The supporters of the amendment did not lack arguments. Elected by universal suffrage, the wielder of the executive power would have a source of authority co-ordinate with the Assembly; yet by the constitution the president was, and was

intended to be, subordinate to the Assembly.
Between these two co-ordinate powers there might
and would be conflict; but there was no legal way
of settling such a conflict. Moreover, there were
monarchical memories, Napoleonic precedents;
dare the Assembly disregard them? To such
arguments Lamartine replied with a speech more
magically eloquent perhaps than any other ever
uttered from the French tribune. True, it was a
time of disaffection; but for that reason were they
to distrust universal suffrage? So doing, they
would alienate it for ever; rather they ought to
reconquer it by trusting it. True, the president
would be popular; but his popularity might be a
much-needed reinforcement to the unpopularity
of the Assembly. 'Though the dangers of the
republic are my dangers, though its fall is my
ostracism and my everlasting sorrow, yet I do not
hesitate to pronounce in favour of the course which
seems to you the most dangerous—election by the
people. . . . Then, whatever happens, it will be
good in history to have attempted the republic. . . .
It will be a dream if you like, but a fair dream for
France and for humanity. . . . If, in fine, this
people would turn back on its own self, would
make light of the blood shed so plentifully in
February and June, would speak the fatal words
. . . let it so speak. We, at any rate, citizens,
will not speak them for it in advance.' There was
no resisting such an appeal. On October 9,
by a majority of three to one, the Assembly

confirmed the clause which gave the election of the president to the people. Republicans who, looking back on the debate, saw in its conclusion the death wound of the republic, have yet generally refused to believe that Lamartine's intervention was prompted by any but the loftiest motives. Unfortunately it is a fact that the sublimest eloquence does not necessarily imply the sublimest self-surrender. Lamartine knew, every one knew, that the vote of the Assembly would certainly elect Cavaignac. But in the spring reports from the country had shown that, given universal suffrage, he could himself count on four-fifths of the total votes cast for the presidency.[1] Lamartine himself must have realised that his popularity had greatly waned since then; but at any rate with universal suffrage he had a chance of election; without it he had none. And what more likely than that his eloquent defence of the popular vote should win back for him the goodwill of the people? Ordinarily it would be difficult to blame the man who advocated a mode of election which favoured his own candidature, and opposed one which was fatal to it. But in this case it is still more difficult to acquit Lamartine of preferring the risk of the extinction of the republic to the certainty of his own defeat.

[1] Normanby to Palmerston, 24th April 1848.—'M. Lamartine told me that . . . yesterday, L. Rollin informed him that the result of his reports from the country convinced him that if there were ten million electors, he, Lamartine, would unite eight millions.'

Louis Napoleon had taken no part in the debate on which depended his whole political future. He had taken his seat on September 26, and had on that day made a short speech in which he disavowed all intrigue against the republic. The Assembly had listened coldly, and the silence with which they received his statement was an evident compound of dislike and mistrust. Since that day Louis had seldom appeared and still more seldom spoken in the Chamber. Once while he was at Ham, a friend who was pleased with the success of his pamphlet on the sugar question wrote advising him to develop his views on French taxation generally. Louis replied by a refusal. 'I neither can nor will,' he wrote, 'make myself a mere pamphleteer. The occasion of my paper was unique, and the origin of the question explained my intervention. . . . Believe me, in my position my intervention should be rare and always intelligible. One must not fritter away one's fortune in small change.'[1]

The man who realised this truth in prison had taken one important step towards success in parliament, where men are more easily forgiven for speaking ill than for speaking often. One of his rare utterances in the Chamber was drawn from Louis by a proposal brought forward immediately after the decisive vote as to the method of electing the president: a proposal to exclude from that office all members of houses that had reigned in

[1] Aug. 29, 1842. From Ham, to Mme Cornu.

France. Even Cavaignac opposed this amendment; urging, with no less justice than generosity, that since the Chamber had decided to trust the people in the matter, it must trust them whole-heartedly, without restriction or reserve. But Louis himself was forced to take some notice of an attack so clearly personal. On this occasion his inability to defend himself in debate was to prove his best defence. Although he could deliver effectively a prepared speech, the prince was at this time quite incapable of improvising an adequate retort to any sudden attack. But the few faltering sentences from the tribune served him better than the most eloquent of apologies; for they once more convinced his foes that he was an opponent beneath their serious notice; the mover of the amendment announced with polite sarcasm that the prince's speech had convinced him of the needlessness of persisting in his proposal. This was on October 9; two days later the laws against the Bonapartes were finally repealed without further discussion. Strangely tempting is the suggestion that the prince in this debate deliberately exaggerated his own incompetence; for it is an undoubted fact that Louis Napoleon, who hardly ever failed to speak well, when speaking well could serve his cause, on the one occasion in his life on which speaking ill could serve him better, did speak superlatively badly.

But here again we must avoid unnecessary subtilties of interpretation. On the whole, in the

analysis of human motives, a healthy appreciation
of the obvious will serve us better than a morbid
distrust of the superficial. In this instance the
prince's breakdown is simply and sufficiently
explained, by the fact that he was called upon
unexpectedly to speak on a point which closely
affected his whole political future, at a time when
public speaking of any kind was still new to him,
and while the French language itself, as spoken by
Frenchmen in debate, was hardly yet familiar to
his ear.

After this oratorical failure Louis Napoleon
became a still more silent and infrequent figure at
the meetings of the Assembly. His cousins were
constant in attendance and frequent in utterance;
he himself, since he lacked distinction of speech,
took refuge in the easier distinction of silence.
This was indeed his obvious policy; his presence
in the Chamber would have exposed him to all the
ordinary knocks and blows of parliamentary conflict,
a conflict in which he could not have succeeded in
asserting any personal pre-eminence. But by remaining studiously in the background, by employing his
cousins as ministers to speak for him, he adopted
already an attitude of semi-royal reserve. So
apparent was his design, that it soon became the
fixed purpose of his opponents to force him to take
part in the debates. On October 25 an unusually
violent attack was launched on him by a deputy,
who accused him of plotting an insurrection which
would place the presidency in his hands. As usual,

Louis was absent; as usual, one of his cousins rose to speak for him. But Prince Napoleon's advent to the tribune was at once greeted by cries for 'Louis,' for 'the other one.' So great was the excitement that Louis Napoleon himself felt bound to take account of it. On the following day he came in person to the Chamber and mounted the tribune. This time he read his speech; a speech in which he formally announced his candidature for the presidency.

He was sorry, he said, that his personal concerns should again be obtruded upon the Assembly, at a moment when all their time was needed for the consideration of grave questions affecting national interests. He defended himself briefly against the general attacks which were brought against him; even from the attack grounded on his taciturnity. 'I am reproached for my silence. It is given to few to express in eloquent words true and wholesome ideals. Is there no other way of serving one's country? Acts, not words, are wanted. . . . I know that it is sought to encumber my path with rocks and pitfalls. I shall not fall over them. Always in my own way I shall follow the line I have marked out for myself, without fear but without anger. . . . I declare, then, to those who would organise against me a system of provocation, that for the future I shall answer no charge, no appeal, intended to make me speak when I would hold my peace.' And to this declaration he adhered. His defence was not a very adequate one, but it did not lack dignity; the attacks to which he was subject were not altogether ungrounded, but they were unmeasured and unconvincing.

On November 4 the constitution was carried. On Sunday, the 12th, it was solemnly inaugurated at the Place de la Concorde. Mass was said by the new Archbishop of Paris, successor of him who had lost his life in a noble attempt to curtail the horrors of the June days. A *Te Deum* was sung, as for some especial mercy vouchsafed by heaven; symbolical figures of Peace and Plenty were there, as well as a plaster personification of the constitution itself. Incense rose in clouds from tripods at their feet to the tricolours above. The whole ceremony, if a little puerile, was more than a little pathetic. The bleak air of a dull November morning, slightly snowing on the assembled deputies, served to give an atmosphere of unreality to the rejoicings; while it emphasised, if it partly explained, the marked absence of any gathering of the people to witness the latest boon which was being conferred upon them. Indeed it was with ill-concealed relief that the country turned from the wrangling debates with which the constitution had been carried, and the mummery with which it had been inaugurated, to the practical and absorbing question which still remained to be decided. Who was to be the first president of the republic? In other words, was the republic to receive the only direct sanction which the people had the opportunity of bestowing, namely, the election of a republican to the presidency?

It was soon evident that the presidency lay between Louis Napoleon himself and General Cavaignac. The general had in his favour the memory of his service in June, the support of the Assembly, and—most important of all—the actual possession of power. But gratitude for his former services was by this time largely counteracted by irritation at his recent indiscretions; the Assembly was so unpopular in the country that its support was a very doubtful advantage; while even the army of functionaries, whose ready response to the voice of authority tells so much in France in favour of the existing power, even the *maires* and *préfets*, were beginning to grow restless under the uncertain hand of Cavaignac. The only assured following which remained to him in the country was the entire body of republican voters; but this force was numerically an unknown quantity. On the other hand, the general retained to the last one great and inalienable advantage over his opponent. By a clause in the constitution it was decided that, unless the successful candidate for the presidency obtained more than as many votes as all his opponents put together, the right of election would revert to the Assembly. And Cavaignac could absolutely depend upon the Assembly to elect himself. Thus he had a very substantial handicap in his favour; for if Louis Napoleon obtained two votes for every one cast for Cavaignac, Cavaignac would still become President. There were several other candidates in the field who, though personally out of the running, were yet bound to be useful to the general. For their votes would count with his towards the total which Louis Napoleon must more than surpass if he would become President.

On the face of it, then, Louis had an uphill task before him. But he too had in his favour many elements of success. In the first place, he had as sources of strength all that was complementary or contradictory to Cavaignac's. Thus, he was detested by the Assembly; but to be detested by a detested body is not to be oneself detested. Politically, the foes of our foes are our friends. Again, as section after section of the party of order was alienated by Cavaignac's ineptitude or offended by his indiscretions, each in turn rallied naturally to Cavaignac's principal opponent. And finally, the fact that Cavaignac was the official candidate of the republican party assured for Louis the support of the whole anti-republican feeling in the country.

Even more formidable were his positive sources of strength; his name, his career, and the monarchical instinct of the French people. Of these the first was the most important, for it carried with it all that shadowy transcendental heritage of which in our opening chapter we endeavoured to give some idea. But it is a grave mistake—

though a very common one—to assume that Louis Napoleon's victory in 1848 was the triumph of a name alone. True, Louis without his name could have accomplished absolutely nothing. But this is not to say that the name without Louis could have effected absolutely everything, or indeed anything at all, in the region of practical politics. On the contrary, there is every reason to believe that had not Louis formulated into a definite creed the vague faith of which it was the symbol, had he not galvanised into substantive action the evasive life that was in it, had he not embodied it in concrete form and personified it in his individual existence — then the name of Napoleon would for ever have lacked a local habitation; and that strange spirit which had risen from St Helena, must have remained 'a beautiful but ineffectual angel, beating in the void his luminous wings in vain.' We may wish that it had been allowed so to remain; for in becoming effectual the angel ceased to be beautiful. Louis Napoleon's faith in his star was about to be justified. But while it is doubtless good for a man 'to hitch his waggon to a star,' it is sometimes less good for the star. We may prefer that Niagara should continue to cast its waters in riotous and glorious waste; we may dislike to see it tamed by human intervention, and turned to servile uses. But though we grudge the engineer his triumph, we must still concede him such praise as is due to his ingenuity. After all, it is just because the process is artificial that we complain; and while we blame the workman for his interference, we cannot consistently deny the skill of his deed on the score that all that has been accomplished was automatic and inevitable.

How little the unaided name of Napoleon could have effected in 1848, we shall better understand if we glance for a moment at the position of the other bearers of that name. When the February revolution broke out, there was actually residing in France one surviving brother of the Emperor, Jerome, sometime king of Westphalia. With him was his son, Prince Napoleon, who in form and feature bore striking resemblance to his great namesake. Yet they remained absolutely unnoticed. The Provisional Government never asked them to depart from Paris; it feared them as little as Louis Philippe had feared them—Louis Philippe who had contemptuously granted them the favour they asked of a return to France, and who at the time of his deposition was actually on the point of granting to this *fraterculus gigantis* a peerage and a pension. King Jerome was, and remained, a nonentity; Prince Napoleon, as soon as he ceased to be unknown, became intensely unpopular. When, after the establishment of the empire, Louis Napoleon, before the birth of his son, adopted his cousin as his heir, he committed one of the most unpopular actions of his reign. An apologist who wished to defend this step could only do so by regarding it as a precaution against assassination; Charles the Second's remark to his brother might have been made by Louis Napoleon to his cousin: 'No one would kill me to make you king.' The only other Napoleonic prince who appeared was Lucien's son Pierre, a turbulent and vicious vagabond who, like the rest of Lucien's sons, had been naturalised as a Roman citizen. Prince Napoleon was eccentric; the other Napoleonic princes with the exception of Louis himself were merely incompetent. But it was not their present lack of ability that nullified the advantage of their name: it was the fact that in the past they had one and all bartered or endeavoured to barter away their birthright; and that not of their necessity for a morsel of meat, but that to their abundance they might add a bounty; readily foregoing their hope of a dynastic future for any handful of silver which Louis Philippe might care to toss them in exchange for it.

Once in a moment of rare provocation Louis Napoleon allowed himself to tax the nominal head of the Napoleonic house with this betrayal of the family cause. Stung by the ridicule which King Joseph had thrown on his Strasburg rising, he wrote to him in 1837: 'Yes, my enterprise has failed. But it has made France hear that the family of the Emperor is not yet dead; that it can still count on the service of devoted friends; more, that its pretensions are not confined to the demand of petty pittances from the Government, but extend to the reconstruction in the people's cause of the fabric that foreigners and Bourbons have destroyed. This I have done; is it for you to cast it in my teeth?'

This was the mere truth. The other members of his family were living in placid or querulous retirement; at best their efforts were directed to the attainment by deferential behaviour of some material benefit from the existing Government. Louis Napoleon alone was sacrificing rest and fortune, was braving ridicule, danger, and discomfort in the faith of a dynastic future. Hence a path lay open to him in 1848 which was quite closed to any of them. For a birthright once sold is not easily recovered.

It is not, then, merely to their intrinsic interest that the circumstances of Louis Napoleon's early life owe their claim to a somewhat detailed examination — though this narrative of them has failed in its purpose if they seem to lack such interest. Nor does their importance consist solely in a fact which would in itself suffice to render them important; that they served to mould and stamp with ineffaceable impress the character of a man who was for some fifteen years the most prominent figure in Europe. Their chief claim to the attention of the historian is after all this—not that they made Louis Napoleon the kind of emperor he was, 'a dreamer and a conspirator,' but that without them he could scarcely have become emperor at all. In other words, without them there might have been no Second Empire. Even Louis Napoleon, who was infinitely the cleverest representative of his name, could hardly have become president in 1848 without the advantage of his past career. While of the other members of the house it is not too much to say that even had they been endowed with all the advantages Louis had so laboriously acquired by eighteen years of labour, still they lacked the dexterity which alone enabled him to make full use of those advantages in 1848.

There remained a third factor in his success, which also has hardly been realised at its true value—the fact that at the time of the election to the presidency, the great majority of the French people desired nothing so much for the republic as its speedy and decent extinction. This is a fact which has been not merely ignored, but deliberately disguised, by many French historians of the Second Republic. There are many to whom the name of a republic has at all times a peculiar virtue; many who unconsciously hedge it about with a divinity no longer accorded to kings; so that while they regard with equanimity the fall of an unpopular monarchy, they condemn almost as an act of sacrilege the destruction of an unpopular republic. By such it is assumed that a republican form of government cannot but have an especial degree of popular approval. This would be in any case a dangerous assumption where the populace is instinctively monarchical; it becomes the height of unwisdom where revolutionary changes are the immediate result not of national movements, but of street-fighting in the capital. For in such cases when an existing government has been swept away by its own unpopularity, unless its opponents are agreed upon some immediate alternative to subsitute for it, a republic automatically ensues. And since in Parisian revolution destruction is easier than construction, by far its easiest outcome is the one form of government which can be reached by a purely negative process. In fine, of governments in general in such a country as France, the republic is the one not least but most likely to have a mere accident as its reason of existence.

But the history of the second French republic in particular has been invested with a wholly spurious pathos. Because it died young, therefore it was loved of the gods; because it was pitiful in its death, therefore it was delectable in its life; because the manner of its execution was illegal, unscrupulous, and indefensible, therefore its death sentence had not been plainly voted by the French people. To these sentimental *non sequiturs* other and more practical inducements were added. It was very natural that in the early days of the Third Republic its eulogists should tell it that it was the one form of government for which France had been pining for the better part of a century; that in 1830 and 1848 no less than in 1815 the country was baulked of its wishes; that it needed the catastrophe of Sedan to give it what it had so long desired. But the Third Republic ought now to be able to dispense with help and defenders such as these; it should no longer need to rely on representations of the past which are as much a perversion of historical truth as those which came to the hand of Louis Napoleon in the Napoleonic Legend. For, considering the relative possibilities of the two themes, the Second Republic has been as successfully idealised as the First Empire; and in one case, as in the other, historical criticism has been postponed to the interests of political propaganda.

Of all the diplomatic agents who were accredited to the Second Republic, there was none who objected more violently or more openly to the method by which it was finally suppressed than the British ambassador, Lord Normanby. Though not a republican, his detestation of the *coup d'état* was so unconcealed that it was found necessary to replace him by a less excitable successor. It may therefore be worth while to notice that however much he grudged Louis Napoleon his success later, he clearly perceived in 1848 how greatly he was being served by the strength of the anti-republican feeling in France. Thus, towards the end of October, before the result of the election had become a foregone conclusion, he wrote that he considered Louis Napoleon's election certain, 'the persecution of the Government since February having identified his success with the overthrow of that of which the people had become so weary.' This even more than the prestige of his name would win him support.[1] A week later, discussing Cavaignac's chances, he adds, 'The general opinion is that General Cavaignac's defeat is assured precisely on the ground on which he rests his hopes—that he is supposed specially identified with the republic.'[2] And on the morrow of the election he comments thus on Louis Napoleon's overwhelming majority: 'The memory of the Emperor is no doubt for something in this impulse, but the hatred of the Republic gives another signification to the name of Buonaparte, and the traditional recollection that it was by such means that the last republic was destroyed gives peculiar force to this mode of protestation.'[3]

On the eve of the elections, indeed, it became evident to the republicans themselves that France was not republican. Many of them confessed it openly; and if regard be paid to their admissions at the time itself, rather than to their memoirs and reminiscences published long afterwards with palpable political object, it is clear that they had already despaired of the republic before the result of the popular vote was made known. Almost alone among the republican leaders Cavaignac himself consistently and incessantly maintained in his every public utterance that the country was indeed republican. 'The nation is seriously, unswervingly engaged to pursue the path of

[1] Normanby to Palmerston, 29th October 1848.
[2] Ibid., 2nd November.   [3] Ibid. 12th December.

republicanism,' he wrote in a public letter to General Changarnier in September. 'To wish anything else would be to betray alike its interests and its wishes.' It has generally been believed that such statements were made in all good faith; the transparent sincerity of the general has been contrasted with the subtle deceitfulness of his opponent. But it is worthy of note that Cavaignac himself, despite his public statements, was really perfectly well aware that the country was utterly opposed to republicanism. On November 27 the general, in a confidential conversation, discussed his chances of success with the British ambassador.[1] Normanby advised him not to appear to advocate the indefinite prolongation of the present unpopular assembly. 'The general's only answer was that new elections for some time to come would destroy the republic. I said: "Then you do not think the country republican?" "Certainly not," was his answer, "and never was, and never was." "And you expect to make it so?" "It is with that object alone that I seek the presidency."' In other words, Cavaignac confessed that he was seeking the presidency with the intention of riveting upon the people a form of government which he knew they did not desire, but to which he hoped in time to accustom them. Louis Napoleon was seeking it with the intention of freeing them from a form of government of which, like Cavaignac, he knew they wished to be rid, and of giving them one which he really believed they

[1] Normanby to Palmerston (confidential), November 27, 1848.

desired. That his ambition was the more personal one, is true; that his method of accomplishing his object was illegal, and worse than illegal, cannot be denied. But if we turn from the means employed to the ends in view, his was perhaps not so very much less legitimate than his opponent's.

It is difficult in regard to the election itself to find any great distinction between the methods adopted by the two candidates. The Bonapartist papers contained violent and unfair attacks on Cavaignac; those which supported Cavaignac contained equally abusive and unfair attacks upon Louis Napoleon. If the prince's agents distributed flattering portraits of him, his opponents were no less prodigal of scandalous caricatures. If his supporters availed themselves to the full of the grievances which can be ranged against any existing power, yet the Government unhesitatingly attempted to bring all the great influence of existing power to bear against their antagonist. 'I cannot doubt that the most unscrupulous use will be made of the powers which centralisation has put into the hands of the Government to influence the result,'[1] wrote Normanby on November 2. On that day a circular was issued to the prefects, directing them to impress upon their subordinates the real interests of the republic. While the Minister of the Interior explained their duties to the prefects, the Minister of Education reminded the schoolmasters that a fund of over a million francs voted

[1] Normanby to Palmerston, 2nd November 1848.

them by the Assembly was about to be distributed; gratitude either for past or future favours should make them good republicans. Cavaignac himself attempted by tardy activities and civilities to propitiate some of the several sections of society which he had contrived to offend. The general was indeed an ideally bad candidate. Not greatly caring if he were disapproved, he disliked and resented the necessity of being 'on approval.' Personally disinclined to make use of his official powers in his own favour, he did not intervene decidedly to prevent his colleagues from using pressure on his behalf. He had thus the appearance of doing hesitatingly what it would greatly have profited him to do with vigour, and greatly have honoured him to leave undone altogether. By this course he sacrificed at once the moral prestige of a dignified reserve, and the material benefit which must have resulted from an unblushing exercise of official pressure.

Towards the end of November he achieved his last public triumph. Many had complained, with reason, of his conduct of affairs since June; it was reserved for a few of the least scrupulous of his opponents to attack him for his actual use of his dictatorship in that month. It was asserted that he had purposely allowed the rising to attain its actual proportions, in order to render his own dictatorship inevitable. On November 25 he answered this charge in the Chamber. There could be no doubt as to the result of a defence made in the one place where his influence was unshaken, on the one point on which his conduct was unassailable; by an overwhelming majority the deputies reaffirmed the vote they had passed on the morrow of the civil war—that General Cavaignac had deserved well of his country.

But by this time it was clear to everyone that the country would have none of him. On the very eve of the elections, by a last act of folly his Government renewed the fears of the supporters of order, by including in a list of political pensioners the heirs of several of Louis Philippe's would-be assassins, among them those of that very Fieschi into whose cell Louis Napoleon had been thrust after Boulogne. The list was withdrawn and cancelled almost immediately, but the impression it created could not be effaced.

Five days later, on December 10, the election took place. Although it was known almost directly that Louis Napoleon had received the necessary majority, it was not until the 20th that the result was officially announced. Nearly five and a half millions of votes were given in favour of Louis; less than one and a half to the official republican candidate, Cavaignac. The other four candidates did not gain half-a-million votes between them; Lamartine, the eloquent defender of the popular vote, obtained from it less than eighteen thousand supporters.

It was on the evening of the 20th that the result of the vote was announced in the Chamber.

Cavaignac resigned his powers; the president of the Assembly announced that Louis Napoleon Bonaparte was duly elected to the presidency. Then in the dimly-lighted Chamber Louis Napoleon himself came forward to the tribune—dressed as on another occasion in black, and bearing on his breast the grand cross of the Legion of Honour which he had worn at his trial before the Court of Peers. He took the oath of fidelity to the republic prescribed by the Constitution, and then amid profound silence he made a short speech in which he expressed in modest language his hope that in conjunction with the Assembly he might be able to found a republic at once just and democratic, neither visionary nor reactionary in its behaviour. Then, accompanied by one or two friends, and escorted by a few officials, he left the Chamber and proceeded to the palace of the Elysée, where a few rooms had been hastily prepared for his use. There that evening he gave his first small dinner-party as President; and his guests were his companions in those mad invasions of Strasburg and Boulogne: Vaudrey and Laity, Bataille, Mocquard and Persigny. What toasts were drunk that night we do not know: but some at least who drank them must have let their thoughts range on; from the delights of old battles which though lost were yet won, to the sterner satisfaction of new conflicts still untried.

Thither in any case we cannot follow them

now,[1] but in his unfurnished palace must leave Louis for the present; already on the footsteps of a throne, yet newly bound by a solemn oath to mount no higher; with the most difficult steps in the ladder already scaled, yet with a barrier in the path of his further progress which could hardly be broken by honest means. If from our study of his early career we seek to explain the causes of his success up to this point, there is one without doubt which stands out before all others. By faith Louis Napoleon, feeble champion of a fallen cause, had triumphed over every obstacle. For among much that is unattractive, and not a little that is actually repellent, there remains in this early career of Louis Napoleon one of the most striking examples of the mountain-moving force of faith that history can afford. It was not, it is true, his sole equipment. That he attempted a task which few would have dared to essay, that he persevered when all others would have desisted, that neither failure, ridicule, nor imprisonment turned him from his purpose, this of course was merely the direct consequence of a faith such as his. But while it could give him the determination to use every opportunity, faith alone could not have given him the discernment to recognise it where it lay hidden, the skill to create it where it did not exist. And this skill was his beyond doubt. He had the power too of attaching to

---

[1] The story has since been continued by the present writer in a volume entitled *Louis Napoleon and the Recovery of France*.

himself devoted friends—though not always of discriminating his true friends from his false. He had the knack of winning the goodwill of the underlings with whom he was brought in contact; of gaining the lasting affection of his personal dependents. Of Louis Napoleon his English biographer and apologist, Jerrold, remarked truly that he was an exception to the rule that no man is a hero to his own valet. Unfortunately, Jerrold himself was no exception to another rule which is equally true—that every man, every biographer at any rate, is inclined to be a valet to his own hero, to dress him up in such guise as seems good to him. This instinct—like all instincts that are universal—is to some extent a right one. It is right that a biographer should portray his subject as a consistent whole, using the light which is available to him for that purpose for the production of something more than a mere photograph. And we confess we are even grateful to him, if in the process he do not attempt by any too ruthless scrutiny to expose after death all the petty infirmities which have escaped ordinary notice in life. There are judgments which even posterity may do well to leave. But we have the right to ask that the guise in which the biographer presents his hero shall not be a disguise; that the figure shall be truly discernible in the light of the completed life. And no one whose task it has been to make his way through the 'lives' of Napoleon III can ignore the fact that, whether in praise or blame, the figure of Louis Napoleon has been heaped with clumsy draperies till its very outlines are unrecognisable. The difficulty of attaining a true picture of the man is in this case aggravated by the fact that, at any rate after his accession to power, Louis Napoleon was consciously posing before history; to some extent he was aware that he must make himself fit a mantle which was not made to fit him.

Lest we should seem to have fallen under our own condemnation, to have read into Louis Napoleon's early actions a consistency of purpose which did not really animate them, to have induced harmony and set design into incidents really chaotic or irrelevant—most of all, lest we should appear to attribute to his own prescience results properly due to the promptings of able friends or the coincidence of fortunate circumstances, we here quote in conclusion a passage in which Louis Napoleon summarised his own reading of his own early life. In 1842 he wrote from Ham to a friend who had complained of the folly of his efforts to attain his object:—

'Your letter troubled me. It proved to me—what, alas! I knew only too well before—that in all the steps which I consider useful or necessary I can count on myself alone. . . . They call me self-willed; I assure you this is quite untrue. I listen to all advice, and after weighing it in my mind I decide for myself. But what would become of me if I acted otherwise? Instead of taking a single influence from me, my friends would all wish to influence me themselves; if I consented I should be drawn in two hundred different ways at once; no morsel of my own self would be left to me. . . . Now you tell me that I am trying to advance my cause by puerile efforts. Heaven knows, success depends on an immense number of infinitely small things, which only at the end attain weight and count for something. If you saw a shipwrecked man alone on a desert island, you would say to him, "Don't trouble to build logs of wood into a raft, which will founder in the first storm; wait until chance sends in your way a ship to rescue you." *I* would say to him, "Employ all your efforts in creating instruments with which you may finally succeed in constructing a vessel for yourself. This occupation will sustain your moral being, for you will always have an end in view. It will develop your character, by the obstacles you will have to overcome. It will prove to you, if you succeed, that you are master of fate. When your ship is ready, launch out in it hardily. If you succeed in reaching land, you will owe your success to yourself alone. If you fail, you have at least found a better end than death by wild beasts or of sheer weariness." No, there is nothing puerile in my efforts, however feeble they be, so long as they originate always from the same motive, and make always for the same end. In 1832 I wrote a treatise in Switzerland in order to gain the esteem of those among whom I was forced to live. Then for nearly three years I devoted myself to a work on artillery, which I felt to be beyond my powers; in order that I might acquire by it some friends in the army, and show that if I held no command I had at least the knowledge necessary to the commander. By this means I arrived at Strasburg. Then I had the Laity pamphlet published; not only in self-defence, but in order to give the

Government a cause to have me expelled from Switzerland. In this I succeeded, and so recovered my freedom of action which I had in a sense lost by my forced setting at liberty. In London I published, against the advice of everyone, the *Napoleonic Ideas;* that I might both formulate the political ideas of the party, and prove that I was not myself merely a reckless adventurer. . . .

Boulogne, it is true, was an overwhelming catastrophe for me. But after all I am pulling myself up from it, by that interest which always attaches to misfortune, by the inherent elasticity of all national causes. In fine, what results from all this series of little acts and cruel sufferings? Why, a consequence of immense importance to me. In 1833 the Emperor and his son were dead; there were no more inheritors of the imperial cause. France knew of none. True some Bonapartes survived, here and there in the backwaters of the world; bodies without life, petrified mummies, imponderable phantoms. But for the people the line was broken: *all the Bonapartes were dead.* Well, I have retied the thread; of my own self with my own strength I have resuscitated it; and to-day here I am, within twenty leagues of Paris, hanging over the Government like a sword of Damocles. In short, I have built my boat, I have raised my mast; now I only ask the gods for a wind to carry me forward. . . .

'In fine, would you know the difference which exists between you and me in certain matters? It is that you proceed by method and calculation. I have faith, the faith that makes men endure all things with resignation, makes them trample under foot domestic joys; that faith which alone is able to remove mountains.'[1]

[1] Ham, 10th June 1842, to M. Vieillard.

This letter, written be it noted before the mountains had been removed, is in itself a sufficient proof that what Louis achieved he achieved by the conscious exercise of his own powers; nor would it be difficult to quote other passages in proof of it, if other proof were necessary.

It is easier to moralise on the past than to prophesy of the future. If, not content with accounting for his success hitherto, we should seek also, from our study of Louis Napoleon's early life, to forecast his conduct of affairs as the head of a great nation, then we should have essayed a more difficult task. We might hope for him that as he had made the uttermost use of talents and opportunities hitherto, so he would turn to yet greater advantage the vastly increased powers now placed in his hands. It is always an attractive argument, that the qualities by which men rise to rulership are necessarily the qualities which fit them to rule. For such an assumption, to whatever department of human enterprise it be applied, provides a royal road to an easy and comprehensive optimism. We are here concerned with the contention only in relation to the capacity of political rule. In this aspect of it, the fact that the comparative accident of heredity continues to produce rulers not notably inferior to those who emerge from the most cunningly contrived systems of election or competition, would alone suffice to give pause to the assumption.

But in the case of Louis Napoleon there would be even less than the usual foundation for hopes so based. For if ordinarily the talents by which a man may most quickly obtain rule are not necessarily the talents which best qualify him to rule, the especial means whereby a pretender attains to power are almost inevitably the actual reverse of the means by which a potentate maintains his power when it is won. To this fact Louis Napoleon was to bear unconscious testimony. We may, as we follow his career further, be forced to the conclusion that this man who has found his way to the rulership over ten cities, was only a two-talent man after all. In any case, the methods of his early years had served him so long and so well that he could not bring himself to cast them aside when they had achieved their purpose. He declined to put away what was childish in his past; because in the past, when no other methods were to his hand, he had successfully availed himself of childish means and trivial instruments. He never recognised the fact that in a pretender alone is persistent self-advertisement tolerable or even profitable; that pamphlets, open letters, secret communications to the Press, while they may help a pretender to a throne, can only stamp a monarch as a pretender. He could not understand that a successful conspirator has no further need to conspire; he never quite realised, now that his long Odyssey was over, that πολύμητις is not the highest epithet to which the statesman can aspire. Hence in taking leave of Louis Napoleon as a private citizen, we must to some extent be prepared to find that the very qualities, which have made him seem a prince among pretenders, will hereafter stamp him as a pretender among princes.

Yet we would not end on this note. Other and more gracious characteristics of his youth clung to him as well. The child who had given away the clothes off his back to a passing pauper never in later life turned a deaf ear to any voice of distress. The boy who had leaped into the Neckar to recover a lady's gauge never quite lost as a man the quixotic gallantry which prompted him to that deed; even as emperor

> 'Believing a nation may act
> Unselfishly—shiver a lance
> (As the least of her sons may, in fact),
> And not for a cause of finance.'

'Hitherto Fate has denied me the happiness of serving my country; . . . but so closely are the destinies of all civilised nations bound together, that to be of use to a free people is still to serve France.' So Louis Napoleon had written in 1835 in the preface to his *Manuel d'Artillerie:* half, no doubt, in apology for the fact that a volume intended for circulation in the French army was ostensibly written for the use of Swiss soldiers, and was signed by the mere captain of a Swiss artillery regiment; but half, it may be, from a wistful desire to convince himself that his existence already was not altogether purposeless. In 1848 the saying was no longer needed for an exile's consolation; for France at last was Louis Napoleon's, and his not merely to serve but to govern. But by this time, however engendered, the belief in an essential harmony — even an essential unity — in the interests of all civilised nations, had become a fixed idea in the mind of Louis Napoleon: to the end of his reign he believed fondly that 'to be of use to a free people was still to serve France.' During that reign he was indeed useful in some degree to France, and he was beyond question of immense service to Italy. But it was in part at any rate his fault that in being useful to France he was not serving a free people: it may, in part, have been his punishment that the immense service he rendered to a free people proved anything but useful to France.

Yet if the curse of the wanderer was upon him, the gift of wonder was his also. Still the author of the *Extinction of Pauperism* had his schemes for the welfare of the working man; schemes which were in some part put into execution. Still the writer on the 'Nicaraguan Canal' sought to civilise the world's waste places; to break down commercial barriers, to unite neighbouring oceans where international jealousies would have kept them asunder. The prisoner of Ham still dreamed of distant glories; of a revival of the Latin races, of a sort of European patriotism not easily conceived of now. Great schemes they were, grandiose, magnificent; sometimes even noble in their failure, magnanimous in their partial success. But while the dreamer gazed on far horizons he stumbled ever more often over the obstacles at his feet, and at last fell headlong, tripped by an antagonist who never lifted his eyes from the ground.

APPENDIX A

SOME EARLY LETTERS OF LOUIS NAPOLEON

ALL the letters quoted in this appendix have been published before at various times. For this reason, and for the saving of space, I have not thought it necessary either to quote the letters entire, or to give them in the original French. Passages quoted in the text are not repeated in this place. For obvious reasons, letters intended for publication have been more sparingly employed than those written by Louis to his near relatives and intimate friends. The extracts given below have generally been chosen with a view to throwing light on the thoughts rather than the actions of their writer; for it seemed unnecessary to reproduce here letters which serve as evidence for statements of fact made in the text. Reference to the most important of these will be found in the Bibliography.

Should any apology be considered necessary for the inclusion in crude form of so much published material, I would plead that light may still be light even when it has not come fresh from under a bushel; that although documentary evidence once published ceases in a sense to be documentary, yet it does not for that reason cease to be evidence. And I would quote in my defence the most just remark of a distinguished English biographer: 'That it is undesirable to make the reader of a biography suffer under the evils, with which legislation by reference has made the student of English law only too familiar in the pages of the Statute Book.'

To his mother, on hearing of the death of Napoleon.

AUGSBURG, 24*th July* 1821.

It is a great grief to me that I did not even see him once before he died; for at Paris I was so young that it is really only in my heart that I retain any remembrance of him. When I do wrong, if I think of *this great man* I seem to feel his spirit within me bidding me make myself worthy of the name *Napoleon*.

To his father, on his twenty-first birthday.

[20*th*] *April* 1829.

To-day I am twenty-one; I am of age; but in this I see but one reason the more for obeying you still, for following your counsels. and so making myself worthy of you.

To his cousin, the Duc de Reichstadt.

[*No date. Probably in* 1830.]

I turn everywhere for news of your health; and the uncertainty in which I am left by indirect reports gives me the greatest anxiety. . . . If the presence of a nephew of your father could do you any good, if the care of a friend who bears the same name as you do could a little lighten your sufferings, the opportunity of being of any use to one to whom I am entirely devoted would make me more than happy.

SOME EARLY LETTERS

To his mother.

CAMP AT THUN, 21*st July* 1830.

We have been at work now for three days. The exercise we take does me a world of good; I have twice my ordinary appetite. Réveillez is at a quarter to six in the morning: then we march, drums beating, to the Polygon. . . . We sup at eight, and then to bed; for one is quite ready for sleep.

To his mother.

CAMP AT THUN, *August* 1830.

We are very quiet in our little corner, while far away men fight for interests we hold most dear. . . . Think of it, the Tricolor floats in France! Happy the men who were able to be the first to give it back its ancient splendour.

To his mother, on hearing that she was ill.

FLORENCE, 18*th December* 1830.

I am much troubled by the news; I hope you will not choose the time when I am away and cannot nurse you to be ill. If you do not write, send me news by Hortense [La Croix ; afterwards Mme Cornu].

To his mother, informing her that he had joined the Italian revolt.

February 1831.

Your affection will understand us. We have accepted engagements, and we cannot depart from them. The name we bear obliges us to help a suffering people that calls upon us. Arrange that my sister-in-law may think that it was I who carried off her husband; she suffers at the idea that he has hidden one action of his life from her.

To his mother.

SPOLETO, 12*th February* 1831.

We have the joy of finding ourselves in the midst of a people who treat us with the greatest kindness, and who are wild with patriotism. . . . Send us all the money you can: this is no time to think of economies.

To his father.

LONDON, *June* 1831.

Ah, my dear father, how cruel this world is! One only lives to suffer and to see others suffer. Truly, I cannot understand how I have been able to survive my brother, the only friend I had in the world, the only person with whom I could find consolation in all possible misfortunes.

To his sister-in-law, Princess Charlotte.

ARENENBERG, 29*th August* 1831.

I have lost the being I loved best on this earth. Since his death I have to force myself not to be indifferent to everything. I never conceived a wish, never formed a plan, in which my brother had not the half of all my thoughts.

To his father, on the disposition of his brother's estate.

ARENENBERG, 31*st August* 1831.

I approve all you have done: naturally your first care should be to carry out his wishes and make all the payments he desired. As for me, I will have nothing to do with money which comes to me from such a miserable source. What I would like is any of his belongings. If you will send me whatever you do not want to keep, as a souvenir of him, I shall be grateful.

To Chateaubriand, after reading his pamphlet, 'De la Restauration et de la Monarchie Élective,' in defence of the Bourbons.

ARENENBERG, 4*th May* 1832.

How happy are the Bourbons in possessing a genius like yours to uphold them. You restore a cause with the weapons that have been used to overthrow it; you find words which vibrate in every French heart. . . . I also, M. le Vicomte, am enthusiastic for all that concerns my country's honour. That is why I have followed my first impulse in expressing to you the sympathy I feel for the man who shows so much patriotism, so much love of liberty. But permit me to tell you that you are the only redoubtable defender of the old monarchy: you would render it national if one could believe that it thought as you do. To make it worthy it is not necessary that you should declare yourself in its favour, but rather that it should prove itself worthy of your opinion.

To his mother.

BRUSSELS, 14*th November* 1832.

Yesterday we visited the field of the battle of Waterloo. You can understand all I felt in seeing the spot where the fate of France was decided, and where the star of the Emperor set for ever.

To his father, who had complained of his writings, of his travelling, and of his choice of friends.

LONDON, 10*th May* 1833.

It is really very painful to me to find you irritated against me at every turn, whether I venture to express my thoughts, or whether in search of distraction I travel from one country to another. I came here to see my uncle Joseph. Having no one else near me, I took Count Arese with me. . . . This young man is of one of the best families of Milan; he is calm, steadfast, and what is more, he is very much attached to me, and I am very fond of him. You must see that I have a right to be a little pained when, after choosing my travelling companion yourself six months ago, you suddenly bid me send away a man I like, and that on the strength of false reports which have been made to you. Remember, father, that I am twenty-five, and no longer a child.

To his father, who had answered his former letter after two months' silence.

ARENENBERG, 9*th July* 1833.

I was delighted to get your letter, it was so long since I had heard from you that I was really grieved. I beg you, dear father, never be angry with me: your anger hurts me too much. I am young, and have a difficult and unenviable position to fill. Forgive me if I sometimes differ from your opinions; and when I do, reproach me, but do not punish me by not writing. Alone here with my mother, with no other bonds save those which attach me to you, obliged to pass my youth without friends, without country, I strive to distract my mind by busying myself about serious matters.

To his father, who is again angry; this time at a reference to himself in the 'Considérations sur la Suisse.'

ARENENBERG, 2nd *September* 1833.

Perhaps, as you say, I was wrong not to have told you in advance; but I thought I could not displease you by one short sentence in your praise. Had I wished to explain your conduct and policy at length, I should certainly not have done so without consulting you.

To his father, who had met his offer to visit him in his illness by a reference to his will.

ARENENBERG, 2nd *February* 1834.

I was delighted with your letter, except where you speak of 'patrimony.' I care little enough for money, and it is only the sight of the poor people who come to me every day that sometimes makes me regret the lack of it. But I am often glad to think that if any ill chance should suddenly force me to work for my living, I should face the change with perfect resignation.

To a French Deputy, on hearing that the Bonapartes were to be excluded from France under the same statute which banished the Bourbons.

[*No date.*]

I say nothing of a cruel and unjust law; but I do protest against a measure which tends to confound the family of the man who was proud to owe everything to the French people with the family brought back by the foreigner, the family which claims incessantly outworn rights which belong to the nation alone. In the name of all my family—and I trust they will not disavow me—I intervene to ask that we be not placed on the side of the conquerors—we, who are the conquered of Waterloo.

To M. Vieillard, on the same subject.

ARENENBERG, 18*th February* 1834.

Yes, as Marshal Soult said in his speech, the Government banish us because the nation is not yet indifferent to us. . . . You are quite right. It is not in gilded rooms nor in the writings of a timid class that we shall find justice, but in the street. Here we must look if we would find noble sentiments. How I pity the narrow-minded people who think themselves strong because they have a *coterie*, a party, a *Vendée*. They do not see that their power would be far greater if, instead of having the support of a few individuals, they had ideas and interests in common with the entire nation. True, with a party you may wage war, but so you cannot consolidate your conquest, having no foundation.

To his mother.

BADEN, 10*th July* 1834.

I am sorry to see you worried by business matters, especially if your anxieties are increased by concern for me. I shall marry soon, and things will all settle themselves. In any case, it is character and not fortune which confers independence. If I had to sell all my luxuries to-morrow—and the only luxuries I have are my horses—and work for my living, I should find myself less pleased perhaps, but not less happy or less independent.

To his mother, on receiving from the Government of Berne a commission as honorary captain of artillery.

BADEN, 13*th July* 1834.

I am the more pleased, as it shows that my name will only find sympathy where democracy reigns. Yesterday I was walking on the Zurich road, when a coach passed full of Bernese marksmen. When they saw me they raised a shout of 'Vive Napoléon!' These friendly demonstrations are so many consolations for an outlaw like me.

To his father, who had complained at the publication of his 'Manuel d'Artillerie,' and at his large subscriptions to local charities.

GENEVA, 7*th February* 1835.

I receive hard words from you so often that I ought to be used to them. Yet each reproach you address to me wounds me as keenly as if it were the first. [Explains that the 4000 francs he had spent on cannon for Thurgau, and the money for the free school he supported at Gallenstein, were sums which had come to him from his brother's estate.] Such are my plans and actions. I see here neither interest nor ambition, but only a wish for quiet occupation, and a desire to be useful to my fellow-creatures. Is it fair that when I am always trying to do good I should constantly be the object of your reproaches ?

To M. Vieillard; on the death of his cousin, the Duke of Leuchtenberg.

GENEVA, 29*th April* 1835.

The *Constitutionnel* had an article on his death which touched me, because of its truth. 'The young scions of the house of Bonaparte,' it said, 'are all dying in exile, like shoots of a tree that has been transplanted into a foreign climate.' To die young is often a good fortune; but to die before one has lived, to die in one's bed of sickness, without glory, that is terrible.

To his grandmother, shortly before her death.

BADEN, *July* 1835.

You can imagine how grateful to me is the blessing of the mother of the Emperor, for I venerate the Emperor as a god, and hold his memory in sacred esteem.

To his mother, on leaving his cousins at Baden.

BADEN, 14*th August* 1836.

It is neither the pleasures nor the society that I regret, it is only that I shall no longer see France on the horizon—France which has been constantly before my eyes for the last month.

To his mother, from prison at Strasburg.

November 1, 1836.

I am in prison with the other officers. It is only for them that I am troubled; for myself, I was prepared for anything when I embarked on this enterprise. Do not grieve, my mother, I am the victim of a fair cause, a cause altogether French; later they will do me justice, and mourn for me. . . . Happily no French blood was shed. That is my one consolation in misfortune. Courage, my mother, I shall know how to sustain up to the end the honour of the name I bear. . . . Good-bye, my dear mother, do not grieve uselessly over my fate. Life is no great matter. . . . Honour and France are everything to me. I embrace you with all my heart.

To his mother.

LORIENT, 18*th November* 1836.

Forgive me if, at the moment of leaving Europe my last prayers are for my companions. . . . As Colonel Vaudrey is not rich, please send his counsel after the trial the amount of his fees, and take it from what is left at my bank. I shall need little in America; I will become a farmer.

To M. Vieillard, from the Citadel of Port Louis.

November 19, 1836.

Against my will, I do not share the fate of those whose existence I have compromised. And so all the world will take me for a fool, a self-seeker, a coward. Before ever I set foot in France I had accustomed myself to the prospect of the two first accusations; but the third is too cruel.

To his mother.

ON BOARD THE 'ANDROMÈDE,
November 1836.

What care I for the cries of the common crowd, who will call me mad because I have failed, and who would have exaggerated my merit had I been successful? . . . On the 29th [of October, the eve of the rising], at eleven o'clock at night, one of my friends came to see me in the Rue de la Fontaine, to conduct me to the place of rendezvous. We walked across the town together. A magnificent moonlight flooded the streets, and I accepted this as a good omen for the morrow. I carefully observed all the places we passed; the universal silence made a deep impression on me. What, thought I, may reign in place of this calm to-morrow? 'However,' I said to my companion, 'there will be no disorder if I succeed: for it is to prevent the troubles which often attend popular movements that I wished to accomplish this revolution with the help of the army. But,' I added, 'what confidence, what a profound conviction one must have of the nobleness of a cause to face, not the dangers we are going to meet, but public opinion, which will rend us in pieces and load us with reproaches if we do not succeed. None the less I call God to witness that it is not to gratify a personal ambition, but because I believe I have a mission to fulfil, that I risk what is more dear to me than life—the esteem of my fellow-citizens.' . . . The night seemed very long. . . . How difficult it is to describe what one feels on such occasions as this: in one moment one lives more than ten years. For to *live* is to use one's senses, faculties, every part of our being which makes for the idea of existence. . . . It is a source of moral strength to be able to say, 'To-morrow I shall be the deliverer of my country, or else I shall be in my grave.' Pitiable, indeed, is the man to whom circumstances have forbidden either alternative.

To his mother.

ON BOARD THE 'ANDROMÈDE,
14*th December* 1836.

A few months ago, when I came back after taking Mathilde home, I noticed as I entered the garden again a tree which had been broken by a storm. I said to myself, 'Our marriage will be broken by fate. . . .' My vague fear has been realised. . . . Do not accuse me of weakness if I indulge myself by telling you all I feel. One may regret what one has lost without repenting of what one has done.

SOME EARLY LETTERS 341

To his mother.
                            1*st January* 1837.

This morning the officers came in a body to wish me a Happy New Year. I was touched by this act of kindness. At half-past four we were at table; as we are 17 degrees west of Constance, it was then 7 o'clock at Arenenberg. Very likely you were at dinner; I thought of you, and drank to your health. Perhaps you did as much for me, anyway I gave myself the pleasure of thinking you did. I thought also of my companions in misfortune. Alas! *I am always thinking of them.* I thought that they were in more unhappy case than I am, and the thought made me in turn far more unhappy than they.

To his mother.
                            10*th January* 1837.

We have just arrived at Rio Janeiro. The *coup d'œil* of the roadstead is superb; I shall make a sketch of it to-morrow. I hope this letter will reach you soon. Do not think of coming to join me; I do not know yet even where I shall settle; perhaps I may find it suit me better to live in South America. Work, to which the uncertainty of my fate will oblige me to return in order to create a position for myself—work will be the only consolation I can taste.

To a friend.
                            NEW YORK, 5*th April* 1837.

I have read all my papers. I had imagined there was as much generosity as policy in the Government's treatment of me. I now see there was only policy. I have been traduced when I was not there to defend myself. . . . And what of their behaviour to my mother? Why did they not tell her I was to be taken first to Rio? I know her; they must have caused her cruel suffering.

To his father.
                            NEW YORK, 10*th April* 1837.

On arriving here I found your letter, in which you sent me your blessing. It was the most consoling thing I could have found here. . . . All my fair cousins have written me charming letters—except Mathilde!

APPENDIX A

To Colonel Vaudrey.

NEW YORK, 15*th April* 1837.

For two months I have sailed in the tropics before a wind from St Helena. Alas! I could catch no glimpse of the historic rock. But always the breezes seemed to float me those last words the dying Emperor addressed to the companions of his misfortune: 'I have sanctioned all the principles of the revolution; I have infused them into my laws and actions. There is not one of them that I have not consecrated. . . .'

To his mother, describing his journey from Norfolk to New York.

NEW YORK, 17*th April* 1837.

On Ap. 2 the captain and officers conducted me to the steamboat that conveyed me to Baltimore. . . . There were two hundred passengers on board. The cabin reaches the entire length of the boat. It is a narrow room about 160 feet in length. . . . About four in the morning, being very hot, I got up and went on deck to get some fresh air. I had hardly reached the deck when I saw a gentleman following me in his shirt, who seemed anxious to speak to me. After having twice made the round of the ship, he at length accosted me. He began with the customary 'Very beautiful night, sir.' Then he said, 'Would you be so good, sir, as to tell me your history?' I nearly laughed in his face. But I restrained myself, and merely told him that the memory of what had befallen me was so painful that I could not comply with his request. . . . From Philadelphia to New York we travelled in the same way. I passed before Point Breeze, my uncle's residence. It is a pretty little house on the banks of the Delaware, but the surrounding country is flat. The only fine features are the width of the stream (since it is agreed that this *is* beauty), and the steamboats, which are magnificent.

To his mother.

NEW YORK, 20*th April* 1837.

When I left the frigate on which the tricolor floated, the ship where men had shown me such attention, I wept as though I were quitting my country a second time. The pleasure of recovered liberty did not make up for the grief of being no longer with fellow-countrymen under a French flag.

To his mother.

ON BOARD THE 'GEORGE WASHINGTON,'
9th July 1837.

A strange place a packet-boat is. All these people whom chance has thrown together appear as fond of one another as though they had planned to travel together. We have a doctor from Boston, and his family; a New York trader, with his wife and child; two ladies, who seem to have dropped from the moon; two capital English actors, an officer of the same country, who has been in garrison in Canada and in the Antilles, two Swiss, a priest, an Italian sculptor who carves in marble at Washington the great deeds of American history; a gentleman, an *innocentin*, with whom I play chess—and the rest—freight.

To his father.

LONDON, 12*th July* 1837.

If you knew, dear father, how wretched I am in the midst of this London tumult, amid relatives who shun me and foes who fear me! My mother is dying, and I cannot carry her the consolations of a son; my father is ill, and I cannot hope to go and see him.

To his uncle Joseph.

LONDON, 12*th July* 1837.

I do not reproach myself in the least for my deed, because I have acted from conviction. Moreover, whatever may be your conduct towards me, mine shall remain unchanged. For I have a religion that guides me, and I am not subject to personal resentments. None the less, if you were not brother of the Emperor and of my father, I should have every right to quarrel with you; I, your nephew, a champion of your cause, went forth in all likelihood to be shot by a Bourbon; and you, uncle, range yourself on the side of his hangmen, wishing to overwhelm me with your blame and reproaches.

To his father.

ARENENBERG, *5th October* 1837.

To-day, at five in the morning, my mother died in my arms. She had received all the consolations of the Church and of filial love. I have no strength to write more.

To his father.

ARENENBERG, *31st October* 1837.

I am bound to spend the winter here in arranging my mother's affairs; they need arranging. My mother has left me many obligations and responsibilities, and an old castle [Gottlieben] half restored. I must finish this work in order to realise something by it. Besides, it will be my one distraction this winter. This new misfortune has induced my family to show me some signs of affection. My uncles Joseph and Lucien have written to me. Uncle Jerome is the only one who has not deigned to do so.

To his father.

GOTTLIEBEN, *10th May* 1838.

I have spent the whole winter in the old castle of Gottlieben. My mother had planned repairs, and I have carried them out. Although it is less finely situated than Arenenberg, I like it better. for here I am not haunted with heartrending memories.

To M. Laity, on the eve of his trial by the Court of Peers.

ARENENBERG, *2nd July* 1838.

So you are to go before the Chamber of Peers, because you have been generous and devoted enough to reproduce the details of my enterprise! In authorising you to publish them, my only object, as you know, was to repel the cowardly calumnies with which the Ministerial organs covered me during the five months wherein I was in prison or at sea. My honour and that of my friends were concerned in proving that it was no mad dream which led me to Strasburg in 1836. They say your pamphlet is a fresh conspiracy; on the contrary, it acquits me of the reproach of ever having conspired. . . . You will be asked, as some newspapers are asking already, Where is the Napoleonic party? Answer, 'The party is nowhere — the cause is everywhere.' The party is nowhere, for my friends are not brigaded; but the cause has partisans everywhere, from the workshop of the mechanic to the council chamber of the King, from the soldiers' barracks to the palace of the marshal of France—Republicans, *Juste-Milieu*, Legitimists, all who desire a strong government, real liberty, an imposing governing authority. All these, I say, are Napoleonists, whether they know it or not; for the Imperial system is not the bastard imitation of English or American Constitutions, but the governmental form of the principles of the Revolution. It is a hierarchy in a democracy, equality before the law, reward for merit; it is, in short, a colossal pyramid with a broad base and a high head.

Say that in authorising you to publish the pamphlet my aim was not to disturb the tranquillity of France, nor to rekindle smouldering passions, but to show myself to my fellow-citizens as I am, and not as the hate of interest has depicted me. But if some day parties were to overthrow the actual Government— and the example of the last fifty years makes this supposition permissible—if, accustomed as they have been for the last twenty-three years to despise authority, they were to sap all the foundations of the social edifice, then, perhaps, the name of Napoleon would be a sheet-anchor for all that is generous and truly patriotic in France. It is for this reason that I insist, as you know, that the honour of the eagle of October 30 shall remain intact in spite of its defeat, and that the nephew of the Emperor shall not be taken for a common adventurer. You will be asked, no doubt, where you obtained all the statements you publish; you may say that you received them from me, and that I certify on my honour that their truth has been guaranteed to me by men worthy of belief.

To his father.

LONDON, *end of December* 1838.

Though absence cannot in any way weaken my regard for you, I am always afraid to write to you. For a long time past not all that comes from me has the good fortune to please you. Suffer me none the less at this season to mingle, with the good wishes of the polite, the sincere good wishes of a son who only asks his father for leave to express all his love and respect.

To M. Berryer, thanking him for conducting his defence after Boulogne.

THE CONCIERGERIE, 6th October 1840.

I do not know if I shall ever be in a position to give you tokens of my gratitude. I do not know if you would ever be willing to accept such tokens; but whatever our respective positions, outside of political life and its dreary obligations, we shall always be able to regard each other with friendship and esteem.

To Mme Salvage.

HAM, 16th October 1840.

By this time I am installed. I have a good bed, white curtains for my windows, a round table, a chest of drawers, and six chairs. You see I have *all that I ought to have.*

To an old friend (Mme Cornu).

HAM, 8th June 1841.

You are right in saying that childhood and youth are two great saints which are only canonised after their death. But let me add that the friends of our early years are like the precious relics of these great saints, and as such are objects of our attachment and veneration. Amongst other flattering remarks you tell me that the only persons really to be esteemed are those who have received the great consecration of misfortune. You quote as your maxim, 'Tell me how you suffered, and I will tell you what you are.' Again, my dear Hortense, I find a surer touchstone for human character; it is to examine men's conduct towards those who suffer.

To M. Vieillard.

HAM, 17th December 1841.

Here is another year nearly over. Accept my good wishes for 1842. I wish you, and your wife as well, all that a friend may wish for a friend. As for me, do not have any regrets; I have no right to accuse fate; my misfortunes are my own making, and to deplore them would be to revolt against myself.

To M. Vieillard, explaining why he cannot support a certain publication.

HAM, 10*th April* 1842.

I have a sacred duty to fulfil, the duty of providing for all those who have devoted themselves to my cause; and unfortunately the pensions I am paying are in excess of my income. I do what I can, too, for the unfortunate people around me; and to meet the cost of all this I am retrenching my expenditure even on my pleasures; for I have sold my horse, and I don't suppose I shall buy another.

To M. Vieillard.

HAM, 10*th June* 1842.

I begin by telling you how grieved I was by the sad end of your poor Finette. No one knows better than I how much the loss of a dog one loves can sadden a man. For I was a very long time in consoling myself after losing a dog I had at Rome. . . . I readily admit that there are in Paris a hundred writers cleverer than me. But ask Bastide, ask Louis Blanc, ask George Sand or any of them, if in developing their political ideas they have ever moved their readers to tears. I am sure they have not; yet I have seen and known a thousand instances where my writings have produced this effect. Do you ask why? It is because the Napoleonic cause goes to the soul: it stirs vibrant memories. And it is always by the heart, never by cold reason, that one moves the masses.

To Mme Cornu.

7*th March* 1843.

Have no fear about my experiments; they are quite harmless, and distract me when I am tired. I cannot read or write long without fatigue. Chemistry is an agreeable relaxation. See the benefits of science! A little copper, zinc, and acid, and for several hours I forget my troubles and am the happiest of mortals.

To M. Desportes, on hearing of the death of the Duc d'Orléans.

HAM, 13*th July* 1842.

To-day every other thought ceases in face of the tragic event which has just carried off the Duc d'Orléans. In spite of the interests of party and of conflicting claims, I personally have been profoundly moved at the sight of a son snatched so suddenly from his mother's love; and my only thought has been for the mourning and misfortune of a French family.

To M. Vieillard.

HAM, 18*th April* 1843.

You tell me that there is much talk of an amnesty at Paris, and ask what I think of this news. I will answer your question frankly. If to-morrow they should throw open the doors of my prison, telling me, 'You are free, stay with us as a citizen,' then indeed my heart would rejoice. But if they offered me exile in exchange for my actual position, I should repel it as an aggravation of my punishment. Better imprisonment in France, than liberty abroad. Besides, I know the meaning of the word 'amnesty' in the mouth of the present Government. [Repeats the story of the Government's attempt to make it appear that he had promised to remain in America.] That was the effect of one amnesty the Government inflicted on me. Do you suppose that after that I could possibly desire a second?

To Mme Cornu.

HAM, 5*th June* 1843.

Headaches, visitors, and hard work have prevented me from writing sooner, but they did not prevent me from often thinking of you. I was very pleased at the reading of my letter by M. Arrago, and at its insertion in the *Bulletin de l'Académie*. I wish I could say that my work on artillery is almost finished; but the farther I go forward the farther I fall behind. When you see the proofs, you will understand how much patience is necessary for such a labour.

To M. Vieillard.

HAM, 22*nd April* 1844.

Apparently, the longer my captivity lasts the more their severity increases. But this is a small matter. By the ill-will of the Government I measure its strength and mine. Here I have an unfailing barometer.

SOME EARLY LETTERS

To a friend at Florence, who was attempting to reconcile his father to him.

HAM, 6*th May* 1844.

Unhappily my father has not judged me as you have often he has attributed the most sordid motives to my actions. I will tell you the thing which wounded me most: it will show you what I mean. In 1834 I was in Switzerland with my mother when I learnt that cholera had broken out at Leghorn. At once I asked for passports so that I could go to my father and look after him in case he had been stricken with the plague. Will you believe me, he answered me in the coldest manner, and read in this proof of attachment motives of self-interest. I have never been able to forget that: it was a thing so foreign to my thoughts that I could hardly even understand the idea of it. Am I not unfortunate to be so misunderstood? *Mon Dieu! I* act from self-interest! Why, to-day I have spent almost all I possess in sustaining in their misfortune the men whose existence I have compromised, and I would give all my heritage for my father's embrace. Let him give his whole fortune to Peter or Paul; it is small matter to me: I will work for my living.

To the same.

HAM, 28*th September* 1844.

My definition of good fortune is almost the same as yours: to command in order to do good, or to obey one whom he loves, that is a man's true happiness. . . . You are right in saying that my poor father is more wretched than me, since I have what he has not, the hope of a better future. . . . Do you know if he has read a notice in the *Revue de l'Empire* which I have written on my Uncle Joseph? . . . My uncle had told me at London that it was not fair that I should support alone all the charges which political life has forced me to accept: he often said that he would make me some return in his will. He has done nothing of the kind. I have avenged myself by writing an appreciation of him, clearing him of the calumnies men showered on his memory.

APPENDIX A

To a friend.

Ham, *6th January* 1845.

Years roll on with a depressing monotony. It is only in the promptings of my heart and conscience that I find strength to stand up against this leaden atmosphere which surrounds and suffocates me.

To George Sand.

Ham, *24th January* 1845.

I desire liberty, and even power. But I had rather die in prison than owe my rise to a lie. I am not a republican, because I believe that to-day, in face of party divisions and of a monarchical Europe, the Republic is an impossibility.

To M. Peauger.

Ham, *3rd February* 1845.

I believe in fate. If my body has miraculously escaped every danger, if my soul is secure amid so many causes of discouragement, it is because I am called to do something.

To M. Peauger.

Ham, *12th March* 1845.

I am glad to find that our characters are so alike: we pass by turns without excuse of reason from misery to joy, from discouragement to hope. I loathe those 'golden mean' persons who are never gay and never sad, because they have no lively sense of any emotion: such persons do not live, they vegetate.

To his father.

Ham, *20th August* 1845.

The Feast of St Louis approaches. In writing to you, dear father, I cannot repeat the banalities common on such occasions. But I will tell you that every evening I address to God fervent prayers for those I love; and in them my first thought is to ask for the lengthening of your days and the realisation of my dearest wish—that of seeing you again, and being able once more to embrace you.

To his father, on receiving his letter, asking Louis to visit him.

HAM, 19*th September* 1845.

Yesterday I had the first real joy I have experienced for five years, when I received the kind letter you were so good as to write. . . . Till then I was resolved to do nothing at all to leave my prison. For I had nowhere to go, nothing to do. Was I to wander alone in a foreign land without friends? Better a grave in my own country. But now a new hope dawns on my horizon, a new object presents itself for my efforts.

To M. Vieillard.

HAM, 8*th December* 1845.

I have found no more despicable rôle in history than that played by Cromwell's son, who deserted his father's cause to become an unobserved spectator at the coronation of the Stuarts.

To Mme Cornu.

HAM, 3*rd February* 1846.

M. Odilon Barrot, acting against my wishes, drew up with M. Duchatel a new draft of a letter to the king. He enclosed with it a very kind letter, urging me to sign it, and eight or ten deputies wrote in practically the same words. I replied yesterday to M. Odilon Barrot with a definite refusal. I told him that I had asked the king for leave to visit my father, because my duty called me to him; but that I had no intention of asking for pardon, and would rather stay in prison all my life than demean myself. This unfortunate step of M. Barrot will divide the deputies and rob me of the moral support which it was so important for me to keep.

To General Montholon.

HAM, *May* 24, 1846.

I thought it better for your own sake to leave you in ignorance of plans which are only a few days old; besides, I am convinced that my escape will be nothing but good for you and the other friends I leave in prison. . . . Believe me, general, I was very sorry not to have shaken your hand before I left. But I could not have done it; my emotion would have betrayed the secret I wished to keep from you. I have taken steps to ensure the payment of your pension. As you may have need of money in advance, I have given Conneau two thousand francs, which he will give you.

To M. Degeorge.

LONDON, *June* 1846.

The desire to see my father once more in this world prompted me to undertake the boldest enterprise I have yet attempted; one which called for more resolution and courage than those of Strasburg and Boulogne. For I had determined not to endure the ridicule which is the lot of persons arrested under disguise.

To M. Vieillard.

3 KING STREET, 17*th February* 1847.

I have been installed for a fortnight in my new house, and for the first time in seven years I am enjoying the pleasure of being at home. I am collecting all my books, papers, and family portraits; in fact, everything of value which has escaped the shipwreck.

To Captain Lecomte, commander of the guard of honour at the final funeral ceremony of Louis of Holland.

LONDON, 4*th October* 1847.

It is not the man whom chance and the fortune of war made a king for a few months that you have honoured with your regrets, but the old soldier of the republican armies of Italy and Egypt—a man who remained but a little time on a throne, who paid for a few years' glory by forty years of exile, and died alone in a foreign land.

To his cousin, who had praised him faintly.

LONDON, 16th *June* 1848.

Thank you for your speech about me. I am only sorry that you felt obliged to blame the enterprises of Strasburg and Boulogne. There was no need to refer to them at all. . . . What would you think, what would anyone think of me, if I went out of my way in a public speech, even after preliminary praise of you, to say that I was sorry that you had made your bow to Louis Philippe?

To the same, rallying him on his habit of signing himself Napoleon, like the Emperor.

3rd *July* 1848.

Personally I always ask people to call me 'Louis,' to distinguish me from my relations. In fact I would gladly be called Louis Napoleon Nebuchadnezzar Bonaparte, in order to have a clearly-marked personal identity. Think it over, and you will see that I am right.

To General Plat.

28th *August* 1848.

There is only one way to make the return of past governments impossible; and that is improve on them. Believe me, one never really destroys a thing until one has replaced it.

APPENDIX B

BIBLIOGRAPHY

THIS bibliography covers only that portion of Louis Napoleon's career which is treated of in this volume, *i.e.*, the first forty years of his life. The evidence for this period, as a whole, is far from satisfactory. The most important authorities are marked with an asterisk. Where the author's name is given in brackets, the book was originally published anonymously. The date of publication is given; where the place of publication is not mentioned, books with English titles were published in London, and those with French titles at Paris. From these two data the bias of the writer may generally be inferred. Most of the accounts of Louis Napoleon's exploits published before 1848 are friendly; for the obvious reason that it was not yet worth while for anyone to attack him, while it was already greatly to his interest to make himself known favourably to the French people. From 1848 to 1851 the President was subject to the ordinary attacks of political life. After the *coup d'état* and during the earlier years of the Empire, all books published in France were necessarily polite; during the same period, books published outside France were almost uniformly hostile. As the reign advanced, moderate criticism became possible in France, while qualified appreciation became more common in Europe. But the writings of the political exiles—books published for the most part at Brussels or Geneva—these naturally remained bitterly hostile. In the closing years of the Empire criticism was unmuzzled in France itself, and after the downfall the great majority of French writers waxed almost hysterical in their abuse of Napoleon III and all his works. It was only after twenty years had passed that some signs of an approach towards historic impartiality began to appear; the latest French writings on the Second Empire show perhaps a slight reaction in its favour.

Almost all accounts of Louis Napoleon's career, published during his lifetime, were mere partisan pamphlets attacking or defending him. Defenders and detractors alike were in many cases capable of tampering with their facts. Hence the majority of the earlier publications cited below are not altogether reliable. But I enumerate them, rather than mere compilations published after Louis Napoleon's death, because they rank as primary authorities, and because they may conceivably have had some material influence on contemporary opinion.

I.—GENERAL AUTHORITIES FOR THE EARLY LIFE OF LOUIS NAPOLEON

EMILE OLLIVIER. *L'Empire Libéral*, 17 vols.; 1895-1915.
Vol. II., chapters i. and ii., cover this period, though not, of course, in any great detail. M. Ollivier's work only becomes of first-rate importance as he approaches the later part of Napoleon III's reign.

*H. Thirria. *Napoléon III avant l'Empire.* 2 vols. 1895-6.
   The first scholarly study of this portion of Louis Napoleon's life. Vol. I. treats of the period covered in this book.
   Only eleven pages on the first twenty-five years of Louis Napoleon's life, but most useful afterwards. It contains many quotations from the French press of the period.
*A. Lebey. *Strasbourg et Boulogne.* 1906.
   On the whole, the best book on this early period. M. Lebey hardly succeeds in proving that these two attempts possessed quite the importance which he ascribes to them, but his study of the subject is illuminating.
F. Giraudeau. *Napoléon III intime.* 1895.
   The chief value of this book consists in a number of Louis Napoleon's early letters contained in it which had not before been published. A further interesting collection of his letters from 1837-48, written to his cousin Prince Napoleon, was published in the *Revue des deux Mondes* of 15th December 1923.

During the Second Empire a constant succession of eulogistic biographies of Napoleon III was forthcoming. As examples of their kind, the following may be mentioned :—

B. Renault. *Histoire du prince Louis-Napoléon.* 1852.
Gallix et Guy. *Histoire complète et authentique de Louis-Napoléon Bonaparte.* 2 vols. 1853.
De Barins. *Histoire populaire de Napoléon III.* 1853.
A. Mansfield. *Napoléon III.* 1860.
E. Fourmestreaux. *Napoléon III.* 1862.

These eulogistic lives do make some slight contributions to our knowledge of Louis Napoleon's early days; the series of diatribes which appeared after the fall of the Second Empire do not. Their authors were generally concerned with the later and greater crimes of Napoleon III; for this reason they claim no notice here.

The authorised English life of Napoleon III, published after his death, was

*BLANCHARD JERROLD. *Life of Napoleon III.* 4 vols. 1874-82.
Though a far from satisfactory biography, Jerrold's book contains much valuable matter. For the disabilities of a professed apologist he had real compensation, in access to important documents in the possession of the imperial family. This period is covered by the first two volumes of the work.

ARCHIBALD FORBES. *Napoleon III.* 1898. A mere *réchauffé*.

F. H. CHEETHAM. *Louis Napoleon and the Genesis of the Second Empire.* 1908.
Save in regard to the Strasburg and Boulogne affairs, this is an accurate and carefully compiled account of Louis Napoleon's early life; an account in which, in the author's phrase, 'the works of M. Emile Ollivier, M. Thirria, and M. André Lebey are largely drawn upon, in many cases their narratives being closely followed.'

PHILIP GUEDALLA. *The Second Empire.* 1922.

II.—AUTHORITIES FOR PARTICULAR EVENTS

The Napoleonic Legend.

The literary foundation of the Napoleonic Legend was laid by the memoirs of Napoleon's companions at St Helena, and so indirectly it was the work of Napoleon himself. Of these memoirs, the more important were :—

O'MEARA. *Transactions at St Helena.* 1819.
,, *Illness and Death of Napoleon.* 1821.
,, *Napoleon in Exile.* 1822.
LAS CASES. *Mémorial de Sainte Hélène.* 1823.
COMTE DE MONTHOLON. *Mémoires pour servir à l'histoire de France sous Napoléon.* 1823.
,, *The Captivity of Napoleon at St Helena.* 1846.
ANTOMMARCHI. *Derniers Moments de Napoléon.* 1825.
GENERAL GOURGAUD. *Refutation of Sir Walter Scott.* 1827.

Hardly less important was the contribution of the whole school of French poets, who, in the generation following Napoleon's fall, made his exploits the subject of their song. Of these, the most important were Béranger (1816 and onwards) and Victor Hugo (1822 and onwards). The Legend was finally incorporated into the works of two of the greatest of French historians. Lamartine's *Histoire des Girondins* (1847), and Thiers' *Histoire du Consulat et de l'Empire* (1845 onwards), succeeded together in presenting Napoleon as a personification of the best work of the Revolution.

But the real literature of the Legend defies the bibliographer, for the true evidence of its growth consists less in the writings of its great French protagonists — poets, historians, ecclesiastics, politicians—than in the innumerable references and allusions to Napoleon with which the entire literature of the reaction abounds.

For a good bibliography of the actual St Helena literature, as well as a capable analysis of Napoleon's own contribution to the Legend, see

PHILIPPE GONNARD. *Les Origines de la Légende Napoléonienne.* 1906.

Parentage of Louis Napoleon.

The story that Louis Napoleon was no son of King Louis of Holland is a tradition of long standing; but it is only the later—possibly the last—stages of the controversy which need here be traced.

In 1893, M. Hachet-Souplet, in his book cited below, stated as a matter of common knowledge the fact that King Louis had never wished to recognise Louis as his son. Like almost all recent supporters of this contention, he maintained that the real father of the future emperor was Admiral Verhuel.

In February 1894, M. Lucien Perey, in an article in the *Vie Contemporaine* entitled 'La Reine Hortense,' by the aid of unpublished letters demonstrated the impossibility of accepting this view.

In August 1894, W. Graham, in an article in the *Fortnightly Review* entitled 'Sidelights on the Second Empire,' revived the statement that in 1831 King Louis wrote to the Pope denying that Louis Napoleon was his son.

In December 1894, M. Fernand Giraudeau, in the *Figaro* (December 8, 12, and 15), published a number of most intimate letters between King Louis and his son Louis Napoleon, proving that in his correspondence King Louis repeatedly recognised the prince as his son.

The author of the English article stated that his discovery was to be followed up by further revelations; but these have not yet been forthcoming, nor has Mr Graham ever produced documentary evidence of the authenticity of the letter from which he quoted. M. Giraudeau, on the contrary, followed up his intervention by publishing in 1895 his work quoted above, in which incidentally he succeeds in showing that M. Hachet-Souplet is a totally unreliable authority.

In 1896 appeared the *Mémoires du Maréchal de Castellane*, which bear out M. Perey's contention that in the summer of 1807 Verhuel was hardly acquainted with Hortense.

Though it has thus been shown to be untenable, a far stronger case was made out for the paternity of Admiral Verhuel than for any of the half-dozen other men on whom scandal has endeavoured to place it. The only one of these others in whose case the contention has even a remote possibility of truth is M. Decazes, a secretary of Napoleon's mother; but a chance remark of his to Thiers, quoted by the latter at Versailles in 1871 (*vide* M. de Baillehache, *Prétendants*, p. 141), seems to show that here too the contention of those who deny the Napoleonic origin of Louis Napoleon is without justification in fact.

In 1924 the Flahault papers, published under the title *The Secret of the Coup d'Etat*, showed that the Comte de Flahault maintained the legitimacy of Louis Napoleon. In fact, by this time the whole weight of the evidence is in favour of the belief that Louis Napoleon was actually the son of Louis of Holland. For this reason, and because the arguments are largely of a physiological nature, I do not summarise the contentions which have been used by advocates of different views of this question. The whole subject is discussed with a certain French thoroughness by M. Lebey, *op. cit.*, pp. 2-14.

Childhood of Louis Napoleon.

LADVOCAT. *Mémoires sur la cour de Louis-Napoléon et sur la Hollande.* 1828.
MLLE COCHELET. *Mémoires sur la reine Hortense.* 1836.
WRAXALL AND WEHRHAN. *Memoirs of Queen Hortense.* 2 vols. 1862.
MME DE RÉMUSAT. *Mémoires.* 1880.
J. TURQUAN. *La reine Hortense.* 1896.

Louis Napoleon's farewell with his Uncle.

Jerrold quotes the story from Renault, *op. cit.*, 1852. Mr Cheetham, following in the steps of M. Lebey, states 'that it dates back at least to 1853, when it appeared in De Barin's *Histoire Populaire de Napoléon III.*' The story is considerably older than this, for it is told in detail in Persigny's *Lettres de Londres*, published at the beginning of 1840. The difference in date is material, for any claim the narrative has to acceptance consists in the fact that it was current before Soult's death in 1851. That Soult did not actually deny it proves nothing; that such a wholly unnecessary risk of denial should have been incurred does, however, seem to show that the story had some basis of fact. Had it been a mere invention, the rôle of sympathetic spectator could obviously have been assigned with greater safety and greater effect to Marshal Ney. For some uses the dead lion is doubly to be preferred. Still, Persigny's book, even more than the 'lives' of Renault, De Barins, Gallix and Guy, etc., is a mere *Tendenzschrift*. Thus, all these official lives state that Louis Napoleon was born at the Tuileries: in reality he was born at No. 8 in the Rue Cerrutti, now the Rue Lafitte. In any case, the parting before Waterloo was not the final farewell of the two emperors of the Napoleonic house, for it seems certain (*vide* H. Houssaye, '1815,' vol. iii., 1905) that Napoleon saw and embraced his nephew after Waterloo, before he left Malmaison for Rochefort.

Youth and education.

GEORGES DUVAL. *Napoléon III : Enfance—Jeunesse.* 1895.
*STÉFANE-POL. *La Jeunesse de Napoléon III.* 1902.

A series of private letters from the prince's tutor, Lebas, to his own relatives in Paris. Most valuable, as containing a perfectly frank contemporary account of the tutor's impressions of his pupil during his term of office, from 1820 to 1827.

The Italian episode of 1830-1.

* *Mémoires de la Reine Hortense publiés par le Prince Napoléon.* 3 vols. 1927.

Queen Hortense published herself, in 1834, her account of the year 1831: her entire memoirs were only released for publication by the death of the Empress Eugénie.

APPENDIX B

Some further details are contained in a notice of Prince Napoleon, Grand Duc de Berg, by E. PASCALLET, *in Le Biographe Universel.* 1854.

Relations with the Carbonari.

M. Ollivier (*op. cit.*, vol. ii., p. 28) maintains that Louis Napoleon was not a Carbonaro; urging (1) that the headquarters of the Carbonari were in Southern Italy, and (2) that the 'engagements' which Louis pleaded in the letter to his mother quoted above (Appendix A, p. 333) referred solely to the prince's promise given to Menotti.

M. Lebey (*op. cit.*, pp. 34-48) discusses the question in some detail, and concludes that Louis Napoleon was a Carbonaro: for (1) note the extremely guarded denial of Count Arese in his letter to Jerrold, quoted by the latter, *op. cit.*, vol. i., pp. 155, 156; (2) this hypothesis gives a natural meaning to the phrase in Louis' letter referred to above; (3) it explains the expulsion of the prince from Rome; (4) it renders intelligible the action of Orsini; (5) it is supported by the fact that several of the prince's early friends were undoubtedly members of the Carbonari.

M. Lebey has clearly the best of the argument, even though he rather curiously ignores the one piece of direct evidence in favour of his contention; viz., Count Orsi's definite statement that in his hearing, at a meeting of Italian conspirators on the night of February 26, 1831, Louis Napoleon declared himself to be a Carbonaro (*op. cit. infra*; p. 179). But the statement cannot be regarded as absolutely conclusive, for it appeared fifty years after the event, and Orsi is not an unexceptionable witness. (See below, p. 367.) In any case, the fact that no documentary evidence of

Louis Napoleon's membership of the Carbonari has yet come to light, is strong presumptive evidence that the society did not possess any written engagements of the Prince.

On Louis Napoleon's visit to Paris in May 1831.

LE DUC D'AUMALE. *Lettre sur l'Histoire de France, adressée au Prince Napoléon.* 1861.

On the Bonapartist plots of the first years of the July Monarchy, and Louis Napoleon's alleged connexion with them.

Mémoires de M. Gisquet, Préfet de Police. 1840.

On Louis Napoleon's meeting with Persigny.

H. CASTILLE. *Le Comte de Persigny.* 1857.

On his subsequent relations with him.

J. DELAROA. *Duc de Persigny et les Doctrines de l'Empire.* 1865.

Occasional notices of Louis Napoleon's life in Switzerland and Italy before his descent on Strasburg occur in the following memoirs:—

LADY BLESSINGTON. *The Idler in Italy.* 1839-40.
MME DE GIRARDIN. *Lettres parisiennes.* 1843.
CHATEAUBRIAND. *Mémoires d'Outre Tombe.* Brussels, 1848-50.
MME RÉCAMIER. *Souvenirs et Correspondance.* 1859.
MALMESBURY. *Memoirs of an Ex-Minister.* 1884.
HENRY EDWARD FOX. *Journal of,* 1818-1830. 1923.

Strasburg.

The most important published evidence respecting the Strasburg affair is naturally contained in the official account of the trial of the seven persons accused of complicity in it. The *Times* for January

APPENDIX B

1837 gives detailed reports of the trial; but for a verbatim report, see

L'Observateur des Tribunaux, January 1837.

*Eugène Roche. 'Insurrection de Strasbourg et procès des prévenus de complicité avec le prince Napoléon-Louis, etc.'

With regard to evidence derived from reports of the trial, it must be remembered that though the Government wished to secure the condemnation of those actually accused, they were still more anxious to minimise the whole affair; hence in their cross-examination of the prisoners they had no desire to bring to light any further ramifications of the plot. And the accused, without seeking to extenuate their own share in the rising, naturally refrained from volunteering information which might compromise others.

The history of the rising from the insurgents' point of view is contained in

M. E. Persigny. *Relation de l'entreprise du Prince Napoléon-Louis.* London, 1837.

*Armand Laity. *Relation historique des événements du 30 Octobre, 1836.* June 1838. Libraire Thomassin.

Both these accounts had a considerable circulation. They agree in almost every particular, but the latter attracted more attention than its predecessor. It was corrected by Prince Louis himself, and may be considered as containing his own view on the rising. Though designed to magnify its importance, these accounts refrain, from obvious reasons, from giving details as to persons involved in the plot who had not actually been brought to trial. See also—

Moniteur, 1837. January 10, 13, 14, 20, and 21.

James Fazy. *De la tentative de Napoléon-Louis.* Geneva. 1836.

*Albert Fermé. *Les grands Procès politiques, Strasbourg.* 1868.

A. Maurin. *Histoire de la chute des Bourbons*, Bks. VI. and VII.

BIBLIOGRAPHY

For Louis Napoleon's own account, see his long letter to his mother, written in November 1836—

Collected Works of Louis Napoleon Bonaparte, 1852. Vol. I., pp. 10-27;

for the curiously sympathetic republican view—

LOUIS BLANC. *Histoire de Dix Ans*, Bk. V., 1844;

and for the Orleanist view—

GUIZOT. *Mémoires pour servir à l'histoire de mon temps.* 9 vols. 1858-68. Vol. V.

America.

JOHN S. C. ABBOT. *History of Napoleon III.* Boston, 1868.
The Daily National Intelligencer. Washington, 1856.
  (*Correspondence*—March 28, April 11, April 15. The Rev. C. S. Stewart, General Watson Webb, and others; reproduced by Cheetham, *op. cit.*, Appendix B.)

Notices of Louis Napoleon's doings in the States appear in—

PIERRE M. IRVING. *Life and Letters of Washington Irving.* New York. 1864.
GENERAL WILSON. *Memoirs of Halleck.* New York. 1869.

The Laity trial.

SAINT-EDME. *Procès d'Armand Laity.* Landois. 1838.
Moniteur, July 4, 10, and 11, 1838.

The Swiss affair.

E. LECOMTE. *Louis-Napoléon Bonaparte, la Suisse et le roi Louis-Philippe.* 1838.
M. le Professeur DE LA RIVE. *Rapport fait au Conseil représentatif.* Geneva. 1838.
JULES LOMBARD. *Le prince Louis-Napoléon Bonaparte et le ministère Molé.* 1839.

APPENDIX B

England.

(PERSIGNY.) *Lettres de Londres. Visite au Prince Louis.* 1840.
PAGNERRE. *Procès de Napoléon-Louis Bonaparte.* 1840.
JAMES BULKELEY. *The Tourney of Eglintoun.* 1840.
J. A. ST JOHN. *Louis Napoleon, Emperor of the French.* 1857.

Several of his English acquaintances make mention in their memoirs of Louis Napoleon's life in London at this period, e.g.—

SIR H. HOLLAND. *Recollections of Past Life.* 1872.
J. R. PLANCHÉ. *Recollections and Reflections.* 1872.
See also DISRAELI's *Endymion.* 1880.

On the Prince's alleged matrimonial designs, see—

BINGHAM (Hon. D. A.). *The Marriages of the Bonapartes.* 1881. Vol. II., p. 327.
Le Figaro, 13th April 1894.
SIR WILLIAM FRASER. *Napoleon III: My Recollections.* 1895.
CHARLES BOCHER. *Mémoires.* 1907.
Blackwood's Magazine, Feb. 1907. 'Lady Burdett-Coutts.'

On his relations with Miss Howard—

GRISCELLI DE VEZZANI. *Memoirs of the Baron de Rimini.* 1888.
DE BEAUMONT-VASSY. *Mémoires secrets du XIXme siècle.* 1874.

and the quarrel with Kinglake in this connexion—

REV. W. TUCKWELL. *Life of A. W. Kinglake.* 1902.

But, according to Mr Graham's article cited above, the Empress herself was the cause of the quarrel.

Boulogne.

Here the evidence is even less satisfactory than that which bears on the Strasburg insurrection. Curiously enough, the trial of Louis Napoleon himself in 1840 excited less attention, and was less fully reported in the French press, than the trial of his accomplices in 1837. The *National* gives adequate reports, while the Bonapartist journal, *Le Capitole*, devoted its expiring numbers to accounts of the trial. This last paper was founded in June 1840, and ceased publication on December 3 of the same year. The most faithful reports of the trial, and so the most important evidence on the affair, is contained in—

*SAINT-EDME. *Procès de Napoléon-Louis Bonaparte.* 1840.
*ALBERT FERMÉ. *Boulogne d'après les documents authentiques.* 1868.

The financial preliminaries of Boulogne are narrated by

ELIAS REGNAULT. *Histoire de Huit Ans.* 3 vols. 1851;

a book generally useful for this period of Louis Napoleon's life.

Contemporary but far from reliable accounts are contained in—

BOHAIRE. *Procès du Prince Napoléon-Louis Bonaparte.* 1840.
Simple exposé de l'expédition de Boulogne et quelques mots sur le prince Napoléon-Louis. 1840.
GALLOIS. *Le prince Louis-Napoléon Buonaparte à Boulogne, révélations historiques et diplomatiques,* par M. de C., ancien ministre plénipotentiaire, etc. 1840.

(The last is a grave attempt to represent the prince as an agent of the Quadruple alliance.)

COUNT ORSI. *Recollections of the Last Half Century,* 1881, contains a graphic account of this affair, in which the count took part himself. Orsi's narrative is always interesting, though sometimes less dependable than might be expected from a man who professed to have kept a contemporary record of the events he narrates in his diary. The same volume contains brief accounts of the Italian episode of 1830-1, of the preliminaries of the escape from Ham, and of Louis Napoleon's excursion to Paris in February 1848.

TAXILE DELORD. *Histoire du Second Empire.* Vol. I. 1869.
   Gives a complete list of the 152 members of the court of peers who condemned Louis Napoleon, and of the 160 who abstained from voting.

On the fate of the historic eagle, really a vulture, see—

La Presse. 21st November 1848.
SUTHERLAND EDWARDS. *Old and New Paris.* 1894.

The imprisonment at Ham.

J. G. G. DE FEUILLADE. *Le Château de Ham.* 1842.
   Ostensibly a guide to the prison; really an appreciation of the prisoner.
   [Cp. a work of precisely similar character, published in 1833 in the interest of Polignac: *Ham, Août 1829 — Novembre 1832, par un attaché à la présidence du conseil des derniers ministres de la Restauration.*]
JÉDÉ. *Abrégé de l'histoire de Ham.* (n.d.)
   A real guide to the Château, with plans and illustrations of the fortress.
M. C. E. TEMBLAIRE. *Revue de l'Empire,* 1842-1845. Gives constant reports of the prince's activities at Ham.
HENRY WIKOFF. *Biographical Sketches of Louis Napoleon Bonaparte. A visit to the prince at the castle of Ham.* New York. 1849.
LOUIS BLANC. *Révélations Historiques.* Brussels. 1859. Vol. II.
A. DE LA GUÉRONNIÈRE. *Portraits politiques contemporains.* 1851.
E. FOURMESTRAUX. *Op. cit.*

A valuable source of information on Louis Napoleon's work at this period exists in the collection of over a hundred letters written by him to his goddaughter, Hortense Lacroix, during his imprisonment, and published by Jerrold, *op. cit.*, Vol. II., Appendix I., pp. 415-61.

The entire correspondence, 297 letters ranging from 1820 to 1872, in parts almost illegible, can now be seen at the Bibliothèque Nationale (Nouv. acq. fr. 1066, 1067).

Traité d'alliance offensive et défensive entre S.A.R. Charles Frederic Auguste Guillaume Duc de Brunswick Wolfenbuttel et S.A.I. le Prince Napoléon Louis Bonaparte.

Nous Charles Frederic August Guillaume Duc de Brunswick Wolfenbuttel et Nous Prince Napoléon Louis Bonaparte convenons et arrêtons ce qui suit.

Art I — Nous promettons et jurons sur notre honneur et sur le Saints évangiles de Nous aider l'un l'autre. Nous Charles Duc de Brunswick à rentrer en possession du Duché de Brunswick et à faire s'il se peut de toute l'Allemagne une seule Nation lui en donnant une constitution adaptée à ses moeurs à ses usus et au progrès de l'époque et Nous Prince Napoléon Louis Bonaparte à faire rentrer la France dans le plan tracé à la souveraineté Nationale dont elle a été privée en 1830 — et à la mettre à même de se prononcer librement sur la forme du Gouvernement qui lui convient de se donner.

Art II — Celui d'entre Nous qui le premier arriverait au pouvoir Suprême sous quelque titre que ce soit s'engage à fournir à l'autre en Armes et en Argent les secours qui lui sont nécessaires pour atteindre le but qu'il se propose et de plus à authoriser et faciliter l'enrôlement volontaire d'un nombre d'hommes suffisant pour l'exécution de ce projet.

Art III — Tant que durera l'exil qui pèse sur nous Nous nous engageons à nous aider réciproquement en toute occasion à fin de rentrer en possession de droit politiques qui nous ont été ravis et en supposant que l'un de nous puisse rentrer dans sa patrie l'autre s'engage à soutenir la cause de son Allié par tout les moyens possibles. —

Art IV — Nous nous engageons à n'outre à ne jamais promettre faire et signer aucune renonciation Abdication ou desistent de nos droits politiques ou civiles mais au contraire à nous consulter et à nous soutenir en frères dans tout les circonstances de notre vie. —

Copy of Draft for Treaty of Alliance between Louis Napoleon and the Duke of Brunswick

Art V. Si par la suite et lorsque jouissant de notre pleine liberté nous jugerons convenables d'apporter au présent traité des modifications dictés soit par notre position respective soit par l'intérêt commun Nous nous engageons à les faire d'un commun accord et à réviser les dispositions de cette convention dans tout ce qu'elles contient défectueux par suite des circonstances sous lesquelles elle a été fait

Approuver les traité ci dessus

Fort de Ham
25 Juin 1845

Napoléon Louis Bonaparte

I hereby declare that this is a correct Copy of a Treaty made by His Imperial Highness The Prince Napoleon Louis Bonaparte & signed in my presence when a Prisoner of Ham in France in the Year 1845.

T. B. Smith

On the alleged opportunities of escape before 1845.

Dr Veron. *Nouveaux mémoires d'un bourgeois de Paris.* 1866.
A. Mansfield. *Op. cit.* Bk. I.
Sir Henry Drummond-Wolff. *Some Notes of the Past.* 1891.

On the negotiations for Louis Napoleon's release.

Odilon Barrot. *Mémoires.* Vol. III. 1875.
S. Poggioli. *Napoléon-Louis Bonaparte retenu en prison.* Simple récit. 1846.
    Barrot and Poggioli were both actively concerned in these negotiations; the latter's brochure was written before Louis Napoleon's escape.

On the treaty with the Duke of Brunswick.

Orsi. *Recollections, op. cit.*
Drummond-Wolff. *Op. cit.*
T. H. Duncombe. *Life of T. S. Duncombe, M.P.* 1868. Unreliable.
    Orsi himself acted as ambassador. Mr G. T. Smith, who accompanied him to Ham, was afterwards T. S. Duncombe's secretary. On the opposite page is reproduced his signed and attested copy of Louis Napoleon's original draft of the treaty.

Louis Napoleon's subsequent relations with the Duke.

Sartorius. *Le duc de Brunswick.* 1875.

On the escape.

The official evidence is contained in the report of Dr Conneau's trial at Péronne, for which see—

'Tribunal correctionel de Péronne, évasion du prince.'—*Gazette des Tribunaux*, 1846.
*(F. T. Briffault.) *The Prisoner of Ham: Authentic details of the Captivity and Escape of Prince Napoleon Louis.* 1846.
    This book was written under Louis Napoleon's direction: in letters to M. Degeorge, editor of the *Progrès du Pas-de-Calais*, and to Vieillard, June 1, 1846, he gives some further details as to his own escape.

GARNIER. *Papiers et Correspondance de la Famille Impériale.* 1871.

Contains Thélin's detailed bill for the prince's disguise, the total cost of which was 25f. 25c.

PIERRE HACHET-SOUPLET. *Louis-Napoléon, prisonnier au fort de Ham,* 1893, adds some interesting details. The author is the grandson of Calixte Souplet, editor of the *Guetteur de St Quentin,* one of Louis Napoleon's republican journalist friends at Ham. The book is unreliable.

On the assertion that Louis Philippe connived at the escape, see footnote to text, p. 242.

England, 1846-7.

As above, for England 1838-40. See also—

J. FORSTER. *Walter Savage Landor: A Biography.* 1869. Vol. II.

On Louis Napoleon's activities in 1848.

COUNT ORSI's *Recollections,* and ODILON BARROT's *Mémoires,* quoted above.

(A. D. VANDAM.) *An Englishman in Paris.* 2 vols. 1892. Contains, though not at first hand, Persigny's account of his part in the events of 1848. He accompanied Louis to Paris in February. This account disagrees in many details with that given by Orsi.

ARISTIDE FERRIÈRE. *Révélations sur la propagande Napoléonienne faite en* 1848 *et* 1849 *pour servir à l'histoire secrète des élections du Prince Louis-Napoléon Buonaparte.* Turin. 1863.

Ferrière was one of Louis' confidential agents at this time. He considered that his services had not been adequately rewarded, and wrote his book to show their importance. It contains information of real value, but certainly exaggerates Ferrière's own rôle. It was he who hastened to Louis on June 13 to announce the crisis of his affairs in Paris.

*ANDRÉ LEBEY. *Louis-Napoléon Bonaparte et la Révolution de* 1848. 2 vols. 1907-8.

In the year 1848 the biography of Louis Napoleon becomes merged in the history of

France, and from this time onwards, though the evidence is still unsatisfactory in some respects, there is at least an abundance of material for all the public actions and utterances of the prince. Of the works on the Second Republic, the most useful in this connexion is perhaps

LORD NORMANBY. *A Year of Revolution in Paris.* 1856.

For the general history of this year—

LAMARTINE. *Trois mois au pouvoir.* 1848.
LOUIS BLANC. *Histoire de la révolution de* 1848. 2nd ed. 1870.
VERMOREL. *Les hommes de* 1848. 1869.
STERN, DANIEL. *Histoire de la Revolution de* 1848. 2 vols. 1850.
*STEIN, L. *Geschichte der socialen Bewegung in Frankreich.* 2 vols. 1850.

Louis Napoleon's writings, until the year 1848.

Rêveries politiques. Un projet de Constitution. May 1832.
Considérations politiques et militaires sur la Suisse. July 1833.
Manuel d'Artillerie. November 1835.
Des idées Napoléoniennes. July 1839.
Fragments Historiques. May 1841.
Analyse de la question des sucres. August 1842.
Projet de Loi sur le recrutement de l'armée. 1843.
Extinction du Paupérisme. May 1844.
Réponse du Prince Napoléon-Louis à M. de Lamartine. August 1844.
Canal of Nicaragua; or, a project to connect the Atlantic and Pacific Oceans by means of a Canal. By N. L. B. 1846.
Études sur le passé et l'avenir de l'artillerie. 2 vols. 1846.

All the works enumerated above were published separately at the dates mentioned; it is worthy of note that many of them had run through several editions, and been translated into several languages before 1848; in other words, it is clear that they had attained a considerable circulation before their author had attained a position which would account for their sale.

The above list does not include essays of Louis Napoleon which made their appearance in reviews. Of these the most important were—

'Examen de la théorie physique et de la théorie purement chimique de la pile voltaique,' published (May 1843) in the *Comptes rendus de l'Académie des sciences*, vol. xvi., pp. 1180, 1181.

'Quelques mots sur Joseph-Napoléon Bonaparte' (September 1844), in the *Revue de l'Empire*.

Besides these more important writings, the prince produced during his imprisonment at Ham a considerable quantity of occasional articles, in which he treated of almost every aspect of French political life; *e.g.*, among his writings in 1843 were articles on 'The Military Organisation of France,' 'The Clergy and the State,' 'Of Governments and their Sustenance,' 'Peace or War,' 'The Duties of the Opposition,' 'The Emperor's Opinion on the Relations of France and the European Powers,' 'Reforms to be desired in our Parliamentary Institutions,' 'The Treatment of Negroes,' 'Of Individual Liberty in England,' 'Espartero and the Conservatives,' 'Recruiting for the Army,' and 'The Destiny of Empires.'

The papers to which Louis Napoleon contributed during his imprisonment were the

Guetteur de St Quentin; Progrès du Pas-de-Calais,

and less frequently to

Le Commerce, La Paix, La Revue de l'Empire, Le Journal de Maine-et-Loire, Journal du Loiret, Almanach populaire de la France.

For a consideration of Louis Napoleon's early writings in the light of his subsequent policy, see

M. G. DE MOLINARI. *Napoléon III, publiciste.* Brussels. 1861.

APPENDIX C

This essay, on the profound effects upon Louis Napoleon's later policy of the prolonged and brooding study of his uncle's career which he made during his early years of exile, originally appeared in a special Supplement of *The Times*, published on the centenary of Napoleon's death.

No estimate of the historical significance of Napoleon can be complete which ignores one necessary consequence of his greatness. Great men, like great movements, have their reactions; they leave a negative as well as a positive legacy to their successors. They influence not only by attraction, but by repulsion; for the only true denial of greatness is indifference. That denial at least Napoleon never suffered, but even in France he has not wholly escaped the tribute of opposition. The century that followed his death has seen not only imitations and revivals of his policy, but also some definite and deliberate deviations from it. It is the function of the present article to suggest that of these deliberate deviations some of the most important have remained unrecognised, by occurring precisely where they might least have been expected— under the régime which has been regarded as one palpable piece of imitation, the Second Empire itself.

Of the innumerable differences between the third Napoleon and the first, the most relevant in this connection is unfortunately the least recognised. The one distinction between the Emperors which has escaped the notice of historians is their fundamentally divergent attitude towards history. Not only because it has been ignored, but because it is important, a word must be said on this divergence here.

To Napoleon history was primarily a storehouse of useful material: an arsenal which might provide an orator with arguments, a legislator with precedents, or a governor in a hurry with excuses for his haste. He did not disdain the contemporary cult of historical parallels; but save in extreme youth he used such parallels carelessly and with a proper contempt. His historical reading, though ravenous, was not really profound; but he was the master and not the servant of such historical knowledge as he had. In providing the wherewithal to adorn a proclamation or illustrate a dispatch, classical allusions might be all very well; but Napoleon was the last man living to be dictated to by the dead. The great figures of history had indeed their function and their service; they could adorn the triumph of a greater than them all. No robe of past magnificence caught his eye or fancy but Napoleon would don it airily, and strut in it for as many paces as might show how far better than its owner he could have worn it if he would. Cæsar, Hannibal, Charlemagne, Alexander, Justinian, Christ—each in turn received this passing token of esteem. But not Cæsar himself—whom of them all Napoleon most nearly

APPENDIX C 375

adopted as his permanent prototype—not Cæsar himself was suffered to have more. *Caesaris Caesari* : and to the part of his favourite model Napoleon did not grudge such momentary sincerity as even great acting demands. But even here he did not allow his dramatic instincts to make him the puppet of his own play. Not for a moment was he deflected from any course he would pursue by the supposed necessities of the part, by the need of repeating or avoiding any feature of the past. What served his turn he used; what he had no use for he flung unceremoniously aside. Had Imperious Cæsar shown signs of taking real control of the stage, he would soon have been reminded of the stop-gap nature of his present business.

Very different was the effect of history upon Napoleon III. He too had read history, and read it widely; but always *au grand sérieux*. For the serious study of it he had some facilities which his uncle lacked—comparative leisure and a considerable knowledge of modern languages. With a good working knowledge of English and Italian, he was as much at home in German as in French (more so, said the unkind). In all these languages, and on all Napoleon's heroes, he had read conscientiously. Of one he wrote, and of more than one he began to write, the biography. But through them all, and more than them all, he had studied the career of the great Napoleon himself, to whom and from whom for his nephew all history flowed.

Now it has generally been assumed that Louis Napoleon's prime object in his study of the institutions of the First Empire was the achievement of as exact a reproduction of them as possible in the Second. In this object it is conceded that he attained a certain superficial and temporary success. But ultimately his attempts to ape the grandeurs of Napoleon are held to have been fatal to a monarch who lacked alike the ability and the resources of his great original. This theory I hold to be psychologically unsound, as based on a misapprehension of Louis Napoleon's entire mental processes; internally unproven, as at variance with his published writings; and intrinsically improbable, as out of harmony with the general conception of history current in his day. What is more important, I believe the assumption to be profoundly misleading, if it is adopted, as it commonly has been adopted, as a clue by which to follow the elusive Louis in the labyrinthine maze of Second Empire diplomacy.

It is obviously impossible within the compass of this article to submit so complicated a subject as Louis Napoleon to any process of post-mortem psycho-analysis. Suffice it therefore to say that both the simplicity and the humility of his traditional rôle are foreign to his character. But from his published writings alone it would not be difficult to show that he rather plumed himself on being no mere copyist. All his early publications, it must be remembered, were of the nature of Imperialist and anti-Orleanist propaganda: precisely the most difficult vehicle in which to convey even the gentlest criticism of the Emperor. But even in the most directly propagandist of them all —*Des idées Napoléoniennes*—Louis makes bold to indicate that servile imitation is unwise even of so great a man as Napoleon. Rather adroitly, in launching the dart he shields himself behind a saying of the Emperor himself. " History," he quotes Napoleon as saying, " can yield us many lessons, but few models." And from this he goes on to denounce detailed imitation of any past government. " As well," he remarked, " might a general giving battle on the scene of one of Napoleon's victories suppose that he could repeat the Emperor's success by the mere process of repeating his manœuvres." In fact, " one *cannot* copy the past, because imitations cannot be relied on to produce resemblances." Hence " En lisant l'histoire des peuples, comme l'histoire des batailles, il faut en tirer des principes généraux " without servile imitation. " I do not systematically defend all the Emperor's actions," he wrote to Lamartine in 1843, " I explain them." " Servile copies," he wrote elsewhere in the same year, " produce results which are invariably pernicious." And on this point his speeches as President echo the sentiment of his pamphlets as pretender : " Ce n'est pas la copie mesquine d'un passé quelconque qu'il s'agit de refaire " was his characteristic utterance on the first anniversary of his presidential election.

If the accepted theory could survive express repudiations such as these, there are other and more general grounds for rejecting it. The whole tone and temper of Louis Napoleon's writings show that as an historian he took himself most seriously. Now historians of his day were generally engaged in justifying themselves to a utilitarian generation by setting up their subject as a school for statesmen ; the gloomy fiction that history is a science had not yet delivered men from the folly of supposing it to be a philosophy. And Louis Napoleon had all the second-rate thinker's pathetic eagerness to be abreast of the latest thought of his age. How completely he was *dans le mouvement* historically, the preface of his *Julius Cæsar* sufficiently shows. The " lessons of history" are to be learned. " Political and social changes " are to be " analysed philosophically." The particular brand of the stuff in this case may be described as a variant on the Great Man theory—the Great Man beset by Pitfalls. It is wrong to " impute mean motives to great men "; but equally wrong to attribute to them " superhuman foresight."

Given then a monarch who boasted in prison that he had " meditated profoundly on the causes and effects of revolutions,"[1] a monarch who from his throne assured his subjects that he would never forget the lessons of history,[2] we are forced, I would submit, to discard to some extent the orthodox conception of his policy. Whatever that policy was, it was not intentionally a policy of mere imitation. For missionary purposes it might be presented as the old gospel; but it was in fact at the least a deliberately revised version. True, Louis had lived long with ghosts, and called up many spirits of the past. But always it was that he might ask them questions. " Was this the lesson or that ? " Certainly there *was* a lesson, if one could only discover it. And in

[1] Ham. *Fragments Historiques*, 1841. Here is a typical reflection on the subject, from an article published two years later. " Qu'ont donc gagné les Français à leur révolutions ? Nous y avons gagné une seule chose, *l' expérience.*"
[2] March 1856.

APPENDIX C 379

the long run one always could discover it, else what was the use of being a philosophic historian ? One ghost, till it had answered one question, Louis could least of all let go. Poring perpetually over every act and utterance of the Emperor, he faced, I believe, the question—as how indeed could he not face it ?—" Why, then, did this hero fail ? " The more one deified Napoleon, the more that question cried aloud for an answer. And it too finally found one : found it in a series of avoidable mistakes into which the uncle had been betrayed, and against which the nephew must at all costs be on his guard. These particular faults it became his fixed idea to avoid. For his boast to his senators was pitifully true ; once he had learned a lesson of history he could never forget it. More easily might Mrs Micawber desert her husband, than Louis Napoleon the Lessons of History. From this fidelity at least he allowed himself no lapses ; and virtue here was its own punishment. For the worst of all the nephew's blunders were efforts to avoid the blunders of the uncle. The accepted view contrives to reverse quite ingeniously the actual sequence of affairs. The alleged cause of Louis Napoleon's undoing was his attempt to imitate Napoleon's successes. What really undid him was his endeavour to avoid Napoleon's failures. Elements of imitation there were, but it was not these that were fatal. The old bottles might have served, but the new wine burst them.

These essays in avoidance were relatively unimportant, so far as Louis Napoleon's domestic policy was concerned ; it was not, he considered, the internal policy of the Emperor that was at fault. " L'édifice à l'intérieur," he wrote of the First Empire, " était solide : ce n'est pas de l'intérieur qu'est venu le choc qui l'a renversé." But from the foreign and the colonial, from the ecclesiastical and the economic policy of Napoleon he reacted deliberately, and on the whole disastrously.

The Second Empire may almost be said to differ from the First in having a colonial policy at all. Napoleon himself, for all his protestations, had eventually allowed his energies to be confined to Europe, had sold Louisiana for a song, and failed to compensate France for the loss of Canada or India. Therefore the new Napoleon would range from China to Peru, would endow his country with a further India in Siam, with a more fertile Canada in Mexico. And so France, which in the Seven Years' War had lost the New World in the Old, proceeded as gratuitously to lose the Old World in the New. A century earlier she had dissipated her energies in Europe at a time when all things were possible in the colonies. Now she was to be entangled in colonial adventure at the moment when all things were possible on the Continent. In 1866 the mere presence of her Mexican armies on the Rhine might have won France a province without a war. And in 1870 French troops were still suffering from surreptitious economies designed to conceal the true costs of that forlorn adventure in world-policy.

Because Napoleon had let himself be limited by his coast-line, his nephew launched out disastrously into the deep. But he could never have embarked upon his colonial excursions at all, had not history first dictated to him a far more fundamental innovation. Which was it of all his foes whose hostility had been most fatal to the Emperor ? Loud and clear came the answer of history. It was England whose ships had swept his navies from the seas, whose pugnacity inspired, whose treasure armed, whose endurance rendered invincible even in defeat that unending series of coalitions which learned at last how not to be defeated. In the end the side England was on, won. Therefore the uncle's foe should be the nephew's friend ; not on this rock also should the Second Empire perish. Other causes contributed to Louis Napoleon's desire for the English alliance : his genuine liking for the English people, and his natural instinct as the most liberal monarch on the Continent. France and England he sincerely believed, and in the first year of his presidency publicly proclaimed, to be " the two most civilized nations in the world." But the alliance was something more permanent and imperative than a natural impulse or a personal predilection : it was a Lesson of History.

As such it probably did Louis Napoleon less harm than any other that history taught him. For it helped him as much in the first half of his reign as it misled him in the second. It was qualified throughout by another historical inference, deduced this time from the reign of Louis Philippe : that subservience to England was only less fatal than fighting her. Until 1856, at any rate, the alliance was wholly beneficial to France. After that date it was largely vitiated by the most important of its own results. By dint of the alliance, France had become once more the strongest power on the Continent. But to be the strongest Continental Power was automatically to be the natural rival of England. And, once France had succeeded Russia in that position, it was French aggrandisement which it became England's chief anxiety to prevent. It was in spite of the wrath of England—and of England alone among the Great Powers—that Louis Napoleon recovered for France her well-earned frontier of the Alps. But long before the annexation of Savoy, it was clear that only by complete abnegation of natural ambitions could he hope to retain the English alliance. Of this fact he had frequent proof. Vainly, for example, as unpublished papers of our Foreign Office show, he endeavoured to anticipate by nearly half a century the Anglo-French Agreement of 1904: proposing that England in return for adequate colonial compensations elsewhere should allow France " to extend her African possessions towards Morocco." Vainly he sought to commend the proposal by urging that "the two countries should forget their former rivalries: instead of being jealous of each other's prosperity each should see in the progress of the other a source of advantage to itself." In all such overtures he was rebuffed. "If," he was told by our Ambassador, "his Majesty could guarantee that all future sovereigns of France would have the same amicable feelings for England that animated his own breast, then indeed we might be asked to look upon the aggrandizement of France without jealousy or apprehension. But that could not be."[1] This was a perfectly clear intimation that

[1] F.O. Paris. Cowley to Clarendon "Most Confidential," 28th December 1856.

the friend of to-day could only be treated as the foe of to-morrow, and that nothing less than a complete surrender of French territorial ambitions could keep the alliance in being. On such terms at that time the English alliance was not worth purchasing ; nor was Louis Napoleon really prepared to pay quite so exorbitant a price for it. On this point Ollivier's defence of his master is neither true nor even necessary : it was no mere " aberration " that impelled him to put more space between Paris and Prussia. But though the facts of geography forbade the price which might have restored substance to the alliance, the lessons of history equally forbade the complete surrender of its shadow. Not by the uncle's methods must the uncle's policy be pursued. To the nephew now, at the height of his power, came the offer of alliance with Russia : a liberal Tsar, sympathetic to Louis Napoleon, had succeeded Nicholas as ruler of a country which had no objection to seeing its ally strengthened, and was even willing to co-operate in a French advance towards the Rhine. That in the last decade of the Second Empire such an alliance was the true policy of France even an Englishman may now be allowed to suspect. Certainly it was the policy demanded by any further pursuit of the natural frontiers. But it was a policy precluded by the lessons of history. Had not Napoleon I at the height of *his* power thought to ignore England and divide the world with Russia ? How then could a second Tilsit with a second Alexander hope to attain a better fate ? The most crazy designs were safe when they had a precedent of Napoleonic success ; the return from Elba justified not only Strasbourg but Boulogne. But the wisest schemes were foolishness when the Napoleonic precedent was failure: where Napoleon I had burnt his fingers Napoleon III dreaded the fire. And so in this matter it was left to the Republic to revert too late to the tradition of Napoleon.

In rejecting the Russian alliance, Napoleon III had refused the most obvious road towards any material strengthening of his eastern frontier. But it was still possible for him to preserve that frontier intact, or even perhaps to better it in detail. So strong were the cards which he had accumulated as a hale man in the first half of his reign, that it took him ten years even as a sick one to throw them all away. On the very eve of the Franco-German War he still held in his hand the elements of a substantial combination, the draft of a triple alliance between France and Austria and Italy. Russia, it is true, was by this time hopelessly estranged; but the forces even of this new combination were by no means despicable. Nothing was wanting to render the alliance operative save Louis' assent to the withdrawal of his French garrison from Rome. On this Victor Emmanuel insisted; but here Napoleon III was powerless to say "Yes." For the first Napoleon had let himself be led into a final quarrel with the Pope. It was a mistake, as the event proved. "Qui mange du Pape en meurt," at least if he bites too often. Therefore Napoleon III would always stop short of any final rupture with the Vatican; till stopping short he lost the gratitude of Italy, to which an overwhelming service had entitled him. Time and again already the logic of his policy had led him to the very brink of a breach; time and again, at the brink of it, he had drawn back: no, to go farther would be to ignore a Lesson of History. Having observed that lesson all these years, it was not to be supposed that he was going to forsake it now. And so, without allies, but with the Lessons of History intact, he headed his country alone to its doom.

By avoiding Napoleon's capital error in regard to England, his nephew could congratulate himself on having avoided also the necessity of any exclusive concentration upon Europe. But besides the loss of the colonies, history showed two other consequences even more unpleasant which had resulted to Napoleon from his struggle with England. That struggle had not only cost him the New World; it had turned against him both the heart and the stomach of the Old. It was England who had raised up against Napoleon the spirit of nationalism in Spain, and it was against England that Napoleon had devised his suicidal Continental System. Here again, as in the matter of colonial expansion, Louis Napoleon was careful to avoid not only the cause but the results of his uncle's failure; and not only to avoid the results, but to reverse them. Not to repeat mistakes was only half the lesson; forces which had worked against the First Empire must be made to work in favour of the Second. Napoleon I had framed the most disastrous system of Continental Protection; therefore Napoleon III should be the greatest continental practitioner of Free Trade. Against the uncle had been ranged the unsuspected forces of nationality. Therefore of nationality the nephew would be the first royal protagonist. The storm that had overthrown the one the other would ride; the opponents of the new Empire should find their old thunder stolen and turned against themselves.

Louis Napoleon's experiment in Free Trade was comparatively unimportant. But such as it was it must be pronounced a failure. The Commercial Treaty with England in 1860 has the distinction of being the only step in his internal administration which did him permanent harm in the provinces. For though it conciliated some interests, it alienated more; and the reversal of it by the Third Republic was both prompt and popular. In fact, this particular reaction from the policy of the First Empire was hardly even attempted except by the founder of the Second. As such it proved a minor addition to his internal troubles, without any compensating benefit abroad. For England, after pocketing the treaty patronizingly as a somewhat clumsy bribe, proceeded the more carefully to show herself unbribable.

Napoleon III's advocacy of Free Trade was only a characteristic episode in his career. But his championship of the principle of nationality was lifelong, and fundamental to his entire policy. The topic is, in fact, too large for even summary treatment here. Fortunately it is in a sense less relevant than most of his minor reversals of imperial policy. For though it was a reaction from Napoleon's practice, it was also a compliance with Napoleon's preaching. Napoleon, in the pursuit of his own aims, had done some indirect and unintentional service to the cause of German and Italian unity. From St Helena an insincere and successful apologetic represented these services as fragments of a deliberate and gracious design, conceived in altruism and frustrated by defeat. It was Napoleon's most proper penalty that his successor also was numbered among his disciples ; that when he preached altruism falsely his own nephew believed in him. Dante could have devised no more fitting torment for Napoleon in Hell, than that (from the circle reserved for government propagandists) he should have lifted up his eyes and seen his nephew taking him seriously. For no country, in the ordinary profit and loss accounts of calculators and economists, had more to lose or less to gain from nationality than France. No ruler knew this better than Napoleon, and none would have been in fact more careful than he to set the interests of his own Empire before the aspirations of its potential rivals. But what was in him a pose was in his nephew a passion ; and to the cause of Italy, of Roumania, and even of Poland Napoleon III postponed solid advantages which a truly Napoleonic policy might have extracted from his dominant position after 1856. That such sacrifices, in serving Europe, may prove in the long run to have served his country also, may well be the hope of all lovers of poetic justice ; and more especially of those who acknowledge gratefully, even at the hands of the Napoleons, some unexhausted fragment of God's deeds through the French.

INDEX

[In the case of contemporaries of Louis Napoleon mentioned in the following index, dates of birth and death have been given, wherever it seemed possible that they might be of service for the purpose of identification, or convenient for the sake of reference. Occasionally brief introductory notices are inserted in this place after the names of Louis Napoleon's more obscure adherents, of whom but casual mention has been made in the text. The abbreviation *n.* in the index indicates that the reference is to a footnote.]

ABBOT, J. S. C., (1805-1877) 365
Acar, M., 216, 217
Adriatic, 62
Aix, 35
Aladenize, Lieut., (*b.* 1813) 172, 173, 176-180, 194
Alexander I, Tsar, (1777-1825) 3, 9, 10, 30, 34
Algeria, 291
Algiers, 54
Alsace, 100, 105
America, 122*n.*, 123, 124, 229, 257, 261, 265, 339, 341
—— United States of, *see* United States
Analyse de la question des sucres, 209, 210, 371
Ancona, 71, 72, 81
Andromède, the, 126, 127
Antibes, 76
Antomarchi, F., (*c.* 1760-1838) 357
Arago, M., (1786-1853) 217, 348
Arenenberg, château of, purchased by Hortense, 37; becomes her home, 40; Louis Napoleon's departure from, 143, 344; mentioned, 44, 46, 85, 98, 106, 112, 139, 140
Arese, Count François [*b.* at Milan 1805, met Louis Napoleon at Rome 1826, spent the year 1831 with him at Arenenberg, served in Foreign Legion in Algeria 1832] accompanies Louis Napoleon on visit to England in 1833, 335; joins him in America in 1837, 131; on his relations with the Carbonari, 362
Army and Navy Club, 258
Artillery, Louis Napoleon on, *see Manuel d'Artillerie*, and *Passé et l'avenir de l'Artillerie*
Athenæum, the, 164, 165
Augsburg, 38, 44, 45, 47, 48, 50

Auguste de Beauharnais, *see under* Beauharnais
Aumale, Duc d', (1822-1897) 363
Austerlitz Barracks, the, at Strasburg, 108, 110-112
Austria, reactionary policy of, under Metternich, 10, 11; prospective share in Polignac's redivision of Europe, 54*n.*; intervenes to quell the Italian insurrection, 68, 69, 71; supports French demand for Louis Napoleon's expulsion from Switzerland, 148; acts with England against France in the Eastern question, 170

BADEN, 37, 38
Baden, Grand Duchess of, *see* Beauharnais, Stephanie de
Baden, Grand Duke of, (1786-1818) 36
Baden-Baden, 105, 106
Baillehache, M. de, 360
Baltimore, 342
Barins, De, 356, 360
Barrot, Ferdinand, (1806-1883) 200
Barrot, Odilon, (1791-1873) 230, 231, 275, 351, 369, 370
Bastide, M., 347
Bataille, Martial - Eugène, [civil engineer, *b.* 1815] 176, 193
Bath, 256
Bavaria, 37, 38, 54*n.*
Bayonne, 21
Beauharnais, Auguste de, Duke of Leuchtenberg, (1810 - 1835) 95*n.*, 338
—— Eugène, (1781-1824) 24, 37, 46, 47, 193
—— Hortense, de, (1783-1837) gives birth to Louis Napoleon, 20, 21; marriage to Louis of Holland, 22; character, 24; political and personal

quarrels with her husband, 25; liaison with Flahaut, 26; birth of Morny, *ibid.*; alleged liaison with Verhuel, 27; with Decazes, 360; her action in 1814, 29; visited by Frederick William of Prussia, 29; befriended by Alexander of Russia, 30; receives the estate of St Leu as a duchy, 31; her husband's annoyance at her use of this title, 67; banished from France, 34; at Aix and Geneva, 35; reaches Constance, 36; visits Berg, 37; expelled from Constance, *ibid.*; goes to Augsburg, 38; settles at Arenenberg, 40; gives Louis Napoleon leave to serve in the Eastern war, 52; goes with him to Italy, 61; present at a family conclave in Rome, 64; fails to dissuade her sons from joining the Italian movement, 65; at Florence, 66; overtakes Louis Napoleon at Pesaro, 70; smuggles him out of Ancona, 72; brings him safely to France, 73-76; interview with Louis Philippe at Paris, 80, 81; arrival in England, 83; returns to Switzerland, 85; parting with Louis Napoleon before Strasburg, 107; hastens to Paris to intercede for her son's life, 122n., 126; illness of, 137; her farewell letter to her son, 138, 247; proposed operation on found impossible, 139; her death, 140; influence of her education on her son, 141; burial at Malmaison, 142; amount of her estate, 159; Louis Napoleon's letters to, 332, 333, 335, 337-343; her memoirs, 361

Beauharnais, Josephine, (1763-1814) 17, 21, 26, 28, 209
—— Stephanie de, 36, 47, 49, 52
Beaumont-Vassy, de, (*b.* 1813) 366
Beauregard, Countess of, *see* Miss Howard
Beetroot sugar, Louis Napoleon's pamphlet on, *see Analyse de la question des sucres*
Belgium, 54n., 62, 84, 94, 245
Béranger, P. J., (1780-1857) 86, 215, 358
Berg, 37
Berg, Grand Duke of, *see* Bonaparte, Napoleon-Louis
Berlin Decrees, (November 1806) 23
Berne, 90, 143, 149, 150, 152
Berryer, P. A., (1790-1868) 189, 193, 194, 346
Bertrand, Abbé, 40

Bingham, Hon. D. A., 366
Birmingham, 172
Bismarck, Prince, (1815-1898) 230
Blanc, Louis, (1811-1882) visits Louis Napoleon at Ham, 218; his account of the Prince, 219, 220, 221n., 365, 368; mentioned, 347, 371
Blessington, Lady, (1789-1849) 363
Bocher, Charles, 366
Bocher, Mlle, 96
Bois-le-Comte, C. J. Edmond, Comte de, (*d.* 1863) 55n.
Bologna, 66, 69
Bonaparte, Charles Louis Napoleon, *see* Napoleon, Louis
—— Charles Napoleon Louis, [Duke of Berg, second son of King Louis] (1804-1831) 20; placed in legal custody of his father, 31; parted from his brother, 35; declines to intervene in 1830, 60; relations with Carbonari, 64; joins in the revolt of Bologna, 66; repels contingent of Papal troops, 67; cashiered, 68; his death, 70; Louis Napoleon on, 334; his final burial at St Leu, 265; account of, 362
—— Charlotte, [daughter of King Joseph, wife of Napoleon Louis] (1802-1839) 334
—— Eugène Louis Napoleon, Prince Imperial, *see under* Napoleon
—— Francis Charles Joseph, Duc de Reichstadt, *see under* Napoleon
—— Jerome, King of Westphalia, (1784-1860) 64, 66, 96, 97, 129, 199, 256, 309, 344
—— Joseph, King of Spain, (1768-1844) protests against the proclamation of Louis Philippe, 60; position under Napoleon's will, 76, 87, 88; introduces Persigny to Louis Napoleon, 98; Louis Napoleon visits him at London, 335; disowns Louis Napoleon after Strasburg, 132; upbraided by Louis, 133, 310, 343; his death, 216; Louis Napoleon's tribute to him, 216, 349, 372; mentioned, 255, 344
—— Prince Joseph Charles Paul Napoleon, [son of King Jerome, known as Prince Napoleon] (1822-1891) 96, 256, 257, 304, 309, 310
—— Letitia, [Madame Mère] (1750-1836) 338
—— Louis, King of Holland, (1778-1846) 20; marries Hortense de Beauharnais, 22; early career, 22; becomes King of Holland, 22;

abdicates, 23; retires to Toeplitz, 24; relations with his wife, 25; annoyance at her use of title Duchess, 67; absent at birth and baptism of Louis Napoleon, 27; did he tacitly or openly disavow his paternity of the child? 28, 358-360; awarded the custody of his elder son, 31; sends for him, 35; threatens to claim his younger son also, 40; friendly letter to him, 43; visited by Louis Napoleon, 45, 47; refuses to allow Louis to serve against Turkey, 52, 53; opposes his son's participation in the Italian insurrection, 66; protests against Louis Napoleon's treatment after Boulogne, 185; ill health, 226; misunderstanding between him and Louis Napoleon, 349; his part in the negotiation for Louis Napoleon's release, 227-229; Louis unable to visit him, 254; his death, 255, 266; his will, 27, 259, 264; his final burial at St Leu, 265, 266, 353; Louis Napoleon's letters to him, 332, 334-336, 338, 341, 343-345, 350, 351; Louis Napoleon's letters to, 46, 332, 334-336, 338, 341, 343-345, 350, 351
Bonaparte, Lucien, [Prince of Canino] (1775-1840) 310, 344
—— Mathilde, [daughter of King Jerome] (1820-1904) engaged to Louis Napoleon, 96; the engagement broken off, 129; married to Anatole Demidoff, 199, 200; Louis Napoleon on, 340, 341
—— Napoleon, *see* Napoleon
—— Napoleon Charles, [Prince Royal of Holland, eldest son of King Louis] (1802-1807) 20
—— Pierre, [son of Lucien] (1815-1881) 133, 310
Bosnia, 54*n*.
Boulogne, reasons for Louis Napoleon's expedition in 1840, 167-170; preliminaries, 171, 172; starting of the expedition, 173; the crossing, 174-175; landing at Wimereux, 176; arrival in the town, 177; the appeal to the 42nd, 178; repulse, 179-182; retreat, 183; capture, 184; |Louis Philippe's triumphal visit to, 186; trial of the prisoners, 187-194; sentence, 194, 195; its financial consequences, 236; Louis Napoleon on his failure at, 325; mentioned, 124, 232, 247, 284; evidence regarding the affair, 366-369

Brault, Eléonore, *see* Gordon, Mme
Briffault, F. T., 352, 369
Brunswick, Charles, Duke of, (1804-1873) 237, 238, 276, 277, 369
Brussels, 250, 251, 355
Bulgaria, 55*n*.
Bulkeley, James, 366
Burdett-Coutts, Baroness, (1814-1906) 261
Bure, M., (*b.* 1807) 259

CALAIS, 83*n*.
Camoscia, 73
Cannes, 76
Canning, George, (1770-1827) 11
Canning, Stratford, (1786-1880) his despatches quoted, 37, 38, 39
Capefigue, J. B. H. R., (1802-1872) 257
Capitole, Le, 160, 161, 367
Carbonari, the, 62, 64; Louis Napoleon's relations with, 362, 363
Cardigan, 7th Earl of, (1797-1868) 161
Carlsbad Decrees, (August 1819) 13
Carlton Gardens, Louis Napoleon's residence at, 157, 161, 166, 172*n*., 173
Carlton Terrace, Louis Napoleon's residence at, 157, 161, 258
Carlyle, Thomas, (1795-1881) 59
Carrousel, Place du, 31
Castille, H., 363
Castlereagh, Viscount, (1739-1821) 11, 38
Cavaignac, General Eugène, (1802-1857) threatens to take steps against Louis Napoleon, 284; appointed dictator, 291; his power continued after the June days, 291, 292; his character, 292; difficulty of his position, 293; repulse of his candidates in September, 294; opposes election of president by universal suffrage, 298; Assembly remain faithful to him, 300; opposes any special disqualifications of ex-royal families of France, 302; strength and weakness of his position as candidate for the presidency, 306, 307; Normanby on, 315; professes to believe that France was republican, 315, 316; insincerity of this profession, 316; his conduct as candidate, 317, 318; his last public triumph, 318, 319; his crowning blunder, 319; his defeat, 319; resigns his powers, 320
Cerrutti, Rue, 361
Champ de Mars, 31, 281
Changarnier, General, (*d.* 1877) 316

Charlemagne, Napoleon compared to, 12; Louis Napoleon on, 208
Charles X, (1757-1836) 54, 55, 119, 223n.
Chateaubriand, M. de, (1768-1848) 334, 363
Cheetham, Mr F. H., 357, 360, 365
Cherbourg, 176
Chislehurst, 261
Clarendon, 59
Civita Castellana, 67, 68
Cochelet, Mlle, (d. 1835) 48, 360
Col-Puygélier, Captain, (d. 1869) 173, 180, 181, 186
Conciergerie, the, Louis Napoleon imprisoned in, 185
Conneau, Dr, [b. Milan, 1803; secretary to King Louis, 1830; doctor of Queen Hortense] urges Louis Napoleon to return from America, 139; prints his Boulogne proclamations, 172n.; tried for his share in the Boulogne expedition, 193; sentenced to five years' imprisonment, 195; imprisoned with Louis Napoleon at Ham, 197, 198, 206; obtains permission to remain at Ham after his sentence had expired, 240; his share in the prince's escape, 241, 242, 246; his deception of Demarle, 251-253; trial and sentence of, 253, 254]; presented by Louis Napoleon with a London practice, 260
Considérations politiques et militaires sur la Suisse, published 89, 371, 336; favourable reception of, 89; possibility of a companion volume on the United States, 135; Louis Napoleon's intention in writing it, 324
Constance, 36, 37, 39, 40, 48, 51
Constant, Benjamin, (1767-1830) 17
Constantinople, 170
Cooper, J. F., (1789-1851) 134
Corfu, 71
Cornu, Mme Hortense, (b. 1812) 225, 301n, 333, 368
Corsica, 293
Cowley, 1st Earl, (1804-1884) his despatches quoted, 30n., 55n.
Cromwell, Oliver, 58, 59
—— Richard, 58; Louis Napoleon on, 351

DALMATIA, 54n.
Decazes, M., (1780-1860) 359
Degeorge, Frédéric, (1797-1854) 352, 369
Delaroâ, J., 363
Delord, Taxile, (b. 1815) 368

Demarle, Commandant, 199, 244, 251-253
Demidoff, Anatole, (b. 1812) 200
Desjardins, Alexander Prosper, [b. 1789, retired captain, veteran of the Napoleonic wars] tried for his share in the Boulogne landing, 192; acquitted, 194
Desportes, M., 347
Dijon, 34
Disraeli, Benjamin, (1804-1881) describes Louis Napoleon in *Endymion*, 157, 366; comparison of his career and Louis Napoleon's, 158-159
Drummond-Wolff, Sir Henry, 369
Duchatel, M., 351
Dufour, Colonel, (1787-1875) 51
Duncombe, T. H., 369
Duncombe, T. S., (1796-1861) 369
Dunkirk, 176
Duval, Georges, 83n., 361

Edinburgh Castle, the, 173, 174, 176
Edwards, H. Sutherland, 368
Eglinton Tournament, 162
Elba, 5, 29, 100, 168
England, generous attitude in 1815, 9; subsequent abandonment of continental liberalism, 11; comparison of growth of Parliamentarianism in England and in France, 57-59; correctness of its action in regard to the Swiss question of 1838, 155, 156; isolates France in 1840, 170; and the 'Spanish Marriages,' 269; effect of the Revolution of 1848 in, 277; Louis Napoleon on the Revolution of 1688 in, 202-205; on English procedure in Parliament, 213; Louis Napoleon's first visit to, (10th May to 7th Aug.1831)83-85; second visit, (Nov. 1832 to May 1833) 98, 133; third visit, (10th to 30th July 1837) 139-140, 343; fourth visit, (25th Oct. 1838 to 4th Aug. 1840) 156-173; fifth visit, (27th May 1846 to 23rd Sept. 1848) 254-294
Ermatingen, 142
Eugène, Prince, *see* Beauharnais, Eugène
Eugénie, Empress, (1826-1920), 53

FAENZA, 71
Favre, Jules, (1809-1880) 286
Fazy, James, (1796-1878) 364
Fermé, Albert, 367
Ferrière, Aristide, [a banker, met Louis Napoleon 1846] 370
Fesch, Cardinal, (1763-1839) 64-66

INDEX 393

Feuillade, J. G. G. de, (1786-1880) 368
Fialin, *see* Persigny
Fieschi, (1790-1836) 185, 186, 319
Finkmatt Barracks, the, at Strasburg, 109, 115-120, 128
Flahaut, Comte de, (1785-1870) 26
Florence, 47, 62, 65-67, 69, 70, 185, 226, 228, 254, 261
Foligno, 67
Fontainebleau, 26
Forbes, Archibald, (1838-1900) 357
Forestier, M., (*b.* 1815) 173, 176
Forli, 69, 70
Forster, John, (1812-1876) 370
Fourmestraux, E., 365, 368
Fragments Historiques, 56n., 202-205, 371
France under the First Empire, 3; in 1814, 2, 29; during the Hundred Days, 4, 5, 31; under Louis XVIII, 54; under Charles X, 54, 55; in 1830, 56; compared and contrasted with England in 1688, 57-59; in 1831, 82; in 1836, 103, 122, 131; and the punishment of Laity in 1838, 145; opinion in regarding the Molé Government's treatment of Switzerland, 148; Louis Napoleon's increased importance in, 156; growth of Napoleonic cult in, 82, 163, 168; political isolation of in 1840, 169, 170; under Louis Philippe, 267-271; the February revolution in, 272; under the Provisional Government of 1848, 273-275; under the executive commission, 278-283; and the June days, 290-291; under Cavaignac, 291-293; and the constitution of 1848, 305; and the rival candidates for the Presidency, 306 - 309; and the Second Republic, 312-316
Franck-Carré, M., (1800-1861) 124, 193, 258
Franqueville, M. de, 104
Fraser, Sir William, (1816-1898) 242n., 243n., 366
Frederick William III, of Prussia, (1770-1840) 10, 29
Freiburg, 107

GALLIX, M., 356, 361
Galvani, M., [*b.* 1786, served under Murat in his Calabrian expedition, 1815] tried for his share in the Boulogne rising, 192; acquitted, 194
Garnier, 370
Gay, Delphine, *see* Girardin, Mme de
Geneva, 35, 98, 238n., 355

Genoa, 76
George Washington, the, 139
Girardin, Mme Émile de, (1805-1855) 363
Giraudeau, M. Fernand, 356, 359
Gisquet, M., (1792-1866) 363
Goethe, (1749-1832) 8
Gonnard, M. Phillippe, 358
Gordon, Eléonore, [née Brault at Paris 6th Sept. 1808, daughter of a captain of the Imperial Guard, made her début as a professional singer, Paris 1831, brought by Persigny to sing at Strasburg June 1836] wins over Colonel Vaudrey, 105; joins Louis Napoleon at Freiburg, 107
Gottlieben, 143, 344
Gourgaud, General, (1783-1852) 357
Graham, W., Mr, 359, 366
Granville, first Earl, (1773-1846) despatches quoted, 91n., 114n., 122, 125
Gravesend, 173
Greece, 55n., 71
Greenwich, 173
Gregory XVI, (1765-1846) 27, 63
Grenoble, 2, 112
Grey, Earl, (1802-1894) 83n.
Griscelli de Vezzani, M., 366
Guéronnière, A. de la, (*b.* 1816) 368
Guizot, (1787-1874) 56n., 102, 202, 268-272, 365
Guy, M., 356, 361

HACHET-SOUPLET, M., 358, 359, 370
Hague, The, 25
Halleck, Fitz-Greme, (1790-1867) 134
Ham, Fortress of, described, 196, 197; Louis Napoleon taken there after Boulogne, 184, 185; his return after his trial, 197; his rooms in, 198; his captivity at, 199-231; effects of imprisonment at on Louis Napoleon's character, 231-234; plans of escape from, 239-242; preliminaries of Louis Napoleon's escape from, 243-246; the escape, 247-254; evidence regarding Louis Napoleon's imprisonment at and escape from, 368-370
Hamilton, W., 185n.
Harryett, Elizabeth Anne, *see* Howard, Miss
Heckingen, 107
Herzegovina, 54n.
Holland, 54n., 156
—— Sir Henry, (1788-1873) 366
Holy Alliance, Treaty of, (26th Sept. 1815) quoted, 10; mentioned, 11

Hortense, Queen, *see under* Beauharnais
Hôtel de Ville, Paris, 56
Houssaye, M. Henri, 361
Howard, Miss, [Elizabeth Ann Haryett, assumed name of Howard] her relations with Louis Napoleon in London, 162; occasion of his quarrel with Kinglake, 162, 366; and of his breach with Miss Rowles, 261; [created Countess de Beauregard, 1853, married Clarence Trelawny, 1854, *d.* 1865]
Hugo, Victor, (1802-1885) 59, 86, 358

Idées Napoléoniennes, the, published, 163, 371; character of the pamphlet, 164; its large circulation, 165; Louis Napoleon's object in publishing, 325
Irving, Pierre M., 365
Irving, Washington, (1788-1859) 134, 365
Istria, Duke of, 226
Italy, attitude towards Napoleon, 63; alleged Bonapartist intrigues in, 64; insurrection of 1831 in, 60-69; Louis Napoleon's escape in disguise through, 70-76; significance of his participation in the rising, 76-78; permanence of his interest in the Italian cause, 60, 61, 77, 78, 86

JEROME, King, *see under* Bonaparte
Jerrold, Blanchard, (1826-1884) 322, 357, 362, 368
Joinville, Prince de, (1818-1900) 170
Joseph, King, *see under* Bonaparte
Josephine, Empress, *see under* Beauharnais

KHARTOUM, 170
King Street, St James, 258, 288, 294
Kinglake, A. W., (1809-1891), 162

LABORDE, Étienne, [*b.* 1782, fought under the Empire in Spain, Russia, Saxony, Belgium, and France; officer of the Imperial Guard, with Napoleon at Elba] tried for his share in the Boulogne expedition, 192; sentenced to two years' imprisonment, 195
Lacroix, Mlle, *see* Cornu, Mme
Lafayette, M., (1757-1834) 56
Laity, Armand, (*b.* 1809) joins Louis Napoleon, 105; takes part in the Strasburg rising, 113, 116; publishes his account of the rising, 144, 364; Louis Napoleon's object in causing its publication, 146, 324; his letter to, on the eve of the trial, 344, 345; trial and imprisonment, 144, 145, 187, 365; returns to France in June 1848, 284; ordered to be arrested, 285; the order rescinded, 286, 287
Lamartine, A. de, (1790-1869) 165, 216, 285, 286, 298, 299, 300, 319, 358, 371
Landor, Walter Savage, (1775-1864) 24, 370
Laplace, Louis Napoleon's warder at Ham, 250, 252
Las Cases, Marquis de, (1776-1842) 357
Lebas, Philip, (1794-1860) appointed tutor to Louis Napoleon, 41; his character, *ibid.*; opinion of his pupil, 43; his scheme of instruction, 43; left in sole charge of his pupil, 44; his system of education constantly interrupted, 44-46; dismissed by Hortense, 47; effects of his training, 48; his letters, 361
Lebey, M. André, 278*n.*, 356, 357, 360, 362, 370
Lecomte, Captain, 353
Lecomte, Elisée, 365
Ledru-Rollin, M., (1808-1874) 300*n.*
Leghorn, 349
Leneveu, M., 225
Leopold, I, King of the Belgians, (1790-1865) 84
Lepelletier, Felix, (1769-1837) 4*n.*
Lesseps, M. de, (1805-1894) 262
Lettres de Londres, 165, 166, 360, 361
Leuchtenberg, Duke of, *see* Beauharnais, Auguste de
Lille, 170, 172
Lombard, Jules, (*b.* 1809) 113, 120, 171, 177, 183, 193, 195, 365
London, 83, 98, 139, 156, 157, 172, 173, 215, 237, 254, 256, 257
Londonderry, Lord, (1778-1854) 229
Loreto, 72
Lorient, 126
Lorraine, 100
Louis XVIII, (1755-1824) 54
Louis Napoleon, *see under* Napoleon
Louis Philippe, King, (1773-1850) becomes King of the French, 56; his attitude towards the Italian revolutionaries of 1831, 68, 69; Louis Napoleon's appeal to, 79, 80; his reception of Queen Hortense, 80; urges speedy departure of her son, 81-83; offers her financial assistance, 84; receives news

INDEX

of the failure of the Strasburg rising, 101-103; his government's affected disdain of the attempt, 104, 105; decision not to bring Louis Napoleon to trial, 121-123; story of Louis Napoleon's promise to him that he would remain in America disproved, 124-126; gift of money to the prince, 127; his government fails to secure the conviction of Louis Napoleon's accomplices, 130, 131; annoyed at Louis Napoleon's return to Europe, 142; his government's attempt to procure the prince's expulsion from Switzerland, 143-154; its complete discomfiture, 155, 156; his concessions to the Napoleonic cult in restoring his effigy to the Vendôme column, 82; and his ashes to the Invalides, 168, 169; his government isolated and humiliated over the Eastern Question, 169, 170; visits Boulogne, 186, 187; Louis Napoleon compares him to the Stuarts, 203-205; his government's concessions to their prisoner, 207; his attitude in the negotiations for Louis Napoleon's release, 229-231; alleged complicity in Louis Napoleon's escape, 242-243n.; summary of his reign, 267-270; refuses reforms in 1847, 271; his abdication and flight, 272
Lowe, Sir Hudson, (1769-1844) 13
Lucca, 75
Lucerne, 150
Ludlow, Edmund, 59
Luxembourg, 54n.
Lytton, Bulwer, (1803-1873) 164

MACEDONIA, 55n.
Magnan, General, (1791-1865) 171, 172, 193
Mainz, Commission of, (1820) 13
Malmaison, 29, 30, 142, 361
Malmesbury, 3rd Earl of, (1807-1889) 50, 51, 225, 226, 363
Mannheim, 49
Mansfield, A., 356, 369
Manuel d'Artillerie, publication of, 90, 371; method and object of its distribution, 91, 92, 104, 324; Louis Napoleon prepares a new edition, 208, 224; preface quoted, 328.
Margate, 173
Maria, Donna, Queen of Portugal, (1819-1853) 94, 95n.
Marie Louise, (1771-1847) 26, 29, 31
Marienbad, 45, 47

Marlborough, 1st Duke of, 59
Massa, 76
Mathilde, Princess, *see under* Bonaparte
Maurin, A., 364
Maussion, Sub-lieutenant, 177, 178, 180, 182
Mehemet Ali, (1807-1865) 169, 170
Menotti, Ciro, (d. 1831) 66, 362
Mésonan, Le Duff de, [b. 1783, served with distinction in campaign of 1809; taken prisoner by the English, 1815; created officer of the Legion of Honour for bravery at the rising of Lyons, 1834; retired prematurely, 1837; wrote to the papers complaining of this treatment, 1838; received letter of condolence from Louis Napoleon, and became his ardent supporter, 1838] endeavours to win over General Magnan to Louis Napoleon, 171, 193; tried for his part in the Boulogne landing, 192; condemned to fifteen years' detention, 195
Metternich, Prince, (1773-1859) 10, 11, 255
Mexico, 262, 263
Milan, 335
Modena, 66
Molé, Count, (1781-1855) 122n., 146, 148, 153, 154, 156
Molinari, G. de, 372
Montauban, Bouffet de, [b. 1794, aide de camp to Prince Eugène, fought through Russian campaign and during the Hundred Days] conduct at trial after Boulogne, 192; sentenced to five years' detention, 195
Montebello, Duc de, (1801-1874) 143, 144, 153, 155
Montigny, M. de, 153n.
Montholon, General, (1782-1853) published his account of Napoleon's captivity, 357; tried for his part in the Boulogne landing, 198, 192; condemned to twenty years' detention, 194; imprisoned with Louis Napoleon at Ham, 197, 198, 240; pensioned by Louis Napoleon, 236; annoyed that the prince had not consulted him as to his escape, 245; Louis Napoleon's letter to, on his escape, 245, 351-352; his release, 245, 254
Morier, D. R., (1784-1877) his despatches quoted, 143, 144, 149, 150, 152, 153n., 155, 156n.
Morny, Duc de, (1811-1865) 27
Munich, 46

INDEX

Murat, Joachim, (1771-1815) 83*n*., 193
—— Achilles, son of above, (1801-1847) 85*n*.
—— Lucien, son of above, (1803-1878) 282

NAPOLEON, (1769-1821); congratulates Hortense on Louis Napoleon's birth, 21; attitude towards his brother Louis, 22, 23; remarriage, 26; apparent hopelessness of his position in 1814, 1; his unpopularity in France, 2; return to Paris in 1815, 31; farewell interview with his nephew, 32, 33, 360, 361; effect produced by his early success and final failure in 1815, 5; contrast between his position at Elba and at St Helena, 6-8; compared by his admirers to Marcus Aurelius, Alexander, Charlemagne, Christ, 12-13; his remark to Las Cases, 15; his re-statement of his own past, 16, 17; difficulties of his successor, 18, 19; death, 44, 342; contrasted with Cromwell, 57-59; with Pius IX, 7, 8, 13; sympathy of Italian nationalists with, 63; his effigy restored to the Vendôme column, 82; translated to Paris, 168, 169, 197; apostrophised by Louis Napoleon, 201, 202; Lamartine on, 216

Napoleon, Louis, (1808-1873); birth, 20, 361; baptism, 26; disputed paternity, 27, 28, 358-360; during the hundred days, 31; farewell interview with Napoleon, 32, 360, 361; banished from France, 34; parted from his brother, 35; at Constance, 36; visits Berg, 37; his home at Arenenberg, 40; his first tutor, 40, 41; described by Lebas, 42; rigorous discipline of, 42, 43; first communion, 43; education at Augsburg, 44; and the death of Napoleon, 44, 332; visits his father, 45; his studies interrupted, 46; faults of his education, 47, 48; romantic temperament, 49; appearance, 49; physical development, 50; athletic powers, 50, 51; military training at Thun, 51, 333; desires to serve against the Turks in 1829, 52; attitude regarding the July revolution, 60, 83, 273, 333; journey to Rome in 1830, 60, 62; present at family conference, 64; relations with the Carbonari, 64, 362; expelled from Rome, 65; joins the Italian insurgents, 66; enthusiastic reception, 67, 333; attacks Civita Castellana, 68; dismissed by the revolutionary leaders, 69; present at his brother's death, 70; illness at Ancona, 71; escape in disguise, 72; passage through Tuscany, 73; and Siena, 74; visits his brother's home, 75; grief at his death, 79, 334; reverses his signature in consequence, 77; enters France, 76; his permanent interest in Italy, 77, 78; letter to Louis Philippe, 80; his request refused, 83; illness and intrigue in Paris, 81; ordered to depart, 82; arrival in England, 83; supposed design on the Belgian crown, 84, 94; return to Arenenberg, 85; refusal to join the Polish insurrection, 85, 86; publishes the *Rêveries Politiques*, 87; and the Duke of Reichstadt, 87, 332; first assertion of his claims, 87; publishes the *Considérations sur la Suisse*, 89; receives civic rights from Thurgau and Switzerland, 89; made honorary captain of artillery, 90, 337; publishes the *Manuel d'Artillerie*, 90; methodical distribution of it, 91, 92; estimate of his own position in 1834, 99; and in 1835, 93; denies rumoured alliance with Queen of Portugal, 95; alleged matrimonial designs in Switzerland, 96; and in England, 260, 261; engagement to Princess Mathilde, 96, 97; the engagement broken off, 129; his attitude in regard to it, 199, 200, 340; meeting with Persigny, 98; preliminaries of Strasburg, 99, 100, 104-106; arrival at, 107; plan of operations, 108-110; reception by the 4th Artillery, 112; at the Finkmatt barracks, 116-118; conduct on this occasion, 128; arrest, 119; in prison, 121, 339; transported to the United States, 123-131; alleged promise to remain there, 124-126, 257, 258; journey, 127, 341; landing, 131; in New York, 132; favourable reception, 134; indignant at his uncle's repudiation of his conduct, 133, 310-311, 343; opinion of the United States, 135, 136; proposed tour abandoned, 137; letter to the president, 139; return to Europe, 139; arrival at

INDEX 397

Arenenberg, 140; his mother's death, 140; her influence on him, 141-142; his letters to her, 332, 333, 335, 337-343; at Gottlieben, 143, 344; French demands for his expulsion from Switzerland, 142-144, 146-156; popularity in Switzerland, 146, 147; causes the Laity pamphlet to be published, 146; object in doing so, 324; assumes responsibility for its publication, 146, 344, 345; elected deputy for Thurgau, 148; secret request for passports to England, 149; announces his voluntary withdrawal from Switzerland, 151; compact with the Swiss war party, 153; completely outmanœuvres French Government, 154; receives passports for England, 155; triumphant departure from Switzerland, 156; arrival in England, 156; described by Disraeli, 157; profuse expenditure, 159, 161; founds two newspapers, 160; his life in London, 161, 162; relations with Miss Howard, 162, 261; at the Eglinton Tournament, 162; charged with the Barbès' rising, 163; publishes the *Idées Napoléoniennes*, 163-165; described by Persigny, 165, 166; reasons for renewed attempt in 1840, 167-170; preliminaries of Boulogne, 171-173; the landing, 174-176; the attempt and its failure, 177-184; imprisoned at Ham, 184; at the Conciergerie, 185; trial by the Court of Peers, 187-194; sentenced to perpetual imprisonment, 195; return to Ham, 197; his quarters in the fortress, 198, 221n.; closely guarded, 199; address to the Emperor's manes, 201; scientific experiments, 202, 216, 217, 347; publishes *Fragments Historiques*, 203; obtains concessions from the Government, 207; proposed life of Charlemagne, 208; pamphlet in defence of beet-sugar industry, 209, 210; relations with republican press, 211, 212; articles in provincial journals, 213, 214; publishes the *Extinction du Paupérisme*, 215; replies to Lamartine's depreciation of Napoleon, 216; publishes an appreciation of King Joseph, 216, 349; and La Belle Sabotière, 217; visited by Louis Blanc, 218, 219; described by him, 220; visited by Henry Wikoff, 220, 221; effect of imprisonment on his spirits, 222, 223; on his health, 205, 223, 232; on his character, 232-234; laborious compilation of a history of artillery, 224, 225; visited by Lord Malmesbury, 226; institutes negotiations for his release, 226-230; refuses to ask the king's pardon, 231; advantage of the negotiation to him, 231; borrows money from the Duke of Brunswick, 237-239; preliminaries of escape, 241-246; escape, 247-250; arrival in England, 254; fails to obtain passports to visit his father, 254, 255; publishes History of Artillery, 256; meets Prince Napoleon, 257; life in London, 258-261; his Nicaraguan scheme, 229, 261-263; secret communications to the *Times*, 264, 276; letter on occasion of his father's funeral, 265; unprepared for the February revolution, 266, 267; hastens to Paris, 273; letter to Provisional Government, 274; return to England, 274; serves as special constable, 277, 278; difficulty of his position in 1848, 279, 280; elected by four departments, 283; propaganda in favour of, 284; arrest ordered by the Assembly, 285; validity of his election recognised, 286; letter to the President of the Assembly, 287; second letter and resignation, 288; consequences of this incident to, 289; Lord Normanby on, 289, 314, 315; resigns his seat for Corsica, 293; elected by five departments, 294; returns to Paris, 294, 295; takes his seat in the Assembly, 301; his reserve, 301, 303; his breakdown in the Assembly, 302; announces his candidature for the Presidency of the Republic, 304; his position strengthened by Cavaignac's unpopularity, 307; by the influence of his name, 307; by his past career, 308-312; by the unpopularity of the Republic, 312-316; behaviour as candidate, 317; elected president, 319; installed at the Elysée, 320; causes of his success, 321-323; his own reading of his early career, 323-325; elements of future weakness, 326-328; early letters quoted, 46, 67, 91-94, 99, 202, 211, 212, 222, 225, 228, 229, 254, 257, 258, 264, 265, 274, 276, 279, 280, 287, 288, 301,

398   INDEX

310, 323-325, 332-353; authorities for early life of, 355-372
Napoleon, Francis Charles Joseph, Duc de Reichstadt, (1811-1833) 26, 31, 59, 60, 76, 87, 332
—— Eugène Louis, Prince Imperial, (1856-1879) 53
—— all other members of the family, *see under* Bonaparte
Navarre, 29
Neckar, 49, 328
Nemours, Duc de, (1814-1896) 95*n*., 104
New York, 127, 132-135, 342
Ney, Marshal, (1769-1815) 361
Nicaragua Canal, 229, 261-263, 328, 371
Nicholas, Tsar, (1796-1855) 30*n*.
Norfolk, Virginia, 131
Normanby, first Marquess of, (1797-1863) his despatches quoted, 119*n*., 288, 289, 293, 300, 314, 315, 316, 317, 371
Nubia, 170

OLLIVIER, M. Émile, 355, 357, 362
O'Meara, Barry, (1770-1836) 357
Orléans, Duc d', (1810-1842) 104, 347
Orléans, Louis Philippe, Duke of, *see* Louis Philippe
Orsi, Count, [a Florentine banker, *b.* 1808, met Louis Napoleon, 1827] 173, 193, 237, 238, 239, 362, 367, 369, 370 (*d.* 1899)
Orsini, Count, 67
—— Felix, (1819-1858) 362
Ostend, 251

PALMERSTON, Lord, (1784-1865) 122, 150, 170, 269; despatch cited, 156
Panama, 262
Paris, and the First Restoration, 3; in 1814, 29; the July Revolution in, 53; Louis Napoleon in, in 1831, 80-83; and the news of the Strasburg rising, 101-104; Louis Napoleon in, in 1836, 121; in 1840, 185-195; February Revolution in, 271-273; Louis Napoleon's visit to, 274; the national workshops in, 281-283, 290, 291; Louis Napoleon's final arrival in, 294, 295
Parquin, Colonel, [*b.* 1787, cavalry officer under First Empire; after serving in eleven campaigns received Cross of Legion of Honour from Napoleon in 1813; saved the life of the Duc de Raguse in Portugal, and of Marshal de Reggio at Leipzic; met Louis Napoleon 1822; married Hortense's reader Mlle Cochelet; and settled near Arenenberg 1824] his part in the Strasburg rising, 111, 115; in the preliminaries of Boulogne, 171; buys a live eagle, 175; sentenced to twenty years' detention, 194 (*d.* 1845)
Parquin, Mme, *see* Cochelet, Mlle
Pascallet, E., 362
Pas-de-Calais, 172
Pasquier, Duc de, (1767-1862) 189
Passé et l'avenir de l'Artillerie, du, 224, 225, 256, 258, 371
Paupérisme, Extinction du, 215, 256, 330, 371
Peauger, M., 350
Perey, M. Lucien, 359
Périer, Casimir, (1811-1876) 81
Peronne, 253, 369
Persigny, (1808-1872) early career, 98; meets Louis Napoleon, *ibid.*, 99, 104, 105; his part in the Strasburg rising, 107, 108, 113, 120; his account of the rising, 364; interviews Morier, 149, 156; publishes description of Louis Napoleon in his *Lettres de Londres,* 165, 366; laudatory and unreliable character of this description, 166, 361; his action at Boulogne, 180; at the trial, 167; condemned to twenty years' 'detention,' 195; goes with Louis Napoleon to Paris in Feb. 1848, 370; consults Odilon Barrot on behalf of Louis Napoleon in March 1848, 276; returns to France in June, 1848, 284; his arrest ordered, 285; the order rescinded, 286-287; accounts of, 363
Perugia, 70
Pesaro, 70, 71
Peyronnet, Cte., (1778-1854) 223*n*.
Philadelphia, 342
Pietra Santa, 75
Piétri, P. M., (*c.* 1810-1864) 283
Pisa, 75
Pius VIII, (1761-1830) 62
Pius IX, (1792-1878) 8, 13
Planché, J. R., (1796-1880) 366
Pleignier,[Sub-lieutenant, 119*n*.
Poggioli, Sylvestre, 226, 227, 369
Point Breeze, 342
Poland, 85, 86
Polignac, Prince, (1780-1847) 55*n*. 197, 368
Portugal, 95
Prince Imperial, *see* Napoleon, Eugène Louis
Prussia, reaction in, 10; its share in proposed redivision of Europe, 54*n*.; supports French demand

INDEX

for Louis Napoleon's expulsion from Switzerland, 148; acts with England in isolating France in 1840, 170; Louis Napoleon's appreciation of its military strength, 214
Putnam, G. P., (1814-1872) 278n.
Puygélier, Captain, see Col-Puygélier

QUERELLES, M. de, (1812-1847) 112, 113, 114

RAMSGATE, 173
Récamier, Madame, (1777-1849) 363
Regnault, Elias, (1801-1868) 367
Reichstadt, Duc de, see under Napoleon
Rémusat, Mme de, (1780-1821) 360
Renault, M. B., 356, 361, 362
Rêveries Politiques, published, 87, 371; character and object of the pamphlet, 88
Rhyn, M. Am., 143
Ripon, First Earl of, (1782-1859) 161
Rio de Janeiro, 127, 341
Roche, Eugène, 364
Rochefort, 361
Rollin, see Ledru-Rollin
Rome, 45, 46, 48, 60, 62, 64, 68, 98
Rosebery, Lord, 59
Rotterdam, 140
Rowles, Emily, 261
Ruskin, John, (1819-1900) 211
Russell, Lord John, (1792-1878) 30n.
Russia, liberal foreign policy of, in 1815, 9, 10; reaction, 11; Louis Napoleon's desire to serve under, against Turkey, 52; Polignac's secret negotiation with, in 1829, 54n.; co-operates with England's action against Mehemet Ali, 170

SABOTIÈRE, La Belle, see Vergeot, Alexandrine
Saint-Edme, 365, 367
St Gall, 36
St Helena, 7, 11, 12, 15, 16, 63, 94, 168, 170, 189, 197, 357-358
St John, J. A., (1801-1875) 366
St Leu, 24, 31, 265
—— Comte de, see Bonaparte, Louis
—— Duchess of, see Beauharnais, Hortense de
St Omer, 153
St Petersburg, 55n.
St Quentin, 249, 250
Saldanha, Marquis of, (1791-1861) 95n.
Salvage, Mme, 346

Sand, George, (1804-1876) 215, 347, 350
Sartorius, 369
Savoy, 35
Saxony, 54n.
Sedan, 313
Sercognani, General, 68
Servia, 54n.
Seymour, E. H., his despatches quoted, 67, 68, 70
—— Miss, 261
Siena, 74
Sismondi, J. C. L. S., (1773-1842) 208
Smith, George Thomas, 238, 239, 369
Soult, Marshal, (1769-1851) 32, 337, 361
Souplet, Calixte, 370
Spain, 21, 23
Spoleto, 67, 333
Stein, Lorenz von, 371
Stéphane-Pol, M., 361
Stéphanie, Grand Duchess of Baden, see under Beauharnais
Stern, Daniel, (Mme d'Agoult) 371
Stewart, C. S., 134, 365
Strasburg, chosen as the scene of Louis Napoleon's first expedition v. Louis Philippe, 100; preliminaries of the rising, 105, 106; arrival of Louis Napoleon in, 107; disposition of troops in, 108-109; design of the insurgents, 110; outbreak, progress and failure of the insurrection, 111-120; reception of the news in Paris, 101-104; Louis Napoleon's imprisonment at, 121; trial and acquittal of other insurgents at, 130, 131, 134, 167; Laity's account of, 144; Louis Napoleon on, 339, 340; other references to, 129, 133, 143, 145, 153n., 159, 160, 168, 179, 187, 188, 192, 193, 232, 236, 257; evidence regarding the rising, 363-365
Stuarts, the, Louis Napoleon on, 203-205
Suez Canal, 263
Switzerland, Louis Napoleon and his mother take up their residence in, 40; opposition of the Allies, and difficulties preliminary to their residence in Thurgau, 36-39; Louis Napoleon's military training in, 51; difficulty of returning there in 1831, 69; his return to in 1831, 85; his book on, 89; receives honorary citizenship of. *ibid.*: returns to in 1837, 140; France requests Louis Napoleon's expulsion from, 143, 144; postpones French demands,

146-148; apparent readiness to fight for Louis Napoleon, 149; Louis Napoleon's 'voluntary' departure from, 150, 151; apparent understanding between Swiss war party, and the prince, 152-154; success of this alliance, 155; Louis Napoleon's triumphant departure from, 156

TALANDIER, Colonel, 118, 119
Talleyrand, Prince de, (1754-1838) 84
Terni, 67
Thélin, Charles, (b. 1801) 131, 207, 244, 245, 246, 248-251, 253, 254, 352, 370
Thiers, L. A., (1797-1877) 59, 86, 268, 358, 359
Thirria, M., 356, 357
Thrace, 55n.
Thun, 51, 53, 60, 333
Thurgau, 37-39, 89, 147, 148, 151
Times, The, 163, 264, 276, 363
Tirmarche, Abbé, 246
Toeplitz, 24
Toulon, 112
Tremblaire, M. C. E., 368
Troyes, 284
Tscharner, M., 153n.
Tuckwell, W., 366
Turkey, 55n.
Turquan, M., 360
Tuscany, 73, 255

UNITED States 123, 125, 126; Louis Napoleon lands in, 131; his residence there, 132-139; proposed tour of, 134; experience of travel in, 342; impressions of, 135, 136; letter to President of, 139; later dealings with, 137; departure from, 139; evidence regarding his stay there, 365

VALENCIENNES, 250
Vandam, A. D., 370
Vaudrey, Colonel, [b. 1786, served in Italy 1806, taken prisoner in campaign v. Austria 1809, Captain 1810,distinguished himself in action before Gronen-Haissen 1813,fought in 1814 campaign and at Waterloo, placed in command of the 4th Artillery 1834] promises his support to Louis Napoleon, 105; joins him at Freiburg, 107; his part in the Strasburg rising, 108, 112, 114, 115, 117; surrenders to Talandier, 119, 120; Louis Napoleon pays for his defence, 339; Louis Napoleon to, 342
Vendôme column, 59, 82
Vergeot, Alexandrine, (La Belle Sabotière) her relations with Louis Napoleon at Ham, 217; [married to M. Bure, 1852; died at Paris, 1886]
Verhuel, Admiral, (1764-1845) 27, 358, 359
Vermorel, 371
Veron, Dr, 369
Versailles, 119n., 360
Vieillard, M., Louis Napoleon's letters to, 93, 126, 135, 146n., 222, 257, 323-325, 337-339, 346-348, 351-353, 369
Vienna, Congress of, 8
Virginia, 131
Viterbo, 67
Voirol, General, 102, 103, 106, 114, 116, 193
Voisin, Jean-Baptiste, [b. 1780, promoted from the ranks at Austerlitz, lieutenant-colonel 1813, retired as colonel 1837] tried for his part in the Boulogne landing, 192; condemned to ten years' detention, 195

WALDEN, Sixth Baron, (1799-1868) 95n.
Walpole, Sir Robert, 270
Warsaw, 86
Wartburg Festival, the, (18th October 1817) 10
Washington, 139
Waterloo, 9, 31, 33, 191, 335
Webb, General Watson, (b. 1782) 134, 365
Wehrhan, R., 360
Wellington, (1769-1852) 4
Wikoff, Henry, 220, 221, 368
William I, German Emperor, (1797-1888) 29
William III, 128, 203, 204
Wilson, J. G., 365
Wilson, Sir Robert, (1777-1849) 91, 92,
Wimereux, 176, 177
Wraxall, Sir F., (1828-1865) 360

ZAPPI, Marquis, 75
Zurich, 150

For Product Safety Concerns and Information please contact our EU representative GPSR@taylorandfrancis.com
Taylor & Francis Verlag GmbH, Kaufingerstraße 24, 80331 München, Germany

www.ingramcontent.com/pod-product-compliance
Lightning Source LLC
Chambersburg PA
CBHW071235300426
44116CB00008B/1046